CRUISIN' WITH THE TOOZ

JOHN MATUSZAK

WITH STEVE DELSOHN

CRUISIN' WITH THE TOOZ

FRANKLIN WATTS   NEW YORK   LONDON   1987

Library of Congress Cataloging in Publication Data

Matuszak, John, 1950–
Cruisin' with the tooz.

Includes index.
1. Matuszak, John, 1950–   2. Football
players—United States—Biography.   3. Oakland
Raiders (Football team)   I. Delsohn, Steve.
II. Title.
GV939.M297A3   1987   796.332′092′4 [B]   87-16153
ISBN 0-531-15055-0

For my parents, Marvin and Audrey;
my lady, Stephanie;
my sisters, Dawn, Karen and Christine;
my grandfather, Leo Walters, and
Susan Schroeder, actress, model, and good friend.
Love you all.
And to my Raiders teammates, 1976–1982.
Thanks for the memories.

Acknowledgments

George Anderson, Mary Kay Anthony,
Ed Breslin, Linda Cosgrove,
Dave Dalby, Al Davis,
Steve Delsohn, Dr. Donald Fink,
Dr. Robert Fremont, Ted Hendricks,
Basil Kane, Earl Leggett,
Al Locasale, John Madden,
Robert Murphy, Terrence Moore,
Phil Musick, Chuck Nevius,
Eric Noland, Kathy Pinkert,
Dick Romanski, Dr. Robert Rosenfield,
Vee Smith, John Vella,
David Vigliano, Phil Villipiano
and Charles Stern

CONTENTS

CRUISIN' WITH THE TOOZ

1

SCORE ONE FOR THE REBELS

New Orleans was wild.

It was midweek, January, 1981. My team, the underdog Oakland Raiders, would meet the Philadelphia Eagles that Sunday in Super Bowl XV. Teddy Hendricks and I were sitting in his hotel room, shooting the breeze and getting pumped up for the game. Suddenly I got a powerful urge. I wanted to check out Bourbon Street, the local strip that rocked all night. New Orleans was one of my favorite cities and that week it was in prime form. I wanted to sample the Super Bowl madness.

The only problem was, it was already two in the morning.

This is not as crazy as it sounds. You have to understand my reasoning. Like any good fan, I had watched every Super Bowl since its inception in 1967. And I had seen what it had done to certain people. Good players, dependable players, had frozen up when they got to the Super Bowl. I don't know why. Maybe it was fear of failure, or the fear of looking like a fool in front of millions of fans. By the time the game came around, they looked almost paralyzed, like their behinds were so tight they could barely run. So my decision to go out that night was actually based on logic: With millions of fans about to watch me, the last thing I needed was a tight behind.

Besides, there was another perfectly valid reason to conduct a mission that night on the streets of New Orleans.

It was Wednesday.

I know, I know. To most people Wednesdays don't mean a whole lot. To me they've always been kind of sacred. Whether I was in Oakland, Miami, even Cleveland, Wednesday was traditionally my evening to cruise, a night to check out the town and blow off a little steam.

Wednesday, as they used to say in Oakland, was always Tooz day.

Why Wednesday? There were two good reasons. First, I reasoned that if I got my, er, explorations out of my system Wednesday night, then low-profiled it the rest of the week, I'd be loose and ready to roll that Sunday. Second, in the practice scheme of the Raiders, Wednesday was always Defense Day, a grueling, full-contact practice that was nearly as intense as an actual game. Our owner, Al Davis, wanted it that way. Wednesday was one day of practice he never missed. If people weren't hitting, Al never said much. He just gave us The Look. Like magic, the practice would heat up. And by the time I walked off the field each Wednesday, I enjoyed going out just to take my mind off my banged-up body.

Although today my life is much more tranquil, when I was younger I had more than my share of scrapes. But you have to keep one thing in mind. If it wasn't for Wednesday, I'd have been a bona fide straight arrow. You'd never know the difference between me and Roger Staubach.

As for that Wednesday night before the Super Bowl, I did actually try and stay in. Quit laughing—I'm serious. I was safely tucked in my bed when the coaches made their curfew check at eleven o'clock. But I wasn't even close to falling asleep. I'm a longtime insomniac. Even when I was a child, my mom says I loved to sleep all day and stay up all night. In the week before an important game, sleeping was a losing battle, and that night wasn't any different. I tried everything. I rolled over to the other side of the bed. I reshuffled my pillows. I tried counting running backs as I threw them over the moon. It was futile. My mind would not stop racing.

By two it was getting ridiculous, so I went by Teddy's room to see if he was still up. As usual, he was. After a few minutes,

I said I was on my way out. Teddy, not exactly Mr. Conservative himself, looked at me like I was lacking a couple of screws. But I even had a destination. I had promised game tickets to Charley Connerly and his wife. Charley used to play quarterback for the New York Giants and he still liked the night life. If I didn't see Charley at the usual Bourbon Street spots, I would drop the tickets off with a mutual friend. Although I'd be out past curfew, what the Raiders didn't know wouldn't hurt me.

"But Tooz," Teddy argued, "it's two now and there's a press conference first thing in the morning."

"It's at nine o'clock," I assured him. "No problem at all. I'll be back way before it ever starts."

At 6' 8" and 280 pounds, I've never been much for clandestine maneuvers. I walked right through the hotel lobby, barreled into a cab and headed out for Bourbon Street. It was wild, even by Bourbon Street's standards. People in New Orleans never need much of a reason to celebrate, but the Super Bowl seemed to fuel their incentive, not to mention their stamina. At two-thirty in the morning, there were mobs of people on every corner.

I stopped in a bar called the Absinthe House for a couple of drinks. Then I had a few dances. Then I hit a couple of other clubs. Before I knew it, I was officially, successfully and irrevocably unwound. Somewhere along the line I dropped off Charley's tickets. After that, well . . . I'd love to give you a blow-by-blow account of the evening, but the rest of the night is basically a blur. In fact, my next recollection is waking up in the bedroom—fully clothed, thank you—of a woman I had met the evening before. As I wiped the sleep from my eyes and avoided any unnecessary movements of my head, we had a brief conversation.

"Morning," I said. "Any idea what time it is?"

"It's 9:35."

"AHHHHH! SHIT! I GOTTA GO!"

I was ten miles from the hotel, and one of the biggest press conferences of the year had started at nine. My head felt like Walter Payton had run a sweep over it, but it was clear enough to know that I had screwed things up pretty good. Reporters from every major newspaper in America would be there, all wondering where the Tooz was. Nice move, John. Why couldn't I do this before an exhibition game?

Into a cab, out of a cab, into the den of wolves. I arrived with ten minutes left in the press conference. Each player had a table of his own to help the massive interview session go more smoothly. The table with the card that read MATUSZAK was conspicuously empty. Meanwhile, I could see by their scowls that the Raiders' coaches were not amused. The flock of reporters who spied me, on the other hand, nearly had the first collective orgasm in media history. They could see they were onto something good. You see, just the day before I had promised to keep a low profile.

"If the boys want to go out this week," I had announced, "they'll just have to go through Ol' Tooz. We're here to win a football game. And I'm going to see to it personally that there isn't any funny business."

That was no time to stop. I was on a roll.

"Yeah, I've had enough parties for twenty people's lives, but now I've grown up. I'll keep our young guys out of trouble—you can bank on that."

Now, late and with my foot imbedded firmly in my mouth, I was pulled aside by one of the coaches. He went straight to the point. I was fined a thousand bucks. I was not to say a thing to the press.

Now wait a minute. I love the Raiders, but this did not seem right. First of all, who would have accepted a "no comment" at that point—with ten minutes left in the session? Especially the way I looked. My blood-red eyes were hiding behind a pair of sunglasses. My hair resembled Don King's, on a bad day. I had on an old pair of loafers without any socks. There was no way around it—I looked like I'd had myself a hell of a bender. But besides all that, since I was already out a grand, I felt I was at least entitled to a little fun. The coaches were staring right through me, but still I couldn't resist.

"Fellas," I groaned, "I'm in pain."

"But Tooz, what happened to all that enforcer stuff you were telling us about yesterday?"

"I am the enforcer," I explained. "That's why I was out on the streets—to make sure no one else was."

————

Thursday's practice got nasty. Wednesday's had been too. About halfway through practice Wednesday, Gene Upshaw, one of our offensive guards, got into a brief but angry brawl with Dave Browning, one of our defensive linemen. They kicked and wrestled and grunted until they got pried apart. On Thursday Gene got into it again, with a lineman named Phil Livingston. Phil was working Gene pretty hard in a drill—I think Al Davis told him to—and Uppy just snapped. He apologized to Phil later, but Gene got a lot of grief from the guys. Livingston had just gotten married and one of Gene's kicks had nearly relieved Phil of his balls. Gene was not usually so volatile, but this was Super Bowl week. Everyone's adrenaline was pumping overtime.

Frankly, no one really minded. They certainly weren't surprised. Football is a violent game and it's best played with a violent frame of mind. Away from the stadium you might be the nicest guy in the world. But once you walk on that field you'd better be feeling angry. You just can't manufacture your rage in the tunnel before each Sunday's game. You have to stoke it all week long. Banging against people at practice who are as big and ornery as you are—even people you like—is bound to cause confrontations. Practice fights are inevitable.

Some coaches even like them. My first role as an actor was in a film called *North Dallas Forty*, for my money the best movie ever made about football. There's a scene where a pair of teammates are kicking the crap out of each other as the coaches stand on the sidelines licking their chops. It's not *all* that far-fetched. I'm not saying that NFL coaches enjoy seeing their players spill each other's blood. Of course they don't. But as long as no one gets hurt, fighting at practice isn't just tolerated, it's seen as a positive thing. Complacency is suicidal in the NFL. Fights at least show the coaches that the team is up. The feeling is this: If a guy is feeling mean enough to go after one of his own, then God help his opponent that Sunday.

I remember when Vann McElroy, now one of the Raiders

starting safeties, first came to the team. Vann's father is a preacher. Off the field Vann is relatively calm. He's a different man on Sundays. Run a crossing pattern in his area and he's apt to cut you in half. When Vann was a rookie he got into a fight one practice with Marcus Allen. The next day he walked around depressed because he was convinced he was about to get cut. Someone who didn't know better might assume that an unproven rookie messing with a star would place you directly on the coaches' shit list. Vann needn't have worried. I doubt if the coaches thought about it twice. If anything, they were probably impressed.

All teams in the NFL have fights during practice. The Raiders may be the only team in history that had two players going at it in the middle of a game. Right on the field. It happened to Matt Millen and Lyle Alzado, in 1982. It was the second game of the year, against Atlanta, one of those hot, sticky southern days that shorten everyone's temper. Matt was calling defensive stunts—Lyle had just come to the Raiders and was still getting used to the system. With the Raiders winning big and early, the Falcons went into their two-minute offense. Steve Bartkowski, Atlanta's quarterback, was calling plays from the line of scrimmage. Matt was forced to do the same. Lyle never responded to one of Matt's calls for a stunt, and after the play they started talking about it. Then they were arguing, which led to shouting. Finally they traded swings. Meanwhile, most of the Falcons just stood there wide-eyed. But a couple of wiseguys were yelling to "let 'em kill each other."

As a Raider, I never had any fights with my teammates. Charles Philyaw, who is 6' 10" and more than 300 pounds, once said he was going to kick my ass but he never tried to follow through. I suppose that was fortunate for both of us.

I did have an ugly altercation when I was with the Kansas City Chiefs in 1974. I had only been there a couple of weeks and was basically minding my own business. I was matched against a big offensive lineman in a pass rushing drill. I don't remember his name, but I do recall he was a milkman in the off-season. I beat him to the quarterback when suddenly I felt this sharp blow to the back of my legs. The milkman had cut-block me from behind. Done from the blind side, cut-blocking is one of the cheapest, dirtiest moves in football and the most frequent victims are defensive linemen. The blocker hits you low, usually at the knees, and "cuts" you to the ground. Doing it from behind borders on sadistic. You can end a guy's career.

This guy could have ended *my* career, all for a lousy drill. I was so enraged my entire body was shaking. I hit him in the face mask with an open hand. He staggered back a few steps and reached for his mouth. I had knocked out a couple of his teeth, and the blood was dripping down his chin. He jumped up and wanted some more. I was happy to oblige, but several of my teammates stepped between us.

I practiced against the milkman for another eighteen months without any incident. But there was always that tension. When we became opponents, after I signed with the Raiders, the milkman figured I was fair game. I could never make a move without watching my back for him. If I would jump in the air to deflect a pass, he would plow into my shins as I'd hit the ground. One time I was climbing off the pack, not really looking around me, when he came flying through the air and speared me in the back. The milkman was a dangerous character.

———

By Thursday night, my Bourbon Street quota for the week was filled. All I wanted was some rest, and some time away from the spotlight. Dick Vermeil made that impossible.

Vermeil was then the head coach of the Eagles. In his five-year stint there, Vermeil had completed an incredible transformation of a team that Bill Walsh once called "the most forlorn franchise in football." Often working twenty-hour days, sleeping in his office on a pull-out cot, by 1980 Vermeil had turned a certified loser into a Super Bowl team. There was absolutely no questioning his drive. But Vermeil had what I considered an unfortunate flaw. He never seemed to enjoy what success he had. Even Vermeil admits it today—he drove himself and the people surrounding him much too long and hard. Just two years after he took the Eagles to the Super Bowl, still near the top of his profession, Vermeil quit coaching for a reason he called "burnout."

After my night on the town, a reporter asked Vermeil how he would have handled me if I had been an Eagle.

"If he were on the Eagles," he replied, "he'd be back on a plane to Philadelphia right now."

Well, exc-u-u-u-se m-e-e-e-e-e! I realize he was only answering a question, but think about it. A guy plays his heart out for you for nineteen games. Then you send him home before the biggest game of his life? Talk about cruel and unusual punishment. This was also not the sharpest move in terms of pre-game strategy. We were already psyched enough to kick the Eagles' butts. Now Vermeil was scrutinizing, in public, the Raiders' tactics when it came to handling their players.

Most of my teammates took my night on the town in stride. That's because I was hardly alone. That week the Raiders set a Super Bowl record that will probably stand for all time—$15,000 worth of fines.

"If Tom Flores sent everyone home who screwed around," as Upshaw put it, "he'd be the only one standing on the side-lines."

Time has tempered my feelings. But at the moment I was angry with Vermeil. He had always struck me as a decent enough person—someone I'd never particularly want to play for, but a man whose good points easily outweighed his bad ones. But send me on a plane back to Philly? I suppose I should also have been sent straight to bed without watching *Leave it to Beaver*. I heard from the reporters what Vermeil had said, and I was asked for a rebuttal. I decided to keep things light. I've never considered Philadelphia a real hot spot for winter vacations. So I countered with this: "Who'd want to go to Philadelphia in January?"

Please excuse my irreverence. I wanted to win that Super Bowl as badly as anyone on either team. I just didn't see any good reason I shouldn't have fun in the process. Some guys play their whole careers without ever getting to the Super Bowl.

I was going to enjoy myself while I had the opportunity. Besides, my "spat" with Vermeil actually added interest to the game. It helped to spotlight the game's most intriguing dimension: the radically different natures of the Raiders and the Eagles.

Just take a look at the week before the Super Bowl. When the Eagles jumped off their bus upon arriving in New Orleans, they were all decked out in identical green jumpsuits. The Raiders were dressed as usual—any way they pleased. All week long the Eagles barely had time to breathe. When they weren't at countless meetings, they were practically imprisoned in their hotel rooms, as if the slightest bit of freedom would translate into missed tackles and overthrown receivers.

As always, Al Davis's Raiders had their own way of doing things. As long as we were prepared and ready to move at practice, the Raiders let us use our free time pretty much as we pleased. Basically, Vermeil took the same approach to the Super Bowl as George Allen had done in Super Bowl VII: He got so caught up in "beating the distractions," that beating the distractions became the biggest distraction.

To some people, Super Bowl XV became a morality play. A clash not just between two football teams, but two completely opposing ideologies. It was the milk and cookie Eagles against the shot and a beer Raiders. The local PTA against the street people. There's a measure of truth to that kind of talk. There's also a measure of hype.

What kind of team were those Raiders? It's true we had more than our share of characters. Hell, we had enough for our entire division. But it wasn't like Al went browsing through the police blotter whenever he needed a player. None of us had fangs or slept in coffins. We all loved our grandmothers.

It's just that Al encourages his players to be *individuals*, both on the field and off it. This is hardly universal among NFL owners. To most, different is a four-letter word. Virtually every team pushes its players to dress alike, act alike, speak alike—all in the name of promoting togetherness. The only thing that kind of nonsense promotes is bitterness toward management. Al has never gotten hung up on bureaucratic garbage. As long as you're ready to win each Sunday, you don't have to file a written report every time you blow your nose.

On the other hand, the Raiders go to as many charity functions as any other team in the league and contribute just as much to their community. It's all a matter of perception. Catfish Hunter once said that Reggie Jackson was the kind of guy who would give you the shirt off his back. Only thing was, he'd call a press conference to announce it. The Raiders don't operate that way. We never wanted to be perceived as clones of Donnie Osmond. No one would have bought it anyway. Besides, we liked playing the bad guys.

People used to ask me if we minded our image as the big, bad bullies of the NFL. Hell no, we cultivated it. Look at our logo—a pirate with a patch on his eye, crossed swords in the background. The uniforms are silver and black. It doesn't take a genius to figure out what type of image we liked to project. We never tried to deny it because we felt it was to our advantage. All week long the other teams would hear about how rowdy and unpredictable we were. When Sunday came around, they were more worried about retaliation than about their own assignments. In the NFL, it's hard to intimidate people. How do you intimidate a guy who can bench press your piano? But if you can just get him thinking . . .

Our quarterback for the Super Bowl was Jim Plunkett. He had started the season on the bench, but moved to number one when Dan Pastorini broke his leg in Game Five of the regular season. I have to admit it, I wasn't very confident when Plunkett replaced Pastorini at quarterback. I was familiar with Jim's past. After a difficult childhood, he had gone on to win the Heisman Trophy at Stanford. But in his first few years in the pros, playing behind some porous New England Patriots offensive lines, Jim had been beaten up badly. He was traded to the 49ers, where he was later cut. The Raiders picked him up on waivers in 1978, and he stuck. Jim was a survivor who wouldn't quit. He was tough.

At the same time, he had never really impressed me as an NFL caliber quarterback. By the time New England traded him to the 49ers, Jim was shell-shocked from the punishment. His confidence was gone and he had acquired a terrible habit—if you gave him any kind of pressure, he would throw the ball before he had to. I remember a game against the 49ers when I beat my man but couldn't quite get to Jim. So I dove at his feet, yelling as loudly and as violently as I could. Sure enough, Jim unloaded the ball even though there wasn't any need. The day Pastorini went down and Jim ran onto the field, I recall thinking, "Oh hell, there goes the whole damn season." A lot of the Raiders felt that way. Anytime Jim went back to pass those first few games, we all got a little nervous.

I'm happy to say Jim proved me wrong. Jim's biggest problem was that he had never played behind a good offensive line. Passing behind a pocket made up of Upshaw, Art Shell, Dave Dalby, Henry Lawrence and Mickey Marvin, Plunkett went on to have an excellent year, helping us to the Super Bowl. There's still a feeling among some people that the Raiders used to win *despite* Plunkett, not because of him. I think that's crazy. His skills today aren't what they used to be, but few people's are at the end of their career. Jim was the winning quarterback in two Super Bowls—XV and XVIII. How do you explain that away?

As for the 1980 Super Bowl, a lot of people never expected us to even get close. Each of the two previous seasons we'd gone nine and seven and missed the playoffs. As 1980 approached, several publications were picking us for last in our division.

You can never count the Raiders out. We finished the year at eleven and five, good for a wildcard spot in the playoffs. Even then, nobody gave us half a chance to go all the way. As a wildcard, in order to win the Super Bowl, we would have to win four games, rather than three as the divisional champs had to. Three of those games would be on the road. History was clearly against us. No team before or since has ever won a Super Bowl from a wildcard berth. But we defied the odds, knocking off Houston, Cleveland and San Diego in the playoffs. Next came the Eagles.

On the morning of Super Bowl XV, our locker room was business as usual—a few guys shooting dice, some playing cards and a handful dancing to a song on the radio. Actually there were about a dozen radios blaring. The Raiders' locker room used to sound more like a disco than a locker room. There are tight locker rooms and loose ones. The Raiders gave loose a new meaning. You'd never know there would be a Super Bowl later that day. I looked around the locker room and I smiled. For once I knew the calm wouldn't last, not today. The nerves would kick in soon.

The Raiders have never been big on pregame pep talks. As a veteran team, the last thing we needed was a string of worn-out cliches. Al Davis, however, is the King of Edges. Any *effective* device to pump us up, he wouldn't hesitate to use. This time he invited some of the old Raiders' superstars into the locker room before the game. People like Jimmy Otto, Biletnikoff and Jimmy Cannon, tough guys Al knew we all respected.

We were ready to go to work.

Ron Jaworski was the Eagles quarterback. A lot of heart, powerful arm, vulnerable to getting rattled if you got in his face. Jaworski's first pass of the game was a lousy one, right into Rod Martin's hands for an interception. Eight plays later, Plunkett's touchdown pass to Cliff Branch gave us a 7–0 lead.

Then we caught a break. With the first quarter about to end, Plunkett was bouncing around in the pocket when he threw a wobbler along the left sideline. Philly's cornerback, Herman Edwards, jumped for the football, somehow missed it, and it dropped softly into the hands of our halfback Kenny King. Kenny ran for an eighty-yard touchdown, the longest pass play in Super Bowl history.

Down 14–0, the Eagles had problems. They were hitting every bit as hard as we were, but it seemed to me they were already starting to press. In the second quarter, Jaworski threw what looked to be a game-tying TD pass. But Harold Carmichael was called for illegal motion. Then, with fifty-eight seconds left in the half and a wide-open receiver in the end zone, Jaworski just plain missed him, by a mile. They finally got on the board with a Tony Franklin field goal. But when they tried to kick another field goal right before half, it was blocked by Teddy Hendricks.

In this book we'll go behind the scenes. We'll look at things that the fan in the seats or watching on TV can't normally see. Like the part I played on Teddy's block. Although it will never show up in any box score, I have to take credit for an assist. Even if I did do it with my mouth.

Teddy's block actually had its roots at a press conference the week before the game. There are hundreds of reporters at every Super Bowl, all of them searching frantically for stories with novel angles. One writer asked me for something fresh, some unprecedented approach to discussing the Eagles. So I complied. I started listing their preferences in cologne. I told him Jaworski wore Brut, Wilbert Montgomery wore Old Spice and on and on. When I got to offensive guard Pete Perot—their designated cheapshot artist with a big mouth to boot—I said that Perot didn't wear any cologne at all.

It wasn't the cleverest quote of my career, but you do have to give me points for originality. Anyway, by Sunday I had long forgotten it. Perot apparently had not. In fact, I'm sure it was posted on the Eagles' bulletin board. As the Eagles lined up for their field goal try, Perot's assignment was to protect the gap in their offensive line between Teddy and me. But when Perot saw who was standing over him—me—his eyes got big and he seemed to forget that a gap ever existed. They were losing, he was pissed and now he was going to stick that cologne remark right up my ass. He drove at me low and hard, so hard he knocked me flat on my back. In the meantime Teddy strolled through the vacated gap and blocked the field goal. I wanted to laugh in Petey's face but I decided against it. Guys who don't wear cologne never have a sense of humor.

The second half was ours. Branch caught another touchdown—taking an Eagle safety to school by coming back on an underthrown pass in the end zone—and Chris Bahr kicked a pair of field goals. Plunkett got the MVP, Rod Martin had three interceptions and we held the Eagles to sixty-nine yards on the ground. I'd like to say I had the greatest game of my life. It wouldn't be true. I played well but not extraordinarily. The one time I was about to sack Jaworski—CRACK—I got leveled from behind by a clip. No call, but that's not unusual. As I'll get to later, the refs and the Raiders have had some unusual moments.

The final was 27–10, but the game was decided well before the final gun. By late in the third quarter, the fire had all but disappeared from the Eagles eyes. You could sense that they were done. In retrospect, I'm not going to say the Raiders won because we took a more adult approach. We won because we had better football players. But the Eagles did look as if they were afraid to make a mistake out there. The old tight-behind syndrome.

In the postgame interview, Teddy was asked to put the game in perspective.

"If we lost today we would have gone back to camp as Eagles," Teddy said. "Now we can go on being Raiders."

After the game, the locker room was threatening to become a scene in itself. Earlier that season, Al had announced our proposed move to Los Angeles. His longtime—but mostly private—feud with Commissioner Pete Rozelle had escalated into a bitter public battle. With Rozelle having to present the Super Bowl trophy to Al, our players were wondering how he would handle it. Some of the guys even brought their cameras from home and kept them in their lockers. I think they wanted to record the look on Rozelle's face.

It was academic. Rozelle was gracious and Al was thrilled to get his second Super Bowl ring. The confrontation never materialized. I, for one, was glad it didn't. We'd been battling what seemed like the world for seven long months. We had nothing left to prove.

The locker room was throbbing with emotion. We were hugging each other around the neck. Some of the guys were crying. As I watched the celebration, it hit me like a slap in the face: The season was finally over. My body would have until summer to heal. No more 280-pound linemen to dance with. I could do what I wanted, when I wanted. I should have been elated, but I wasn't. I had the same feeling I did at the end of every season. I was in no rush to peel off my uniform. I didn't want to leave my friends.

When I creaked over to my locker, I realized how sore my body was. No major injuries, but I felt like I'd been in a gang fight. The Eagles may have been tight, but they gave as good as they got. I took off my equipment slowly, laying each piece by the side of my locker. No quick movements for now, maybe not for a couple of days. I ripped the tape from my ankles, then took a rag and carefully mopped my forehead where my helmet had rubbed it raw. Then I took a long hot shower.

The shower felt fantastic—I was finally, gradually, beginning to unwind. The muscles in my neck and shoulders no longer felt like knots. As I stood beneath the water, I let my mind drift. I began to reminisce.

It was 1981, so much had happened to me since I'd joined the NFL eight years ago: out of a nation full of college football players, the number one pick in the NFL draft; my rude awakening with the Houston Oilers; my controversial jump to another league; my trade to Kansas City, where I nearly partied myself right out of the NFL; picked up and then released by the Washington Redskins; passed over by every team in the NFL; on my way to play in Canada, rescued by that last-minute call from Al Davis. Now this, a starter on my second Super Bowl champion.

It had been a wild, improbable journey. Sometimes funny as hell, sometimes frightening.

2

ME AND MISTER MADDEN

My first game as an Oakland Raider was in September 1976, against one of my former employers, the Kansas City Chiefs. After the game the local-beat writers were crowding around my locker. The writers always do feature stories when a player comes back to face his former team. If a guy should rip his ex-bosses, they've got something hot for the morning papers. They grilled me with the standard questions. Was I mad at the Chiefs for trading me? Did I think I could reform? What was it like to be a Raider?

My first few years in the league were fraught with turmoil. You'll read about it a couple of chapters from now. By the time I got to the Raiders, I was weary of controversy. All I wanted to do was play football. Now, as the reporters continued to pepper me, Monte Johnson, one of our linebackers, walked by. Monte could see that I was uncomfortable.

"Look," Monte told the pack, "John's a Raider now. He's going to stay a Raider and he's going to be fine. You guys just leave him alone."

I'll always appreciate Monte for that. He didn't even know me, yet he was already looking out for me. It made me feel wanted, something I hadn't felt in a while. Monte had some great years with the Raiders before a knee injury cut his career short. He's got a beautiful wife and children and he lives in

Nebraska now. If you're reading this, Monte, thanks again, pal.

Monte wasn't the only one who made me feel at home. I found out later that one Raider gave me a vote of confidence before I even joined the team.

In the course of the 1976 exhibition season, the Raiders lost three starting defensive linemen—Horace Jones, Art Thoms and Tony Cline—to season-ending injuries. Out of necessity, they decided to play a 3–4 defense. In a 3–4 you want your three defensive linemen to have size and power, so they can control the line of scrimmage. This enables the linebackers to rush up and make a majority of the tackles. I fit the bill, but there was a catch. John Madden, then the Raiders coach, knew I'd recently been traded by the Chiefs to the Washington Redskins. He knew I'd then been waived by the Redskins and was now available. But for the same reasons everyone else had, John was apprehensive about picking me up. One day John saw Teddy Hendricks, a man whose judgement he trusted, in the locker room.

"Hey, Ted," John said, "what do you think about this Matuszak? I hear he's pretty wild and crazy. Do you think he'll fit in here?"

Just then Skip Thomas and Otis Sistrunk walked by. A bowling ball has more hair than Otis Sistrunk's head. On national TV, Alex Karras once kidded that Otis was from the University of Mars. Skip's nickname was Doctor Death. He was a motorcycle fanatic who thought he was the black Evel Knievel. Good guys, not your basic yuppies.

"Wild and crazy?" Teddy repeated. "Fit in here?

"Look around you, John. What's one more going to hurt?"

John looked at Skip and then Otis. He scanned the rest of the locker room.

"Yeah," John said, "I guess you're right."

Shortly after the Raiders signed me, I was called to John's office.

"I've got three rules," John began. "Be on time, pay attention and play like hell when I ask you to."

I waited for the fall. Teddy had told me about his conversation with John. Considering John's initial reservations, I figured he would now feel obligated to play the heavy. I was ready for the old "you better watch your ass around here" lecture. It never came. John shook my hand and said he was glad to have me.

I soon found out that John Madden is very much like the guy you see on your TV screen every Sunday in the fall—totally without pretension and a hell of a good time to be around. You never wanted to play hard for John because you felt obligated to, although as a pro you *were* obligated to play hard. You wanted to play well for John because you admired him.

The fraternity of NFL coaches is like any other. There are bullshit artists and those who shoot straight. If there was one thing that most endeared John to his players, it was his honesty. Players can smell a phony in a minute, and it turns them off. Who can trust a fake? John never played any mind games, never told you things just because he thought you wanted to hear them. Some coaches will put a disfavored player in their "doghouse." When a player is in the doghouse, he might as well be invisible, at least until the player who's in front of him screws up worse than he did. John had a doghouse, but it was for his dog. If John was upset with you, he'd call you to his office and you'd have it out. Simple. Honest. Adult.

Rules never bothered me when I was playing. I never obeyed them, so they never bothered me. Kidding aside, I actually thought rules were fine, as long as there was a sensible reason behind them. Most coaches didn't share my sense of logic. A rule, even a moronic one, was a rule, and that was good enough. John was different. He never believed in discipline solely for discipline's sake. If a rule had nothing to do with winning football games, then John didn't have it. For a time when I was a Chief, we had to wear matching sports coats whenever we traveled. I liked the Chiefs—I liked them a lot—but forty-nine large men wearing bright red sports coats offended my sensibility. How was that going to help us win? Besides, we looked ridiculous. You've heard of the Dolphins' Killer Bees? We were the Killer Beets.

As long as we didn't show up in our underwear, John let us

wear whatever we wanted, partly because he never liked to dress up himself. John is a big man—6′ 4″ and at least 260 pounds—and he likes to be comfortable. He also said that the guys who looked good in the hotel lobby might not be worth a damn come third and ten on Sunday.

For all its computerized game plans and high-tech jargon, the NFL is still a haven for superstition. John was no different. John's hang-up was clothes. He had to wear the same light blue pants and dark blue shirt to every game. *Had* to. One of the Raiders' staff tells of the time the dry cleaner forgot to deliver John's pants the Saturday before a game. On Sunday morning the cleaners were closed. John was frantic. A change of attire could lead to disaster, not to mention fumbles and interceptions. John didn't want to lose, so he felt as if he had no choice. He called the cleaner at his home. He persuaded him to drive to his shop and open his doors. John got his pants in time for the game. And, yes, the Raiders won.

Some coaches demand their players' respect without even trying to earn it: I'm the coach and you'll respect me. Period. It usually blows up in their faces. Playing dictator was never John's style. He was too smart for that. That stuff might work with an inexperienced team. A team of veterans like the Raiders wouldn't buy it. Which is not to say that John got pushed around. He had a temper and he flashed it when he felt he had to. On more than one occasion, I was the recipient.

Much has been written about the way I gradually "mellowed out" during my seven-year stint with the Raiders. This is basically true. I came to them as a twenty-five-year-old kid, and I retired as a thirty-three-year-old man. Age is a consideration that is generally ignored when people criticize the ways of pro athletes. I'm not talking about veterans. I'm talking about the younger players. They certainly look like adults, but they're just out of school. Think about it for a moment: How well-grounded were *you* when you first got out of college?

I experienced a lot during my career in the NFL, both hard times and prosperity. In the process, I matured. At first I felt I had to be the biggest and the baddest at anything I did. Whether it was football or fighting or hanging around the bars, John Matuszak had to be the best. Eventually, I stopped trying to live up to the John Matuszak legend. I just started to be myself.

It's strange: When people expect you to be wild, talk about you being wild, encourage you to be wild, you begin to *be* wild. It's almost as if you *become* your image. There were times when I tried to live up to other people's expectations, be the life of other people's parties. And I wound up getting hurt for it. But I don't want that misconstrued. Ultimately, anything I did was my decision. The responsibility was mine.

I still had some growing up to do when I first came to the Raiders. There were times when I tried John Madden's patience. Whenever I did slip up, I would work my ass off at practice and the games to try and make it up to John. I think John appreciated that. Then, I'd screw up again and it was like I was right back to square one.

I was with the Raiders all of two weeks before I made John angry. It was the Saturday before the third regular season game, against the Oilers. We were practicing in the Astrodome. Kenny Stabler was hurt and we were working in Mike Rae, a new, inexperienced quarterback. We had to go over things, thoroughly, that we would usually gloss over. It was a long, tense practice.

Finally, we were running short yardage plays near the other team's goal line. That usually signaled the end of Saturday practices. We were wrapping up the final play of the afternoon—or at least I thought we were—when I turned to my defensive teammates.

"All right guys," I said. "Let's make this last play a good one."

John blew up. He became this big, red, raving monster.

"I'm the coach around here," he screamed. "And I'll tell you when it's the last play. And don't ever forget it."

John was right in my face, and his veins looked like they might burst through his skin. He was flailing his arms around, just like he does in those Lite Beer commercials. Only this time, he was seriously ticked off. In my few weeks with the club, I'd never seen John lose his temper. I didn't say a word, just kind of jumped back until the explosion ended. All the guys were laughing at me. I think I officially became a Raider that day.

That was nothing substantial, a simple misunderstanding. One week later there was real trouble. It was after a game against the New England Patriots, a game in which we had been destroyed, 48–17. You remember Charles Philyaw, the humongous defensive lineman who threatened to fight me? I liked Charles. He was like a big, innocent kid framed by a very adult body. I don't think Charles was as scattered as everyone thought he was, but he would say some incredible things at times that would break everyone up. He was also one of those players who always came up with phantom injuries. You could never tell when Charles was truly hurt or if he was just being melodramatic.

Late in the New England game, Charles collapsed on the field after getting blocked in the knee. He was howling and carrying on like he was in excruciating pain. It looked real; everyone feared he had broken his knee. They called for a stretcher and carried him off the field to an ambulance. Back then, the Patriots didn't have X-ray facilities at their stadium. Charles and Doctor Rosenfeld, our physician, drove to a small hospital twenty minutes away. When the doctors X-rayed Charles, they found no broken bones. Since he was still yelping in pain, they put him in a wheelchair anyway.

By the time the doc and Charles got back to the airport, they had held up the flight back to Oakland by over an hour. Nobody was mad. A man was injured and that was all that counted. As the doc was wheeling Charles past the airport bar, Charles spotted a bunch of us having a beer at the counter. Charles jumped out of his wheelchair. I repeat, Charles jumped out of his wheelchair.

"Hey, wait for me," he yelled. "I want to have a beer too."

We're talking about some severely arched eyebrows. It was like the entire coaching staff let out one big "Hmmmmmmmm."

How does this all relate to me? Charles had not had one of his better games that day. The Patriots had run on him all game. We both played defensive end. Charles had started the game, but I had done well in the short time I played. After Charles had the quickest recovery in medical history, right in front of the coaches, I had a distinct feeling I'd be starting the following Sunday. I felt bad about the loss, good about the future. Too good, it turned out.

It was a five-hour flight back to Oakland. Some of the guys decided to have a couple of beers before we jumped on the plane. I could never sleep on planes. I rarely slept easily anywhere. I thought if I had a couple of beers I would get drowsy and hopefully sleep through the flight. The logic of my plan was good, the execution lousy. A couple of beers turned into several. Before long I was flying just fine all by myself. I began talking with two attractive women. They had just dropped off a friend and were now considering a short vacation themselves. They said they didn't go back to work for a couple of days. This gave me an inspired idea.

"Have you ever been to Oakland?" I asked.

"No."

"Would you like to visit?"

"Sure."

"Would you like to go right now, on the plane with the Oakland Raiders?"

(Pause. Exchanged glances. Temporary insanity.)

"We'd love to," the older one replied, "if you can get us on."

That was all I needed to hear. These women definitely had the right attitude. I walked up to John Madden, who was standing by the ramp to the plane. With a woman beneath each arm, I asked John if I could take them back to Oakland. John looked at me like I was nuts, which, at the moment, I may have been. Jack Tatum saw what was happening and told me to lighten up. I cleverly told Jack to mind his own business. John remained cool. I have a pretty good idea of what he was thinking, but all he said was a simple, "No." I said goodbye to the women and walked on the plane. Way to go Tooz. Nothing like making a good impression on your new employers.

By the way, John didn't hold a grudge. I did start the following game against San Diego, and every game for the rest of the season. Things went just as smoothly for the Raiders. After that loss to New England, we won our last ten games of the regular season, finishing at thirteen and one. After beating New England and the Steelers in the playoffs, we faced the Minnesota Vikings in Super Bowl XI. It was an amazing turn of events. One year with the Raiders and I was already in a Super Bowl. Maybe I'd even write a book someday.

The Super Bowl was being played in the Rose Bowl, in Pasadena. In the seats would be more than 100,000 fans, plus eighty million more watching on TV. This was what it was all about. The night before the game we stayed at the Los Angeles Hilton. I woke up Sunday morning and I bolted out of bed. I felt fantastic. I was ready to kick some ass. I was ready to dominate. I was ready to take Fran Tarkenton and bounce him on his nose.

I was late for the bus to the game.

Even though I was running a bit behind, I still had a couple of minutes to spare as I stepped into the hotel elevator. John had announced the day before that we'd be leaving the hotel for the Rose Bowl at 9:30 A.M. It was only 9:20. But the hotel was packed and the elevator was stopping on every single floor. *No, I thought, this was not really happening. I was not going to be late for the Super Bowl.* By the time I got downstairs and ran outside, the bus was history. I couldn't figure it out. It was only 9:25.

This was no time for indecision. Standing outside the hotel was a guy dressed as a pirate, waving a sword. I've read a few detective novels in my day, and I quickly reasoned that this guy was pulling for the Raiders. I pleaded with the guy to drive me to the stadium. He was happy to do it. When I got there, I thought I was in for a fine and a Madden tongue lashing. But when I slinked into the locker room, I was told that three other players had missed the bus too. In all the confusion, John had instructed the driver to leave ten minutes too early. I was tempted to give John a fine. But I realized that nobody's perfect.

As a coach, though, John was closer than most. In his ten years as coach of the Raiders, the Raiders won 103 games, tied seven and lost only thirty-two. During that time they went to the playoffs eight times, won seven division championships, an AFC championship and a Super Bowl in 1977. John was the first coach ever to win 100 games in ten seasons with one team. He was an excellent motivator and a pretty good psychologist. We had a lot of eccentrics in those days. It took a secure guy like John to deal with us all.

John could react on his feet, roll with the punches as they say. No one proved that more than Teddy. For a while, several of the guys were coming late to practices or meetings. John got tired of it. He gave us a lecture on the importance of punctuality. Soon after there was a special teams meeting and John was taking a form of roll call. He would yell out the spot on the special team and each player would yell out his name. As he was going through the punt-return team, one of the coaches interrupted.

"John," he said. "You've got an important phone call."

John didn't want to be bothered but the coach looked earnest. John walked to a nearby phone and picked it up.

"Hendricks" is what he heard over the line.

It was Teddy, confirming his spot on the return team. He knew he was going to be late, so he called from a nearby pay phone.

One day, a pair of the rookies got into a fight in training camp. John let it go for a moment and then stepped in to try and pry them apart. In the excitement, he got knocked to the ground. When he got back up, his face was all red and his hair even more tossed than usual. There was silence. No one knew what to expect.

"Uh, John," Teddy said gently, "did you forget to take your salt pills today?"

Just about everyone on the Raiders had a nickname. It was a sign that you were accepted by the team. Dave Casper's was The Ghost. I'm sure it was originally coined from the cartoon character. But Dave's nickname was perfect for another reason. Dave was the whitest human being in the history of man. He looked like a pillow case with eyes. Everyone called Mark Van Eeghen Black Blood. Mark was white but his hair was a kinky afro. For obvious reasons, another player was called The Whore.

John's nickname was Big Red or Pinky. We used to call him Pinky because he'd always flush bright red whenever he was upset. He was fair skinned and freckled to begin with, but anger would really accentuate it. One day at practice, Biletnikoff made a mistake. Fred almost never screwed up, but this time John got on him about it.

"I'm tired of this shit, Pinky," Fred muttered beneath his breath.

All the players heard it. Everyone was biting his lips, trying to keep from cracking up. We thought John might have a tantrum. He cracked up harder than anyone.

John wanted us to have our fun. It was a long season and he knew it was good to blow off some steam. When Phil Villipiano was the commissioner of our annual training camp Air Hockey Tournament, he always used to ask John for an extended curfew the night of the big event. John always said yes. One season, we lost our first three preseason games and Phil didn't know what to do. He wanted to have the tournament, but the atmosphere around camp had been tense. He didn't know if it would be appropriate for us to have so much fun when we were playing so poorly. He had postponed the tournament for a couple of days when Madden walked up to him in the locker room.

"What the hell is the matter with you?" John bellowed at him. "Why haven't you had the tournament yet? What kind of a commissioner are you?"

Phil and John liked each other. They were both the type of people who were incapable of acting phony. One game, the other team was driving for the go-ahead touchdown when John objected to an official's call. He was chasing the ref down the sideline, really going after him, when he got whistled for a fifteen-yard penalty. It moved the other team down near our goal line. Penalties called on coaches are almost unheard of, especially in such a crucial situation. John was still upset, and now he was also embarrassed. If the Raiders were going to lose, John didn't want to be one of the reasons. The next play was a pass. Phil leaped up, intercepted and ran the ball all the way back to midfield. The lead was secure. When Phil ran off the field, John trotted up to him.

"Thanks for saving my ass," John said.

The next time you watch a game, check out the coaches as they react to the action from the sideline. Every one has a different style. Don Coryell used to look like he was arguing with his in-laws. Tom Landry is Mr. Icewater. Mike Ditka looks like he's about to suit up. John let it all hang out. As he ranted and raved along the sideline, John would be jumping up and down, his shirt untucked and his hair flapping in the wind. John wasn't showboating, he was just 100 percent into the game. Sundays were his favorite day, and he didn't care who knew it. I remember one game against the Rams. It was a hard-fought game. Each team would take and then lose the lead. A great game for the fans, heart attack material for the players and coaches. We had just scored a late touchdown to tie the game. The defense was about to run out on the field to try and protect the lead.

"Man," I heard John's voice from a few feet away, "this is going to be a real ball breaker."

I looked over at John and he was grinning. He was having the time of his life.

As I said before, John made himself accessible to his players. But if you had something to say, you'd better get it said before Sunday, the one day of the week John would never talk to you. He was so worked up he didn't want to make us nuts. At times, he would go over and sit next to Kenny Stabler in the locker room. I swear they never said a word to each other. They'd just sit there for a couple of minutes immersed in thought. Then John would get up and walk away. I think they got strength just by sitting next to each other.

In terms of excitement, team meetings are on a par with yawning conventions. Show me a player who enjoys team meetings and I'll show you a guy who's caught too many stiff arms. With all his jokes and expressions and gyrations, John made them pass a little quicker. You know the Lite Beer commercials where John is moving a few dozen miles a minute? The Raiders had already seen them. We got a sneak preview at every team meeting.

Right after John was offered a part in his first commercial, he approached me one afternoon. He had already left the staff, but had come by to watch one of our practices. I had already acted in several films and TV shows. John wanted some advice. As usual, he was all enthusiasm.

"Tooz, Tooz," he asked me almost like a little boy, "they're sending me to New York. What should I do? How should I act?"

"Coach," I said, "if I were you, I'd just get out there and be yourself. If you do that, you're going to be a hit."

He did and he was.

John also made his presence known in the locker room. John was not overly big on halftime oration. There were never any "Gipper" speeches. But if we were playing poorly enough, John could definitely get fired up. One game, we got abused in the opening half. It was halftime, we were stinking out the place, and John was steaming.

"I'm sick and tired of this crap," he screamed at us in the locker room. "Let's go out and play some football."

There was momentary silence. Then, in case anyone wasn't listening, he picked up a huge garbage can and threw it halfway across the room into a pack of players. Guys were scrambling out of the way to avoid getting hit. John made his point. We rallied to win the game.

One of the advantages John had in dealing with his players was that he had once played the game himself. Born in Minnesota, raised in the San Francisco Bay area, John was drafted by the Eagles in the twenty-first round of the 1959 draft. He was an offensive guard. In one of his first practices as a rookie, he blew out the ligaments and cartilage in his knee. As John might say—BOOM—his career was in jeopardy.

While he was rehabilitating, John tagged along with Eagle quarterback Norm van Brocklin. From Norm, John began to learn the intricacies of the game. He decided to become a coach. After working at several colleges in the West, John became linebacker coach of the Raiders in 1967. Two years later, John was promoted to head coach. He was only thirty-two years old, one of the youngest head coaches in NFL history.

Except for a handful of exceptions, Steve Ortmayer of the Raiders being a notable one, I disliked playing for coaches who had never played football before. They were useless. They couldn't relate to your suggestions, and they had no idea what really went on out there every Sunday. It's like having a guy who never performed surgery teaching you how to be a surgeon.

I was lucky with the Raiders. I got to play with two of the finest defensive coaches in the game, defensive coordinator Charlie Sumner and defensive line coach Earl Leggett. One of the reaons Al Davis never worked too much with the defensive line was the total trust he had in Charlie and Earl.

There's a funny story about Charlie when he was playing for the Chicago Bears. The other team had a player named Monte Stickles who was notorious for hitting late. On the final play of the game, Charlie ran over to Monte. Then he kicked him in the ass and started running off the field. As the crowd was filing out of the stadium, there was Monte chasing Charlie down the sidelines.

Do coaches intrude too heavily on players' lives? Some do, some don't. A few players need to be constantly watched, but those are rare exceptions. One of my teammates said he used to play for a team whose coaches would call up the players' homes late at night. If a guy was out after a certain hour, he'd get fined. This was in the *off-season*.

Once, during a defensive meeting in Santa Rosa, my whole body felt terrible. I started getting those queasy chills, the ones you get right before you're about to throw up. I stood up, walked to the washroom and began getting reacquainted with my intestines. One of the coaches followed me to the restroom. As I stood there getting ill, he screamed that I should never, ever, leave one of his meetings without first asking.

Besides coaches who won't let you vomit in peace, one of my other pet peeves is coaches who make their players look shabby for their own benefit. This is the worst form of scapegoating. Bill Walsh is one of the brightest coaches in the NFL. One of his actions, though, made me question his ethics.

It was in the fall of 1982, the season after the 49ers won their first Super Bowl. The 49ers were struggling and you started reading in the newspapers these vague insinuations from Walsh that maybe his team was losing because of problems related to drugs. I saw the same quotes in several newspapers. Now wait a minute. That January his players had won the Super Bowl. They were the greatest group of guys in the world. No problems, everybody loves each other. That fall they lose a few games and now they have a drug problem? Was Walsh saying that the very same players who were healthy enough to win the Super Bowl had suddenly developed drug problems several months later? I thought it was illogical, and entirely disrespectful to his players. You didn't hear any players suggesting it was Walsh's coaching that caused the slide. Coaches and owners are always demanding loyalty from their players. It's only fair that it should be reciprocated. By the way, primarily the same cast of 49ers won the Super Bowl again three years ago.

After I read that stuff about Walsh, I recalled a story I'd heard about him from one of his players. He was a veteran starter on the defense who is now retired. When I first heard it, I didn't know whether or not to believe it. After that drug garbage, I figured it could be true. This player said that when Walsh first became coach of the 49ers, he had a great desire for his players to carry him off the field following a win. He really wanted it badly. They were playing regular season games, not a Super Bowl or anything, so of course no one carried him off. Still, Walsh was determined. After a while, he offered a hundred bucks apiece to any of his players who would carry him off the field. A couple of the guys accepted and Walsh got his wish.

That reminds me of the time John Madden got carried off the field. It was seconds after we'd just won the Super Bowl against Minnesota, and we wanted to show John our appreciation. We had already made a plan when it became apparent that we had the game won. If the offense was on the field when the game ended, then a few guys from the defense would carry John off the field on their shoulders. And vice versa. The defense was on the sideline when the final gun went off. Since John isn't exactly Pee Wee Herman, we figured we'd better get some of our biggest defensive players to do it. Charles Philyaw, Teddy and I were elected. We somehow got John balanced on our shoulders and were doing fine. At least until a row of photographers started tripping all over each other. One of us—I think it was Teddy—tripped over one of the falling photographers. I remember thinking, *here is John Madden's proudest moment, and we're going to screw it up.* First Teddy went down with a crash. Then Charles. Then me, but not quite. I fell to one knee. Just as John was about to hit the dirt, I regained my balance and managed to keep him from falling. One of the great clutch catches in history.

For all the fun I had with John, there was one time when I let him down. And not just John, but the entire organization: Al, my teammates and the fans. It was one of the lowest points in my life, an experience I've never related to anyone but my closest friends before.

On New Year's Eve, 1977, the Raiders were readying to play the Denver Broncos the following morning in the AFC Championship game in Denver. The winner would go to the Super Bowl. I got a couple of magazines, some iced teas, a few sandwiches and was in my hotel room by eight o'clock. After I read a little, I tried to go to sleep around nine. No such luck. My body was tired but my mind wouldn't cooperate. I was too pumped up for the game. The previous Saturday night, I'd had the same problem before we had beaten Baltimore in the opening round of the playoffs. Tossing and turning and still no sleep. Finally, I took a couple of sleeping pills and slept like a baby. The next day I played well against the Colts. In fact, I had one of the best games of my career.

Now, on New Year's Eve, it was getting later and I was growing nervous. The last thing I needed was to be lacking sleep in a championship game. Insomnia is a catch-22 disorder. The more you fret and grow anxious, the harder it is to relax and fall asleep. I felt as if I had no choice. I took the same medication I used in Baltimore. This time the results were disastrous.

When my wake-up call came in the morning, I felt like I was in some kind of dream world. My body felt thick and slow. I could barely stumble out of bed. Perhaps it was the mile-high altitude in Denver. For whatever reason, I could not shake my lethargy. I drank some coffee and walked around. I took an ice-cold shower. I drank some more coffee. I paced some more. Nothing helped.

I got pushed around badly in the opening half. It was like the world had suddenly been speeded up. I worked as hard as I could but my reflexes wouldn't respond. I'm lucky I didn't get trampled out there. As if the situation wasn't grim enough, the field was frozen like ice. I felt helpless as I skidded along.

I started waking up in the second half. I began to hold my own. We lost, though, 20–17. The Broncos went to the Super Bowl. I approached John Madden after the game. I wanted to apologize and explain what happened. When John looked up and saw me, his face was twisted by fury. He didn't say a word. He just turned and walked away. He probably figured I'd been up all night partying. I wasn't, but he had no way to know that.

I felt like the loneliest person in the world. It was the only game in my career when I wasn't prepared to play football. Yes, I used to play hard off the field. But anyone on the Raiders will tell you that I was always all business when it came to games and practices. I'm not so arrogant to think that I was the only reason we lost to the Broncos. I do know that I had the worst performance of my life in a game for a chance to play in the Super Bowl. I had not held up my end. For a long time I blamed myself for that defeat. I was haunted by it. I whipped myself with guilt.

They say if you look hard enough you can find something good in even the worst of moments. For several months after that game, I would never have believed that. But eventually I did find something positive.

The grief I felt after that game made me realize, irrevocably, how much playing football meant to me. If I had screwed up, felt bad, then forgotten it a week or two later, then obviously I wasn't that committed to begin with. But the hurt and regret I felt was genuine. I began to see that football was more than just the way I made my living. It was my passion, what I was all about.

The Denver game made me see something else: that my feelings for the Raiders ran deep. By playing so poorly, of course,

I had let myself down. But the thing that bothered me the most was that I felt as if I'd let down the Raiders. The Raiders had signed me when my career was in shambles. When the rest of the league felt I wasn't worth the trouble to have around. For that they deserved my best.

Even though my actions had been purely accidental, I still felt lousy. Over time, that game would have a profound effect on me. It made me more serious about my job, clarified my priorities. It helped me grow up.

————

In 1979, John Madden retired. Some people suggested that he retired because he was tired of Al Davis looking over his shoulder. That's nonsense. Al and John were one of the most successful owner-coach alliances in NFL history. They didn't just respect each other's knowledge, they enjoyed each other as friends. Al never looked for yes men and that's one of the reasons he admired John. When John thought Al was wrong, he wouldn't hesitate to tell him. They made a super team.

The season before John quit, the Raiders failed to make the playoffs for the first time in seven years. John developed a bleeding ulcer. He was practically living on Maalox and Rolaids, but his ulcer wasn't responding. I didn't know John was ill at the time because he never told us. I knew something was bothering him though. He seemed weary. He still jumped up and down and carried on, but only once in a while. He'd lost some of his joy for the game.

The ulcer wasn't the only reason John retired. He missed spending time with his family. One of the things that burns the coaches of the Raiders is the perception that the team just gets out there every Sunday and wings it, as if we played sandlot football or something. I know for a fact that the coaches of the Raiders work as hard as or harder than any staff in the league. If you work for Al Davis, you damn well better be prepared. Tom Flores says that his friends are always amazed when they call him for lunch and he doesn't have time to go.

John has a beautiful wife and two sons. He wanted to get reacquainted. John tells about the time his wife reminded him he had promised to buy his son Mike a truck when he was old enough to drive. John said fine, but what's the rush? Mike wouldn't be 16 for four more years. Virginia informed him that Mike would be 16 in four more months.

There was one more factor in John's decision. On August 12, 1978, in an exhibition game against the Patriots, Darryl Stingley ran a crossing pattern over the middle of the field. Steve Grogan overfired and Darryl leaped through the air to try and make the catch. Just then Jack Tatum smashed into Darryl. Jack is the fiercest hitter I've ever seen. It was the kind of legal yet crushing hit I'd seen him deliver many times in the past. Although an official was standing right there, he didn't call a penalty. Because there hadn't been one.

Darryl didn't get up. He lay there on the ground, unmoving. I was on the field that play. I turned around just as Darryl got hit. I was praying that he would get up. He couldn't. His neck was broken in two places and his spinal cord was seriously damaged.

Darryl Stingley and I played in the All-Star game together when we were both rookies. He's a good man and he was a brilliant receiver. I pray for him whenever I can. But Jack Tatum did not hurt Darryl intentionally. It was an accident, a tragic accident. Later in this book I will discuss the violence of pro football. For now I will say that Jack Tatum did that day what he'd been taught to do since high school: to hit. That's the business and that's the game. It's also why he made All-Conference three times. Guys who can hit are valuable commodities.

Jack got brutalized by the press after the injury, partly because everyone thought he never went to see Darryl in the hospital. My understanding is that Jack did try to see Darryl in the hospital but was told that he couldn't. Jack got the idea that Darryl's family didn't really want him around. Some folks said Jack didn't show any remorse. Of course he did. Jack was extremely shook up after that game. He walked around in a daze, and I'm sure he has never gotten over it since. Every player on the Raiders was terribly disturbed and heartbroken.

But no one more than John. After Darryl got injured, John was at the hospital immediately after the game. Darryl stayed at that hospital in Castro Valley, California, for the next two months, and John visited him constantly. Darryl's wife, Tina, would come to the Madden's home for dinner. A few weeks after the tragedy, the day we lost to the Broncos in the regular season opener, John flew directly back to Oakland and went to visit Darryl.

Along with his health and his family to consider, Darryl's injury confused John even more. It pained him to see such a fine young man confined to a wheelchair. John said he just couldn't see going through another season. On the day he retired, John called a press conference.

"I'm not resigning," he said, "quitting to do anything else. I'm retiring. I'll never coach another game of football. I gave it everything I had for ten years, and I don't have any more."

It was one of the saddest days in the history of the Raiders. John was one of a kind.

John's replacement was Tom Flores. Tom had been with the organization as a receivers coach since 1972. Except for when he was injured, he was the team's starting quarterback from 1960 to 1967. The first year was difficult for Tom. Not only was he trying to succeed a legend, but one with a radically different style. Tom is a softspoken man. His emotions rarely show. While John would bluster on the sidelines, Tom always remained impassive. Arms folded, intently staring straight ahead. The players had some trouble adjusting. We missed the Madden fire.

Tom and I never established much of a bond. John had a soft spot for the men who played in the pit. Even today as an announcer, he goes out of his way to mention the offensive and defensive linemen. John was a guard himself and I guess he feels a certain kinship. Tom was a quarterback and then a receivers coach. He was closer to the players on offense. Under John, our practices had always been tough but fun. There was a lot of yelling and whooping by the defense. One practice with Tom I was yapping away, trying to get the defense fired up. Tom looked at me and told me to shut up. I was making too much noise, too close to their huddle or something. So I just shut up. A few minutes later Tom looked at me and said, "Well, you don't have to be that quiet." For a while I resented Tom. I thought he was out of line for telling me to shut up in front of my teammates. We were never the best of friends after that.

I had respect for Tom, though, which is all a coach really needs from his players. Tom was always fair and honest with me. Although it's hard to tell on the surface, Tom hates to lose. It's one of the reasons Al hired him. And in his eight years as head coach of the Raiders, he's won two Super Bowls. In football, winning is the bottom line.

3

I WASN'T BORN THE TOOZ

When people hear about my first few years in the NFL—the controversies, the rebellions—they automatically assume I must have been a little mad dog when I was a child. The reality of my youth was something entirely different. I was a peaceful kid. I never saw a day of reform school, and the only time I used a knife was to cut a steak. I got into a couple of fights in the schoolyard but only if I was seriously provoked. Trapped inside a big, awkward body was a shy young boy struggling with his self-esteem. Looking back, I suppose my childhood could best be described as bittersweet. There were great, uncomplicated times I'll cherish forever, but there was also heartache.

I was born on October 25, 1950. I was the oldest child, followed by three younger sisters. My family lived on the south side of Milwaukee until I was ten. It was an urban area, close to downtown, and to me it always seemed so alive. Milwaukee doesn't have the commerce or cosmopolitanism of Chicago— which is ninety miles to the south—but with more than 611,000 people it's the eighteenth largest American city. One of Milwaukee's greatest charms is its ethnic diversity, its neighborhoods. Although Poles and Germans predominate, there are smaller doses of Italians, blacks, Irish, Jews, Latins and almost anything else you can think of. I loved the south side of Milwaukee when I was a child but I never really thought about why. Now I know. It was blue-collar, hard-working America. It was real.

My world caved in when I was ten. My mom came home one day and announced that we were moving out of the city. She said we were buying a house in Oak Creek, a woodsy suburb about fourteen miles from the city. My father—who worked at the electric company power plant—had been transferred to the plant in Oak Creek, and moving would cut down the drive. Besides, my parents had always wanted a house, and there was a cozy one for sale that would suit us perfectly. So we were moving. And that, basically, was that.

Oak Creek? *Oak Creek?* What the hell was that? When we got to Oak Creek, my fears were confirmed. Milwaukee may not have been Manhattan, but at least it was City. Oak Creek was fourteen miles away but it seemed to me like Siberia. Oak Creek was country. Rural. Boring. Here I was this city kid, and now I'm supposed to be some kind of Huckleberry Finn. In place of the cheese and sausage and beer shops downtown, there was one little general store. There was no downtown. There were wide open spaces instead of gravel playgrounds. Worst of all, it was so damn quiet. Would somebody please make some noise?

I should have been happy for my parents. Owning a home is the American dream, and they had finally made it. And I knew, all too well, how hard my father worked. But like most children, I had tunnel vision. All I could think about was leaving my friends. For a long time I resisted the move. I would take my old Schwinn bicycle and ride all the way back to visit my pals in the city. It was an agonizing ride, fourteen miles of mostly hills, but I was too irate to care. Who wanted to live in the country?

Today I can see that moving to Oak Creek was good for me. For one thing, it was harder to get into trouble. Milwaukee has its share of gangs, and I'm not certain I wouldn't have gotten mixed up with them as I grew older and more wild. Oak Creek really was a nice place to be a kid. The air was clean, and people were warm and happy with what they had. We even bought a dog. Moving to Oak Creek also got me heavily involved in sports. There was nothing much else to do.

At first, though, I hated it. You see, there were other complications entering into my life. Just after we moved to Oak Creek, my body started growing at an extraordinary rate. Every time I would get comfortable with it, it would go and shoot up on me again. Children are always hung up about their appearance. My insecurities came from my height.

Physically, I matured much earlier than the other kids. I was six foot one by the time I was twelve, 6′ 4″ by the time I was fifteen. When I first realized I was taller than all of my classmates, I began to take note of adults who were unusually tall. I didn't like what I saw. They always seemed to be too thin or too fat. And they always hunched over when they walked, like they were embarrassed and regretful about their height. There was one adult in our neighborhood who was extremely tall and everyone called him Tiny. I thought that was terrible. I never wanted to look or feel like some sort of freak. I actually prayed that I would stop growing.

But I just kept getting taller. And the taller I got, the more I felt isolated from my schoolmates. Figuratively and literally, I always stuck out from the crowd. I wasn't just tall, I was very, very skinny. My body made me uneasy—I always felt people were staring at me, making fun of the way I looked. Some of the slights were probably imagined, but a lot of times they were real. Kids would come up and call me stringbean, ask me how the weather was up there, ask me what it was like to be the Jolly Green Giant. One day, after several children had made fun of me at school, I ran home and locked my bedroom door. I remember staring into a mirror and agreeing with my tormentors: I really did look unusual.

I didn't want that much out of Oak Creek, just to be one of the guys, the way I used to be in Milwaukee. It never worked out that way. When there would be pickup football or basketball games, at times the other children wouldn't let me play because they thought I was so much older. Or their mothers told them I would hurt them. They made me very aware of the fact that I was somehow different. When I got older, I liked the idea of being different; I considered it a strength. As a child, all it did was hurt me.

There were other things to divide me from my peers. My father is Polish and my mother is part English and part Irish. They're both from Wisconsin, both Catholic, my mother converting when they were married. In Milwaukee they had sent me to a Catholic school. There was a rule: Whenever the priest would walk in at the start of class, all the children were to stand until he was seated. I got conditioned. When I moved to Oak Creek my parents enrolled me in a public school. The principal walked in our class the first day of school, and I stood straight up in my seat. I stayed there until he sat down, then I sat down. The room broke out in hysterics. I felt like a clown.

Things got worse before they got better. That summer I got chosen in a sandlot baseball game. With my height they probably figured I could kill the ball. But I had never played baseball in my life and I was lost. The first time I came up, the pitcher purposely threw the ball three feet over my head. I swung and missed. Everyone thought that was funny as hell. He pitched the ball over my head two more times. Two more times I swung and missed. I struck out all three times I batted. Not so much as one foul tip. Each time the kids all laughed. I was getting sick of it. I ran all the way home and did what I normally did when I needed someone to console me. I looked for my mother.

In some ways my mom was my closest friend when I was a child. No matter how consumed I became by fear or anger, she was always there to listen. Every time she saw me slouching, she would admonish me to stand up straight. Whenever I was feeling down, she would pump me back up. My mom had her own worries, but she'd put them aside to listen to mine.

I got my spontaneity from my mom, also the side of me that's extroverted. My mom is one of those people who loves to try new things and she's extremely outgoing and chatty. And she genuinely cares about other people.

Part of the reason I always confided in my mother is that she was usually around to confide in. Now she works in a drug store, but then she mostly took care of the children. My father was always working like crazy when I was a kid. His presence was always felt—there was always the knowledge that there was a man in the house—but much more of my time was spent with my mother.

When I was twelve, my mom came through again. I was watching a Steve Reeves movie—it was *Hercules*—and I couldn't believe how strong and good he looked. I figured if I could somehow get tall and muscular, rather than scrawny, my height would be a plus instead of a nightmare. It was Christmas time and I asked my mother for a set of weights. My father wanted to buy me some history books, but my mom talked him into getting me the weights. Along with the weights, my parents also bought me some protein drinks which I drank every day. After just two months, I was astonished—as I looked in the mirror I began to see a different person. Suddenly I had muscles, my legs and arms no longer looked like sticks. Girls who had never given me the time of day were now checking me out. Guys who had been all over my ass now were curiously friendly. Buying those weights was one of the turning points of my childhood. They helped me begin to like myself.

As my body grew, so did my interest in sports. The first time I played football was in eighth grade, and it didn't take me long to see that I had tremendous potential. It all seemed to come together on two consecutive plays, in a game at the end of the season. We were on offense and our quarterback threw a pass that was about a foot over my head. I leaped up, caught the ball, stiff-armed a defender and ran eighty yards for a touchdown. On the next play I kicked off and the ball sailed all the way to their goal line. Their deep man caught the ball and started upfield. I sprinted downfield, shed a couple of blockers, grabbed the ballcarrier with one hand and tackled him at the fifteen yard line. I couldn't believe it myself, it was almost scary.

After the game, I was walking off the field when a couple of girls ran up and started talking to me. They were pretty and bright, eighth grade girls I recognized from school. I'd never even dreamed of starting a conversation with them. Now they were walking up to me!

At Oak Creek High I kept getting better. My senior year, starting at tight end and defensive end, I caught about twenty-six passes, scored six touchdowns and was the only player on my team to be named all-conference. High school football was another giant step in establishing my sense of worth. As a stranger moving to Oak Creek, I had felt like a loner, like I was always on the outside looking in. Now everyone courted my company. Their motives didn't matter. When you're a teenager, you don't care much *why* people like you, you're just relieved that they do. I was searching for some identity and respect, and I began to see I could get it from playing football. I had no idea how far the sport would eventually take me, but I liked what it had done so far. I became obsessed with improving.

For all the respect I was getting at school, my life at home still had a large, gaping hole. For my entire life, if there was one person I wanted to impress, it was my father. I suspect most men feel the same way. But when I was a child, my father's admiration never came.

Much of it came down to a fundamental difference of opinion. I felt that my future, or at the very least, my present, lay in sports. Although my father never said it in so many words, I could see he thought I was living a pipe dream. He felt I would be much better off concentrating on my schooling. When I look back, I realize how sound my father's thinking was. So many children devote their time to sports instead of school and wind up paying for it the rest of their lives. I was the incredibly rare exception to the rule. My father was doing what he thought best—trying to help me make something of myself. Now I can see that. At the time, my thinking was not so clear.

My father was never a talkative man, and it seemed to me the only conversations we ever had were about my grades. If I had been a better student, that would have been great. My father would have had something to be proud of. But I wasn't. I graduated from high school with a grade point average of 1.7, which is equivalent to a C−. As a result, my performance at school was the last thing I wanted to discuss. I'd come home all pumped up and happy about the touchdown I'd scored that day, and my dad would tear into me about the D I got on my history exam. All that talk about my failings made me feel incompetent and humiliated. I resented my father for constantly bringing it up.

I felt bad about my grades too. Mainly because I knew I was bright and capable of doing better. I had always loved to read so I knew that wasn't the problem. My greatest fault was that I rarely paid attention during lectures. I was too much of a dreamer. In some ways it was good. I've always believed that you'll accomplish much more if you're not afraid to shoot for the stars. In the summer I would sit and stare at the clouds, fantasizing about all the great things I'd make happen in the future. Some of those dreams have come true. The problem was, I'd do the same thing in class. I'd be following the teacher when my mind would begin to drift. I'd start dreaming about making some spectacular play on the football field or on the basketball court. Class would end and I hadn't digested a thing.

Sports were so much different, the one area where I could feel good about myself, where I didn't have to apologize or make excuses. If I couldn't make my father proud of my school work, I at least wanted him to feel good about my prowess as an athlete. I was like any other young boy: I wanted to be able to share something with my father. I wanted to come home after practice and throw the ball around with him in the yard. I wanted him to come to my games and cheer for me. While I was in high school, I also played on the basketball and the track and field teams. I averaged twenty-four points a game in the second half of my senior basketball season, and the same year I was state champion in the shot put and discus. There was talk that I could have thrown the discus someday in the Olympics, but I was too preoccupied with football. All of this was lost on the man who mattered to me most. During four years of high school sports, my father came to one of my events, a football game. One event in four years. That hurt me. My mom was often there—she would follow me everywhere—but it wasn't enough. After our games, I used to watch the other players as they embraced their mothers *and* fathers in the parking lot. I wondered if *they* wondered where my father was.

I didn't just want to impress my father, I *needed* to. I knew he was working hard, I knew he didn't want to show any interest in my sports because he felt I was wasting my time. I knew all of that, and still I felt rotten. There was a terrible void in my life, one I feared I would never be able to fill. In retrospect, I think my father's absence affected me later when I became a young man. It left me angry, frustrated, maybe a little mean. It put a chip on my shoulder that would be difficult for me to lose.

Much of my father's own childhood was stolen from him—he was an adult before he knew it. Two years before the Korean War, my father and his twin brother were stationed in China with the United States Marines. They were only seventeen. When they returned from the Marines, they learned that their father had divorced their mother and was now living in a tiny apartment that had no room for two young men. As they scrambled to find the money for an apartment, there were nights when they slept in their car.

My father's childhood made him hard. And like his own father, my father would become a man who rarely showed affection toward his children. In that respect, he wasn't that different from my friends' fathers. Today, times have changed, but back then men showing affection was largely considered a sign of weakness. I knew my father loved me, but I could see he never felt comfortable trying to express it. For affection I went to my mother.

My father was hot-blooded before he ever put on a uniform, and the Marines just reinforced that. When he wanted to, my father could project a serious sense of menace. He was 6′1″ and 180 pounds, not all *that* big, but he had a temper that could frighten people much larger. When he was mad he was the quickest man I've ever seen. Usually he was mellow and that temper didn't surface often, but when it did it would scare the hell out of me. He would explode so *suddenly,* it was like watching another person.

When I was twelve, my father and I were driving past a construction site. One of the construction workers shouted something obscene at my father for no reason at all. Maybe he was a little drunk. My father slammed on the brakes.

"Who said that?" my father yelled out the window. "Did someone say something to me?"

Then my father was out of the car. There were about five guys, all pretty tough looking, but I was more worried for them than I was for my dad. My dad had that look in his eyes. My father walked right up to them. His back was turned to the car and I never heard what was said. But the expressions on the faces of the men told me everything I needed to know. They looked absolutely intimidated. They had my father badly outnumbered, but nobody said a word to him. And nobody made a move when he turned and walked back to the car.

That memory stayed with me, and it was the best damn reason I could think of to keep myself in line. When I did screw up, my father would beat my behind with a strap. Or he would suddenly snatch me and hold me up against a wall. Those times were infrequent though. Had I been a wiseass kid I'm sure I would have spent most of my childhood with a sore behind. As it was I rarely got hit, probably because I was never dumb enough to talk back to Dad or my mom. I recall my father getting really mad at me once, but I don't remember what it was for. He kicked me in the ass as I was walking up a flight of stairs and I swear I flew up a couple of steps. I was about twelve years old and I walked around the house wearing a pout. Some time later my father came to my room and he sat on my bed. He said he hadn't meant to kick me so hard, but sometimes children needed to be reminded of their manners. He told me I was still a little boy and when I was thirteen years old I would be a man. When I was thirteen, my father promised, he would never hit me again. He never did. Not once.

Even before then, I knew my father had a warm side. I used to see it whenever he was with my sisters or my mother. My mother and father were deeply in love. I know a lot of people who are still disturbed by memories of their parents fighting. I was fortunate. In the seventeen years I lived with my mom and dad, I can recall just one argument. Now that's an amazing statistic. My mother was pregnant and needed the car, and my father was off somewhere using it. My father never cared for liquor, but that night he came home smelling of it. My mom tied into him pretty good, and I heard my dad say he was leaving. I was cowering in my bedroom trying to fight off the tears. I ran downstairs and hugged my mom. I told her not to worry, that I would take care of her and the girls. Later that night my father came back home and everything was back to normal.

I had a lot of authority figures when I was a child. My father, the priests at Catholic school, my high school coaches. I was extremely lucky—they were all the salt of the earth. I know full well that I'm a better person for the values they gave me. But when I was younger—a child with ideas of his own— they represented authority. And even if they said something I disagreed with, I kept my silence because that's what children were taught to do. I've been asked by many writers: Once I got out on my own—distanced from those authority figures—was some of the trouble I got into a delayed act of rebellion? It's a good question, one there's no easy answer for. I mean, I didn't go around thinking, "All right Dad, all right Father, all right Coach, this fuckup is for you." I never *consciously* tried to strike out at anyone. Subconsciously, well, it's impossible for me to say.

———

The distance between my father and me was in many ways un- avoidable. He was always so busy working. For many years he worked twelve, sometimes sixteen-hour days. He used to work two jobs, and he'd still take overtime whenever he could get it. His primary job was at the electric company, where he's worked for the past thirty-five years. He also used to work at a tire store. Some days he'd come home from the power plant and go right back to work at the tire store.

Today my father is a supervisor at the electric company, but when he began there he worked on the turbines and the boilers. My father used to work on what's called a shift system. For one week he'd work from seven in the morning to three in the after- noon. Then we'd get to spend some time. For the next week he'd work from three in the afternoon until eleven at night. Then I'd never see him. The next shift was from eleven at night until seven in the morning. He'd sleep during the day. When I'd come home from school, we'd all have to be quiet so we wouldn't wake him up. I wouldn't see much of him then either. Working those kinds of shifts was murder on the employees' systems. Their body clocks were constantly in a state of chaos. The families complained for years, but the electric company said it couldn't do anything about it. Roughly four years ago, the company began giving the men steady shifts. It wasn't soon enough. Many of the men had already suffered heart attacks.

My father was one of those men. He had his first heart attack a few years ago. Then he had another and, finally, a triple bypass surgery. I was so frightened I felt as if I couldn't move. There were so many things I still wanted to say to him.

My father recovered beautifully. Today I see a change in him. He's much more relaxed with himself. It's terrible, but it seems like so many men begin to mellow only after they've experienced a failure of their health. This was only partly true with my father. Even before his heart attacks, my father was already learning how to unwind. His children were all grown up and the financial pressure on him wasn't so great. Today he takes a three-mile walk in the country every day. That's something I never saw him do when I was younger. I think it's fantastic. He's finally got a chance to breathe.

My relationship with my father has a happy ending. In the last ten years, we've been making up for all that lost time. Our relationship began to warm up when I graduated from college with a B average. That made my father feel as if I'd accomplished something important, as if all of his lectures hadn't been wasted. He tried to make up for all those games of mine he missed in high school. He and my mom once drove all the way to Iowa to see me play in a junior college game. Sitting beneath nothing more than a small piece of plastic, they watched the entire game through a pouring rain. I was worried about them catching a cold, but I was also so happy I wanted to burst. Later, when I became a pro, my mom says she couldn't pry Dad from the set whenever the Raiders were on. It took a hell of a long time, but today we can finally share in each other's success.

I've got tremendous respect for my father. He's one of the most relentless providers that I've ever met. I see now that his working habits were certainly not by choice. Money was in short supply around my house; vacations and luxuries were something we rarely knew. Primarily, my father worked so hard for one painful reason: to pay the family's hospital bills.

My family has a history of cystic fibrosis, an inherited disease that interferes with breathing and digestion. Basically, the disease builds up so much mucous that the lungs can't perform their vital functions. CF is the leading genetic killer of children and young adults in the United States. Today the average lifetime expectancy of a person with CF is nineteen years. But this is a gain that's been made only in the past decade. Before then it was closer to nine or ten.

My two little brothers were hospitalized and eventually died from CF. My sister, Dawn, who is 25, also has CF. She's been in and out of hospitals, fighting it all her life. People don't come any tougher than Dawn and she's absolutely precious to me. So are my other sisters Karen and Christine. They all know I'd do anything in the world for them.

When my first brother, Christopher, was born, I was seven years old. I was beside myself with joy. I had always wanted a little brother. I couldn't wait for him to grow up so I could teach him how to play sports. Christopher died when he was two months old.

After Christopher's death I became confused. I spent a lot of time alone, up in my room, trying to figure things out. It was the only time in my life I started to question my belief in God. I had always believed what they told me in church, but now I had so many questions. The priests said that God was just, that He watched and protected all His children. If my family was so devoted, then why was He punishing us? Why had He stolen away my only little brother? And why had He broken my parents' hearts? I felt so helpless. It all seemed so unfair.

Five years later my parents had another son. His name was David and he had beautiful blond hair. He used to knock on my door and want to listen to records with me. Ninety-nine percent of the time I'd let him in, but a few times I wanted to be alone and I would tell him to come back later. The entire family was delighted at David's birth, but deep down I think all of us were a little scared. David died of CF when he was two. After he died, I beat myself with guilt. I could never appreciate the good times. All I could think about were those times I wouldn't let David into my room.

David had an open casket at his funeral. When my dad looked inside, he saw that his little shoes were old and all scuffed up. My dad didn't want David to look that way. He asked me to walk to a nearby store and buy David some shoes that would fit. When I got to the store, the owner looked at the shoes and said that my brother was obviously growing too fast, and that's why the shoes were worn out. He told me I'd have to bring my brother in if I wanted him to get a pair that would fit right. I just told him I couldn't and would he please give me a pair one size larger. As I walked back to the church with the shoes, I broke down crying. Why would God hurt my family twice?

For many years it would pain me to be around children. I loved their company but afterward, when I was alone, I would get depressed. Then one year with the Raiders I played Santa Claus at the Children's Hospital in Oakland. One by one these tiny little children would come and crawl on my lap. I was just one big bundle of emotions, but it was the sweetest feeling in the world. Ever since then I've spent a lot of time working with charities and children.

Although I now live in Los Angeles, I go back to Oak Creek to see my family for about two months out of every year. I own four and a half acres of farmland just outside of Oak Creek, with a beautiful ten-room house sitting in the middle of it. My sister Christine lives there, with her husband and my two little nephews. Sometimes when I see her little boys, I think of the little brothers I had for such a short time.

But I still thank God for what I've got—two loving parents and three beautiful sisters. And a family that sticks together through anything.

4

COLLEGE KID

When I graduated from Oak Creek High in 1968, I had more than just a big body. I had big ambitions. The NFL was still a distant vision but I felt I was good enough to play major college football. The future looked bright.

During my senior year I had been approached by several small schools and a pair of big ones, the universities of Wisconsin and Iowa. My first choice was Iowa. I wanted to leave the state of Wisconsin, explore what else was out there. Iowa was about 400 miles from home, close enough to visit frequently, but far enough to have some freedom. And the people in Iowa were interested in me. At least, that is, until they saw my grades. A 1.7 grade point average, they told me, doesn't cut it at a Big Ten school.

I was crushed. After hundreds of hours in the weight room and at practice, it was all in danger of leading to nothing. I was scrambling for ideas when I got a call from one of the coaches at Iowa. He told me about a junior college named Fort Dodge. He said they would offer me a scholarship. He said I could play football there and also improve my grades. After a year, he said, I could transfer to a larger school. I didn't jump out of my seat, but I also wasn't about to turn it down. My parents were always there when I needed them. With a scholarship I had a chance to help ease their financial burden. And whether it was

Notre Dame or Penn State or Fort Dodge, it was still college football. I had only one question—where the hell was Fort Dodge?

Fort Dodge is in central Iowa. It is a sedate, simple little town, by then something I was used to. In my year at Fort Dodge, I was like any other college freshman: The pursuit of beer and coeds was never too far from my mind. But most of my time was spent concentrating on football and school. I knew I'd have to do well at both if I wanted to leave central Iowa. And I did. I got a B average at Fort Dodge and I played good football. I was all-conference tight end and (small school) honorable mention All-American. Toward the middle of my freshman season, the big-time schools came shopping around.

Although I was still leaning toward Iowa, Dan Devine and the University of Missouri was pursuing me heavily. They would fly coaches to Fort Dodge and take me out for beautiful steak dinners. That's exactly where the generosity ended. There were no long cars, no hundreds stashed in brown paper bags, no blonde bombshells responding to my every whim. A lot has been made lately about illegal recruiting in college. And it's definitely out of hand. I, however, cannot add anything lurid to this particular topic. My recruiting was all by the book. Dan Devine had his share of faults, but as far as I know, his recruiting methods were squeaky clean. I never received a penny as a college athlete.

I decided to play for Missouri and Devine.

Dan Devine is a complicated man, a difficult person to get a handle on. He was nothing like John Madden, a what-you-see-is-what-you-get type. With Devine, you never knew which side of him to expect. Would it be the theatrical, fire-and-brimstone extrovert who threw temper tantrums to get his players motivated? Or the unapproachable brooder who was about as passionate and affable as a loaf of bread? The man was obviously intelligent and capable. He could also be terribly distant. Joe Moore, one of his players, put it best. He didn't know Devine one bit better when he walked out after four years, as a graduating senior, than he had the day he first walked into Devine's office as a freshman.

At first my relationship with Devine was smooth. But once the honeymoon ended, he wasn't the same smiling man who had recruited me. On the practice field he was prone to sudden fits of anger. If they were justified they never bothered me. One time he went off for no reason. That was the time he hit me.

I was playing tight end and we were working on a running play. The halfback was coming through my hole, I missed my block, and he got nailed by the tackler I missed. I felt bad, but it wasn't the first or the last time I would make a mistake on a football field. Mistakes are part of the game. Devine felt differently. He came rushing down from his coach's tower as if I'd just insulted his mother. He ran up and slapped me—fairly hard—on the side of my head. I was shocked. I wasn't hurt, of course, but who the hell was this guy to slap me in the head? Even my father never slapped me in the head.

Devine was oblivious to my anger. He went on yelling and eventually returned to his seat. The matter was quickly forgotten, as it should have been. I mean, it wasn't that big a deal. But if I had done the same thing to Devine, Walter Cronkite would have led with it on the evening news.

Some coaches are consistent in their approach to motivating players. Not Devine. Sometimes he'd say virtually nothing before a game, other times he'd make these grandiose speeches. Some of them were pretty comical. *Sports Illustrated* ran a story about the time Missouri was preparing for a game against Nebraska in 1967. The year before, Nebraska had routed Missouri by more than thirty points. Adding insult to injury, the Nebraska band had played the same song over and over the entire game: "There Is No Place Like Nebraska." Before the rematch, Devine played the song all week in the locker room. He was trying to annoy his players, get them so irritated they would destroy the Cornhuskers. On the day of the game, Devine walked into the locker room with a 45 record in his hand. It was "There Is No Place Like Nebraska." He told the guys that he never wanted to hear that song again as long as he lived. With the players watching his every move, Devine took the record and flung it to the floor. But it didn't break. So he did it again. Again, it remained intact. By now he was manning a sinking ship. Finally he took the record and, with all his might, tried ripping it to shreds. He never quite broke it, but he eventually managed to bend it a little. Finally he threw the record out a window and stalked from the dressing room an embarrassed shade of red. The Tigers won that game, by the way, 10–7. If there's a moral in there somewhere, please don't ask me what it is.

My own feelings toward Devine were becoming increasingly muddled, particularly after our game against Notre Dame. Never in my life had I been so pumped up for a football game. Notre Dame's football program has taken a beating in recent years, but this was back when the Irish were thriving. Just beating them could make another team's season. For me, playing Notre Dame was more personal. Almost every Catholic football player dreams of playing for the Irish. I never even tried because I knew my grades weren't good enough. But it was a huge thrill just to play against them.

As we were about to run onto the field, Devine strode into the locker room. He had this very solemn look on his face, his pep talk look. The room fell quiet as the players crowded around.

"Boys," Devine began, "I had a dream last night."

Already there were smiles spreading across the locker room. Everyone knew what was coming next. He'd had this dream, and in his dream we beat the crap out of Notre Dame. But we were wrong. This time Devine outdid himself.

"And in my dream," he continued, "I spoke with God. And boys, God told me we were going to beat Notre Dame today."

Devine paused for effect.

"Now go get 'em boys."

Well, this was the biggest bunch of garbage I'd ever heard in my life. A few minutes earlier, everyone had been wearing his game face. Now we were biting our lips to keep from laughing. A few guys looked like they might wet their pants.

Devine's remarks startled and angered me. It wasn't that I felt I was holier than thou. It was the realization that Devine would obviously go to any lengths—including forfeiting his credibility—to try and win a football game. It was the most bizarre statement I've ever heard from the mouth of a football coach.

I was also disappointed in Devine for a more selfish reason. He didn't have me starting. Although I was only a sophomore, I felt I was the best tight end they had. At first, so did the coaches. Throughout spring practice I ran with the first team offense. Then I got demoted one day at practice. Diving for an overthrown pass, I landed directly on my shoulder. This was no minor bruise, this was the real thing. I knew I was hurt. But I didn't want to give up my starting position, so I kept it to myself and continued playing. I found out later that I had suffered a minor separation of my shoulder. It was an injury that would plague me for years. And it would not be the last foolish decision I made regarding my body.

Trying to hit people when your shoulder is on fire is difficult, at best, and my blocking suffered accordingly. Since I was afraid to tell anyone about the injury, I guess it appeared to the coaches as if I just wasn't hustling. After an unsuccessful block, my tight-end coach started yelling at me.

"You're second team now, pal," he snapped. "You can just start lining up with them."

When we played Colorado in the third game of the season, I was still second string. I wasn't discouraged though. I knew I was better than the guy in front of me, and it was only a matter of time before I would return to the starting lineup. In the meantime, I'd make the best of the playing time I got. Besides, it was October 25, my birthday. You have to be up for your birthday.

Late in the game Devine put me in. They immediately called a running play through my hole. There was a big defensive end lined up over me. I knew I'd have to deliver my block just right if I was going to move him. On the snap of the ball I fired out of my stance. I made a beautiful block. I straightened him up and had him rocking back on his feet. Then I did what the coaches always harp on—I kept on driving him out of the ball-carrier's path. I drove him hard, right onto his back. Most guys, when they get their butt kicked, are content to try and do better on the following play. Not this guy. Maybe he was trying to save face in front of his teammates. Maybe he was just nuts. He jumped up and took a swing at me. There's a cardinal rule in sports. Never take the second punch. It's the only one the refs ever see, and it's the one that always gets the penalty. But there's a serious flaw in that thinking. When someone is messing with your face, the last thing on your mind is cardinal rules. So I swung back. I missed, the refs did not. I was tossed out of the game for flagrantly throwing a punch.

I was still steaming after the game when Devine ran up to me in the locker room. He could barely spit out the words.

"Any more incidents like that," he hissed, "and you're removed from this team. We don't care for behavior like that at the University of Missouri."

I stood in silence because I didn't want to say something I would later regret. But I was livid. Fights happen every day in football games. We used to have fights at practice a few times a week, and Devine never seemed too upset. I was perplexed over his sudden attack of self-righteousness. It was okay to fight at practice, it was fine for a coach to crack one of his players in the head, but it was unacceptable to fire back against a guy who'd just taken a swipe at you. After the Notre Dame game, I began to think that maybe Devine was a hypocrite. Now I was sure of it.

It wasn't the best way to start a birthday, but there was nothing I could do about what had already happened. I figured I'd try and make up for it at practice the following week. I belonged to the Sigma Chi fraternity and our house was cohosting a party that night with another fraternity. I would be going with my girlfriend and I knew she would boost my spirits. The game had gone all wrong, but it looked as if I could at least enjoy the last few hours of my birthday. I've never been more wrong.

We were at the party about thirty minutes when my girlfriend said she had to use the restroom. I glanced around the room to see who I recognized. When I swung my head back toward the restroom, I saw this guy talking to my date. He was clearly hammered on cocktails, weaving back and forth and lurching over. After my girlfriend continued to the restroom, I didn't give the guy a second thought. A lot of people get drunk at frat parties.

When she walked back out, I couldn't believe what I was seeing. The little bastard had reached out, and was pawing at my girlfriend's groin. She was trying to back away, but he had her cornered.

I didn't think, I reacted. I ran over, pushed him away, and then I hit him. I caught him twice, with a right and then a left. He collapsed in a corner, and when he didn't get up, I went back over to my girlfriend. I figured the little pervert would have a bloody nose, maybe two black eyes, and would deserve every bit of it. Who the fuck did this guy think he was?

In the morning the news was terrible. I had done a hell of a lot more than just bloody this guy's nose. The attacker, who I learned was an air force cadet, had eighteen fractures in his face, and it took ten hours of surgery to put him back together. He was planning to press charges.

I sat in my room and wanted to cry. What on earth had I done? I balled up my fists and I stared at them. They looked frightening, even to me. I was nineteen years old. I knew I was big, but I never dreamed I could hurt a man so badly with just two punches. Now it was too late. My anger toward the cadet turned to remorse. I vowed that no matter how much anyone provoked me in the future, I would just walk away. And, for the most part, I did.

I'd like to point something out right here. As an athlete, my size and strength were tremendous assets. But in my dealings with people on a day-to-day basis, they've often caused me serious problems. It seems as if some people love to challenge bigger people, especially if they're well known. Almost any athlete will tell you the same. They say the heavyweight champion of the world gets provoked by strangers all the time.

I know what you're thinking: Someone would have to be crazy to start a fight with someone as big as me. That's exactly the point—there *are* a lot of crazies out there. They'd probably enjoy a good beating. Or else they figure it's a no-lose situation. If they should somehow clean my clock, they've got something to brag about for the rest of their lives. And if I so much as raise my arms to defend myself, they go and file a nice fat lawsuit. I once got sued for telling a guy to shut up. Of course, his version, which was thrown out of court, was a little different.

Even so-called normals have started up with me for no good reason. Maybe it's to pump themselves up, make them feel better about their own insecurities. For whatever motives, I used to get challenged by people all the time. Complete strangers would walk up and pinch me, punch me in my arms, tell me I was nothing but a big asshole. Some idiots would actually take a swing, just so they could go back and tell their friends that they'd tested John Matuszak. When you're feeling good, it's easy to brush that garbage off. But if you're upset about something personal, or if your body is aching from football, it's harder to ignore. It's one of the curses of celebrity.

I'm not going to bore you by telling you about all the fights I've been in. Let's just say I've had my share. My biggest problems have been the times when I didn't walk away because I had too much pride. I remember when I was small I used to spend a few weeks every summer with my grandfather, Leo Walters, my mom's father. He was a cop and later a Justice of the Peace. Like my own father he was tough. My grandfather used to tell me something often: "Don't let anyone push you around, Johnny. If they push you too hard, just punch 'em in the nose." This was back in the Fifties, when times were so much simpler. And if my grandfather had any idea of how powerful I would later become, I'm sure his message would have been totally different. As it was, his voice would stay with me for years: "Just punch 'em in the nose, Johnny."

This is not my excuse for fighting. I should have been wise enough *always* to walk away. That I didn't was a sign of immaturity on my part. But I mention all this for a reason: I'd like people to know that I'm not some kind of walking time bomb. When I was younger I had a reputation for violence, and it bothers me to this day. But for every fifty times I've been provoked in my life, I retaliated about once or twice. And those were the times when I got my reputation.

My girlfriend had been attacked, and I had reacted too harshly. I was in the wrong and I felt miserable over it. Still, I was unprepared for the depth of hostility I received after the incident. The school paper ripped me to shreds. They emphasized over and over that the guy was much smaller than I. In my eyes, that didn't give him the right to paw my girlfriend. When you see some drunk with his hands all over your girlfriend, you don't think about size. You think about protecting her.

I was suspended from the football team for the remainder of the season. Devine called and said he knew the newspapers had not been very fair, but that he'd have to suspend me anyway. He promised he'd reinstate me the following season. He called my parents and told them the same thing. This seemed reasonable to me—I had hurt a man badly and deserved to be punished. Looking back on Devine, for all the doubts I had about some of his ways, on this I felt he gave me a fair shake. He could have fried me in public, but he never did.

Then fate intervened. Devine quit Missouri that January. He was to become the new coach and general manager of the Green Bay Packers. Al Onofrio, Devine's successor as head coach, summoned me to his office. It wasn't to give me a pat on the back. He said he wanted to start off with a clean slate and I would not be allowed back on the team. As far as football was concerned, I was finished at the University of Missouri.

Maybe I should have crawled into my bed and stayed there. I mean, what else could go wrong? The past two months had been hell. After the fight I had been placed on two years' probation by the local courts. My girlfriend's attitude toward me had cooled and we had broken up. The fraternity had asked me to leave. The worse part was the looks I received from the other students, people who had once respected me. Now I could see the fear and mistrust in their eyes. It hurt like hell. I was an emotional wreck.

I wasn't just short on friends, I was also low on money. My parents had been giving me about twenty dollars a month, but it wasn't going very far. After I was tossed from the frat, I didn't have the deposit money to secure an apartment. I was living on Big Macs and french fries. I didn't want to ask my parents for any more because I knew they had their own problems.

Then, one of my friends introduced me to some long-haired students, then referred to as "hippies." Although they barely knew me, these people let me stay in their home for free. I slept on their living room floor with several other people I didn't know. They never tried to impose on me their lifestyle or their politics. They read the school paper and they knew I was in trouble. The recommendation from my friend was enough for them.

Living with people who are different from you can teach you a lot about others, but even more about yourself. All my life I had hung around jocks. All we ever talked about was football or girls. In our smug little circle, we thought people who dressed or spoke differently from us were somehow not as hip. We were wrong. Some of the so-called hippies were highly intelligent. They read the newspapers every day, they studied, they argued about current events. They knew what was happening out in the world, out in the real world. Much of their discussions centered around the war in Vietnam.

This was the end of 1970, and the spectre of Vietnam was everywhere. Via TV, the brutalities of the war were beamed directly into the nation's living rooms. Colleges were erupting in protest. I had been raised in a relatively conservative environment, but in my heart I knew Vietnam was wrong. Young men were getting slaughtered for a war that wasn't theirs. For political reasons—not moral ones—they didn't understand.

There had been sporadic demonstrations at Missouri throughout the school year. It wasn't like a Berkeley or—thank God—a Kent State, but there was a growing awareness that the war was misguided. There were football players at the University of Missouri who were disturbed by the war. Some of their closest friends had been drafted. But they would take no part in any protests. They weren't allowed to. At the height of the demonstrations, one of our coaches said that if any one of us were found participating in a demonstration, our scholarships would be revoked on the spot. For players like me, whose families had little money, that was warning enough.

I don't know that I would have gotten involved in the protests anyway. On the one hand, I thought they were good, because a lot of people were in the dark about the reality of Vietnam. The Nixon administration had been clouding the issue with distortions, trying to downplay the magnitude of the war. Actual body counts were grossly reduced, our involvement in Cambodia was flatly denied. The protests helped shed light on the truth.

At the same time, I had some doubts about certain student leaders. Some seemed to be inspired by bogus motives. They were looking for confrontation in any form, more concerned with screwing the establishment than ending the war. *Ending the war*—that's what it should have been all about. But it seemed like some protesters just used the war as a convenient vehicle to make some noise. I didn't sense a genuine concern. Regardless of all that, I felt it was wrong that I wasn't given a choice. It smacked of totalitarianism, the precise thing we were supposedly trying to thwart in Vietnam.

I was fortunate. I wasn't drafted initially because I received a student deferment. By the time I graduated from college, the draft had ended. But I originally had a very low lottery number. Had I not been in college I would have been one of the earliest people picked. As big a target as I would have made, I don't even like to think about what might have happened. Because for all my reservations about the war, I would definitely have gone if I'd been drafted. I loved the country too much to say no.

While I was in college, the war in Vietnam was hardly the only disturbing issue of the day. It was an era of assassinations, distrust in government, rejection of traditional standards. I think anyone who went to school in the late sixties came out with at least a latent suspicion of anything that smacked of the establishment. As I said earlier, I began asking questions after my family suffered personal tragedy. Going to college, especially in the sixties, encouraged me to continue.

After Onofrio's edict, I was tired of the University of Missouri. Mostly I was weary of being looked at as a bully. I knew I had brought much of the animosity on myself. I also knew I wasn't the terrible person the papers had made me out to be. I decided to leave. I had made a big mistake, now I wanted a second chance.

The University of Nebraska contacted me, but I would have to redshirt an entire year before I'd be eligible to play again. The University of Tampa wanted me too. Tampa was an "outlaw school," a college that welcomed athletes who'd had trouble elsewhere. Something like a collegiate version of the Raiders. UT was also then an NAIA member, a "small college" school that required transfer athletes to sit out one semester, instead of one full year. I transferred to Tampa that January.

At Missouri I had always wanted to play defense. The coaches wanted me at tight end. When I got to Tampa, there was a guy named Alex Edlin playing tight end. Edlin was excellent and the coaches felt I had little chance of beating him out. So they switched me to right defensive tackle, directly over the offensive guard. It was a whole new world and I was somewhat wary. I had always thought of defensive linemen as guys with big hairy arms and legs, ugly tattoos and not a lot of teeth. Guys named Billy Bob.

But I loved the switch to the defensive line. And I was glad to say goodbye to tight end. Tight end is a bastard position. You're not really a receiver and you're not really an offensive lineman. Linebackers were constantly trying to remove my Adam's apple. But at practice I was made to run sprints with skinny wide receivers. I'm an aggressive person and playing defense was better suited to my temperament. On offense you know exactly what you're going to do because you know the play. You have to exercise more self-control. On defense you have to improvise, be more spontaneous. It's more of an attacking man's game. You still have responsibilities, but they're not as narrowly defined. On defense you can cut loose.

Football in the South gets nasty. I learned that in one of my first games, against the University of Tennessee at Chattanooga. I got into a shoving match with a player on the other team's sideline, and the next instant I was attacked by a horde of his angry teammates. They were all over me before I knew what hit me, sticking their fingers beneath my face mask, trying their damndest to gouge my eyes. I didn't know if I'd get out of there before they tore my eyes out. By the time I fought my way back to the field, I had big ugly scratches around both eyes.

In my senior year, Tampa was granted major college status. We certainly had a major college coach in Earl Bruce, who's now at Ohio State. Bruce was not the kind of guy to mess around with, but he was fair and he worked as hard as his players. When Earl said NOW, he didn't mean in fifteen minutes. Earl loved tough guys. He was an ass kicker, and he turned us into an ass-kicking team.

My senior year we went 10–2, including a 7–0 win against the University of Miami. Miami had people like Chuck Foreman and Ruben Carter and they were expecting to beat us like a rug. I had one of my greatest college games. With Miami at our eight yard line in the opening quarter, I caused a fumble that killed the drive. I stopped a fake punt to smash another drive. I wound up with nine unassisted tackles and five more assists. I was named the Southeastern Defensive Player of the Week. The NFL scouts had already begun to take notice. Now they had few doubts.

There were more honors after the season. I was voted Most Valuable Player in the American Bowl, a North-South all-star game, which drove up my stock considerably. I was named by *Time* magazine as an All-American. But I still considered myself an "almost" star. I hadn't been the Most Valuable Player at Oak Creek High my senior year and I hadn't been MVP at Tampa. Gary Huff, the Florida State quarterback, had also edged me as Florida Amateur Athlete of the Year.

I had worked my ass off and gotten good coaching—and I knew the NFL would be intrigued by my speed and size. But when the draft came up in January, I wasn't expecting the world. I hoped I would go in the first round, but I wouldn't have been shocked if I didn't. After all the turmoil I'd been through, I was ecstatic just to be going anywhere.

On the morning of the draft my stomach was playing games with me. Tom McEwen, the editor of the *Tampa Tribune*, persuaded me to follow the draft from the *Tribune* office. When I got there, Huff was also waiting. He and Bert Jones of LSU were two of the most highly touted quarterbacks and both were expected to go early. A lot of experts thought Jones would go first, to the anemic Houston Oilers. If not Jones, then Miami's Foreman.

We were standing around the UPI wire machine. When someone yelled that the first pick was coming over, I was nothing more than curious. I knew I wouldn't be number one. When I crowded over the wire, my mind could not accept what my eyes were reading: I was number one! Out of an entire nation of college football players, I was the top pick in the NFL draft!

I went numb and I felt like I needed a seat. People were screaming and laughing and pounding on my back. First there was a call to the Oilers, then my mom, then there was a conference call with a hundred reporters stationed in New York. Then I had to go and buy a suit because I didn't own one. That night I was flown to Houston to meet my new employers. Waiting for me at the airport was a helicopter to fly me to Oilers headquarters. It was the first time I'd ever been in a helicopter. It was the first time I'd ever been to Texas.

That night I flew to New York to do the "Today" show with Gene Shalit. As I was walking off the set, I was excited to spot Barbara Walters. I wanted to introduce myself, maybe ask for an autograph. But when I approached her with this big, happy grin on my face, she shot me an ice-cold stare. Like, what right could I possibly have to be so happy? I was pissed. What did Barbara Walters have against me? Then I let it pass. I was in too good a mood to worry about something like that. I was ready to join the big boys.

5

EXILED IN HOUSTON

Before I get into my imprisonment—I mean my wonderful experience—with the Houston Oilers, I'd like to talk about the relationship between athletes and the press. Dealing with the press has become an integral part of being an athlete. In a sense it's like an erratic marriage. When it's good it can be a lot of fun. When it's bad it can get ugly.

One thing you quickly learn about dealing with the press: Think before you speak. Athletes can get in serious trouble with their teammates, coaches and the fans, just by uttering one poorly thought-out statement. And you'd be amazed at how the press can pop up anywhere, without any warning.

I spent the 1980 off-season at my parents' home in Oak Creek, and was asked to speak at a sports banquet at a Catholic school in nearby Whitefish Bay. It was a small room, only about fifty people attending. I was sure my speech was for their consumption only. Somebody asked me what I thought of Tom Flores as a coach. This was after the 1979 season, Tom's first, in which we'd finished nine and seven and missed the playoffs for the second straight year. As I said before, some Raiders felt Flores was too passive after those high-intensity years under Madden. I said that Tom was a good coach and a fine person, but a little too bland for my own personal taste. I likened his personality to "cold dishwater." What I failed to realize is that one of those fifty people was a reporter. Realizing he had a scoop, he called one of the wire services. The next morning it was national news: Matuszak Calls Flores Cold Dishwater.

My comments on Flores were not meant for print. If I had any idea that my remarks were going beyond that little room, I never would have said them. But once again, my foot was firmly imbedded in my mouth. Tom was deluged by writers for a response. As usual he was entirely diplomatic, and he never said anything to me about it, but I'm sure it didn't help our relationship.

Larry Merchant, now at HBO, embarrassed the hell out of me once. I actually liked Larry at the time, thought he was a pretty good sportscaster. It was in 1976, after I'd had all that trouble at Houston and Kansas City. Before we went on the air, Larry seemed like a real nice guy. Once the cameras rolled, I wasn't so sure.

"John," he said out of the blue, "have you ever considered seeking professional help?"

No, Larry, have you ever considered taking a long walk on a short pier? Of course I didn't say that. Though I felt about two feet tall—no matter what I said, the damage was done—I played it cool.

"No I haven't," I replied. "That's what you have your friends for, to talk about your problems."

When it comes to astonishing people on camera, Howard Cosell has no peers. Howard invited me on one of his shows immediately after I signed my first pro contract with the Oilers. I was nervous but I thought I was well prepared. I was sure Howard wanted to talk about football, and that shouldn't be too painful.

"John," he opened, "how do you feel about people who say that athletes are overpaid?"

Howard, can you give me a break? I mean, it was his very first question. I had just played almost five years of college football for free. My signing bonus with the Oilers was $55,000. If I were the number one pick in the draft today, it would be $1.5 million. The last thing I expected him to ask me about was money. I suppose it was a good question. But I at least expected some verbal foreplay first.

In answer to Howard's question, I explained how hard I had worked in college and that I felt true sports fans would never begrudge a man making a good living playing football. That seemed to satisfy him and then we moved on. After the show Howard and I talked as we shared a cab together. Howard's command of the English language is extraordinary, and he doesn't mind if you know it. There were multisyllable words bouncing all over the cab. But I like Howard. To me he has always been a perfect gentleman.

A writer from a national magazine once ran around Milwaukee with me for a couple of days. Since it was a "cruising" story, he wanted to join me in the trenches for a firsthand account. We had a good time and there weren't any incidents. When the story came out, it was funny and offbeat. He did omit one item: The one night he went out by himself, some girl smashed a beer bottle over his head. I think he said something that she might have considered offensive. That's what you get for *not* cruising with the Tooz.

I've found that if you're friendly and honest with the media, you'll get treated fairly about 90 percent of the time. To me, sportswriters are just fans with pens in their hands, reporting to other fans. They're not the enemy. But with a few writers, the lousy ones, there's just no winning.

The one time I really got buried by the press was when a national magazine in New York sent a writer out to see me. It was a female writer. I don't mention her gender because I have anything against female writers. Some are excellent. I mention it because of something she said to me just after we began the interview.

"You know," she told me, "Warren Beatty tried to pick up on me when I interviewed him. I thought it was really tacky."

In the context of our conversation, this wasn't from out of left field, more like Jupiter. I should have seen then that this lady was strange. I didn't say anything, just halfheartedly nodded my head. She asked me several questions off the record, which I answered. She asked me several more questions on the record, which I answered. I was excited as I waited for the article to be published. I was with the Chiefs and it was the first time a national publication had ever written me up. I alerted my parents and my grandmother, and they must have told every last person in Oak Creek.

Jesse James got better write-ups. I wanted to drive around Oak Creek and see if I could buy every last copy before anyone read it. The piece was painfully shallow. She made a big deal out of the fact that I wasn't wearing any underpants at the time she did the interview. You know, stuff that was real important to the story. Worse, she printed several items that she assured me were off the record. My mom read the story and immediately went out and bought me twelve pairs of underpants. She was afraid I didn't have any. I guess I really do owe that writer some thanks. I didn't make the Pro Bowl that season, but I did lead the league in underwear.

Some writers play favorites. They admire a particular athlete so much they make him bigger than life. There was one writer in Oakland who loved to write about the marvels of my physique. This guy let his imagery run away from him. One time he wrote that I had "arms like the map of Asia." Now this is flattering and all, but it's the kind of stuff your teammates salivate over. As soon as I read the story, I knew I would be fair game for the rest of the guys. That afternoon, Teddy Hendricks was waiting for me as I tried sneaking into the locker room.

"And here he is," Teddy announced as if he were Ed McMahon, "the one and only John Matuszak. The only man on earth with arms the size of Asia."

Then there were about forty guys sticking their fingers down their throats, as in "gag me with a spoon." Every time the writer entered our locker room for the next few weeks, you'd hear cracks across the room about Asian-sized arms.

I was doing an interview once with several reporters in Santa Rosa. We were outside, on the grass, and I was seated in a chair. The grounds were wet from rain. As I weighed my response to one of their questions, I started leaning back . . . and back . . . and back. Then I was lying *on* my back. My chair had fallen squarely into the mud. Still, I didn't miss a beat.

"It's a fact," I continued while gazing up at the Santa Rosa sky, "that the Raiders do not have the greatest chairs in the world."

The boys got a kick out of that.

I think the more insightful players see that the press can be an excellent PR tool. The average NFL career is roughly 4 years long. If you play six years you're fortunate; eight, somebody up there likes you. Ten, you must be a punter. If you're interested in becoming a marketable personality after you retire, you'll establish your identity while you can. All the fans see when you're out on the field is a big body in a helmet and shoulder pads. Only by talking to the press can you transcend that.

The most daring thing I ever did with the press was the time I posed for *Playgirl*. Hey, big guys can look good too. And that's one of the reasons I did it. *Playgirl* had already done similar layouts with Dan Pastorini and Bob Chandler, both Raiders, both pretty boys, and I wanted to show that defensive linemen can have sex appeal too. I confess, I was flattered by their interest. And they offered me $10,000 for six hours of work. This was back in 1982, near the end of my career, and I didn't want to reject that kind of money. I also thought it would be good, uh, exposure.

As I was having dinner at my parent's home, Pastorini called to say that *Playgirl* was interested. When I hung up the phone I told my family. My mother turned as green as her broccoli. My father was skeptical too. But when I told them I needed the money and promised not to show my private parts—no frontal nudity—they grudgingly gave their blessing. Very grudgingly.

The shoot—that's Hollywood talk for a photo session—was done at a beautiful home in Hollywood Hills. I was nervous when I arrived but relieved to see that the crew was small. Just two men and two women, and I figured the women would leave the room when we actually did the shooting. Wrong. One of the women was the photographer! The first few times she told me to "look sexy," I felt so awkward that I looked about as sexy as a catcher's mitt. Then I made a discovery. If I pretended I was looking at a beautiful woman, instead of into a camera, I was much more natural. By the end of the session I was feeling pretty suave.

As part of our deal, *Playgirl* also lent me a car to use for the night. I had my choice between a brand new Porsche or to be chauffered around in a limo. The Porsche sounded like more fun, but I couldn't get my lineman's legs underneath the wheel. I took the limo. I felt very cool that evening, I must admit, and I played the model role to the hilt. I put on a tux, a fancy shirt, the whole nine yards. But as I went cruising around that night, I couldn't find a single woman who even wanted to drive around with me. Big-time model can't even get a little companionship. My ego settled neatly back to earth.

I didn't get as much grief from my teammates as I expected (maybe Teddy never saw it). Even my parents liked it because it was done tastefully. From what I understand, Oak Creek never sold so many copies of *Playgirl*. I didn't have a steady girl-friend at the time, but the women I knew thought the layout was great. So did a lot of women I didn't know. My intake of mail suddenly tripled. I was getting packages from women containing their underwear, their phone numbers, and all kinds of personal photographs. Not the kind of shots you'd see in *Field and Stream*.

———

My NFL initiation came in the summer of 1973 when I was invited to play in the annual All-Star game. Defunct since 1976, the All-Star Game used to pit the Super Bowl champs against a collection of college stars. It was played every August at Chicago's Soldier Field and it was part of the league's tradition. The late George Halas had helped create it in 1934 when football was struggling to survive and was searching for a show-case. In later years, not everybody thought the game was such a good idea. With all those high-priced rookies, some owners didn't want to risk their investment on a meaningless exhibition. I thought the All-Star game was wonderful. On our college team were Bert Jones, Ray Guy, Rich Glover, Wally Chambers, Joe Ferguson, Sam Cunningham, Chuck Foreman, Otis Armstrong and some other greats. It was a huge honor just to play with people like that.

Every team that wins the Super Bowl is special, but we had the chance to play against one of the best teams in NFL history. The 1972–73 Miami Dolphins had finished seventeen and zero, the only undefeated team ever. Larry Csonka and Jim Kiick, two men I admired, were the starting running backs. Along with

Joe Namath and some other mavericks, they helped redefine society's perception of what an athlete should be. They were tough, hard-nosed winners all the way. But they were also outspoken and irreverent. They helped make it acceptable for athletes to have minds of their own.

(Csonka once pulled a fast one on *Sports Illustrated*. He and Kiick were featured on the August 7, 1972, cover as "Miami's Dynamic Duo." With his right hand draped across his shin, Csonka is shyly slipping the world his middle finger. *Sports Illustrated* never caught it—at least I don't think it did—and that's the picture they ran).

For most rookies the All-Star game was a rude education. The thing that surprised me most was all the holding. In college everyone played primarily by the rules. In the pros they're playing for money, and the guys will bend those rules when they feel they have to. Some of the rookies were frustrated and ready to fight when they got held. I thought it was no big deal.

The All-Star game was traditionally intense. The timing of the game didn't help. August in Chicago is hot, humid and buggy. By August the pros had already been in camp for several weeks, and their patience and boiling points were running short. It was also their first contact against people other than their teammates, and most humans would rather pound a stranger than a guy who passes you the potatoes at dinner. Also, a Super Bowl team losing to a bunch of rookies would be the ultimate embarrassment, so the pros hit with added incentive. The pros knew they'd be seeing the rookies for the next several years, and they wanted to establish their authority from square one. Can't have some rookie getting cocky on you. When Floyd Little played in the All-Star game, Ray Nitschke greeted him by breaking his nose. Nice to meet you, Floyd. Welcome to the NFL.

I was sweating before the game and not just because of the heat. When you're in college you think NFL veterans are a bunch of Sherman tanks, only faster. I must have told myself every cliché in the book—these guys put their pants on one leg at a time, on any given day anyone can beat anyone, etc., etc. Then I thought about Csonka and the rationalizations went out the window. I decided just to go out there and play.

I never did get a decent shot at Csonka. He ran so hard and

so low to the ground that it was nearly impossible to get any leverage on him. We lost, 14–3, but that was impressive considering who we were up against. I only played the second and third quarters and I never quite got into my rhythm. I played well but not great. It was good for my confidence though. I had gone up against the world champs and I had survived. I was eager to join the Oilers at camp.

Some people might wonder why. In the three seasons before I came to the Oilers, they were the worst team in pro football, winning just eight out of forty-two football games. The year before they drafted me they were one and thirteen, including a season-ending 61–17 disgrace. I wasn't discouraged though. I was honored to be the first pick in the draft, and I went into camp with my eyes and my hopes wide open.

But, first I had problems signing my contract. The Oilers were playing hardball. They immediately made a statement that I wasn't going to get as much money as a first round quarterback would. I thought that was nonsense. If they thought a quarterback was so important, then why didn't they draft one? Their initial offer was terrible, a little less than Barry Smith had just signed for with the Packers. But Smith was the twenty-first pick in the draft and I was the first. We declined and the Oilers wouldn't budge. Bob Woolf, my agent, and Sid Gillman, the Oilers general manager, were later sitting near each other at a B'nai B'rith dinner in Boston. Bob asked Sid if they could get together soon to talk about my contract. Sid said he was too busy. Too busy to sign your first-round pick?

About that time Bob got a call from the Toronto Argonauts of the CFL. They wanted me to play for them. By then Sid wasn't even returning Bob's calls, so Bob and I flew up to Toronto. They offered me more money than the Oilers had, a lot more. But I was still intent on playing against the best, and that meant playing in the NFL. By chance, a wire service photographer snapped a shot of me, Bob and a Toronto official. The photo ran all over the States. When Bob returned to Boston, there was a message to call Sid. Mysteriously, he was now ready to get down to business.

The Oilers offered me about 50 percent more than they had

originally. I still thought they were out of line, but I signed because I was eager to play ball. I signed a four-year contract for $25,000 the first year, $30,000 the second, $35,000 the third and $40,000 the fourth. And I got a $55,000 signing bonus. This was a lot of money for the average professional. In NFL dollars it was not.

After we came to terms, there was a press conference. The reporters asked me what I thought of my contract.

"If the Oilers are happy," I said, "then it can't be too good. But since I'm happy, then it can't be too bad. So overall I'd say I'm satisfied."

A perfectly inoffensive statement, right? Gillman didn't think so.

"Okay, okay," Sid interrupted, "let's break this up. That's enough questions for today."

I should have seen right there what I was in for. I didn't. I was in the NFL and nothing could possibly ruin that. I soon found out I had a lot to learn.

There are myths about life as an NFL rookie, and I believed all of them. First and foremost, there's the cliché about the naive rookie relying on the compassionate, grizzled veteran for guidance and reassurance. That stuff may happen in the movies. In the NFL it doesn't wash.

Sure, there are exceptions. Some veterans will help a rookie right away if they really like him personally. When that does happen, those are usually the friendships that last a lifetime. And veterans do like to help their younger teammates. But that doesn't happen much until a player's second year, or at least toward the end of his first one. First a rookie has to prove he's worthy.

It also depends on the veteran's stature on the team. An established star who knows his job is secure will be more helpful to a rookie than a veteran on the borderline. Generally, though, there's a rule of thumb: Veterans will not give much aid to rookies who play the same position they do. The Oilers who were on me the most were the veteran defensive linemen. It was nothing major, mostly little things. Hitting you after the whistle, making fun of the way you dressed, giving you shit when you were in the locker room. Little things, but little things that pissed me off.

I didn't like it much at the time, but when I became a veteran myself I understood. Behind all their bravado, football players constantly battle their fears: fear of getting injured, fear of making a fool of themselves in front of millions; in the case of veterans, fear of becoming expendable, of losing their jobs to younger players. So while management looks at young, tough rookies with lust, veterans have mixed emotions. On one hand, they like to win, and they know fresh talent can help them do that. On the other hand, they don't want to watch that winning from the bench.

No rookie has it easy. For starters, they're learning a system that's many times more complicated than the one they used in college. And most of them were stars when they were in college. But when they get to the NFL, everyone else is as big and as strong as they are. Now they can't push everyone around and they become frustrated. When you've experienced failure, the frustration is easier to live with, but the rookies have always had their own way, so they don't take failure very well. I've seen guys who were big shots in college destroy themselves with doubt once they got to the pros. That's the NFL though. If you don't have humility when you get there—just wait a practice or two.

Every year you see more than a couple of fights between rookies and veterans at camp. Not all of them are from the heat of the moment, some of them are calculated. A smart rookie knows if he's gutsy enough to take on a veteran, his courage— or insanity—will be remembered by the coaches. Because they have very little time to make an impression, rookies also tend to hit harder during camp. So while the veterans are generally looking at camp as something to endure, the rookies are popping them like there's literally no tomorrow. The veterans sometimes respond with their fists.

For a rookie, I was in a unique position. I was under pressure too, but a different kind. As the top pick in the draft, my every move was scrutinized. I felt an awful lot of eyes on me during every drill. First-round picks are considered "impact players" who can help turn a bad team into a good one. And the Oilers certainly needed a shot in the arm. So, besides the pressure I have always put on myself, I had pressure to justify the Oilers' faith in me. I also got pressure from some veterans. I was the new kid on the block and they were resentful. It happens to most high draft choices. They haven't played a down in the pros, and they're making more money and headlines than the veterans who have already proven themselves. It's human nature.

Unlike most of the other rookies, however, I had some job security. The Oilers had spent dozens of hours evaluating my potential. When they did make me their first selection, it came wrapped in a package of publicity. To cut me would have been like shouting to the world that they didn't know their jobs. I could have shown up at practice wearing a mini skirt and nobody would have said much as long as I made some tackles.

Big-name rookies and proven stars are the exception to the rule at training camp. They know they've got a job. For most rookies, and for every fading veteran, training camp is do or die. Just one screw-up, just one, and they might be cut.

Those were the players who were constantly stealing glances at the coaches, always asking their teammates how they looked that day. Off the field they would try and laugh and be loose like everyone else. But I could always see that it was forced. The desperation showed in their eyes.

When I became a veteran, I thought training camp was sad, and a little unreal. At the beginning there would be about ninety guys, and by the end there were forty-nine. A lot of the guys you never got to know. Maybe you'd knock into them at dinner reaching for a Coke and exchange excuse me's. The next morning they'd be gone. Sometimes I used to wonder what the hell happened to those guys. I used to see the same guys year after year at camp. They'd get time off from their normal jobs to try and become a free agent. Year after year they'd go home disappointed.

A tribal rite among NFL veterans is making the rookies sing their college fight songs. I suppose it's to encourage camaraderie, but all it does is make a nervous rookie feel worse. I've always felt it was stupid. One night the veterans told me to sing the song from Tampa. If Tampa had a fight song, it was news to me. So I told them I didn't know it. They told me to sing something else. I'm a football player, not Wayne Newton. I didn't know any other songs and I wasn't in the mood for games. It had been a long, dusty day of practice. I sat back down in my seat. A couple of assholes got all hot but most of the guys couldn't care less. When it comes to abusing rookies, there's a pattern: Players who are comfortable with their careers and themselves have no problems with rookies. The guys who doubt themselves look for others to rag on.

I've got some vivid memories from my rookie year. I remember the first time I tackled Franco Harris. The first time Franco ran toward me I braced myself for the impact. It was a one-sided collision—Franco fell down the moment I made contact. I was shocked and disappointed. I'm not saying Franco wasn't a great runner. He was. His instincts, both for finding the hole and utilizing his blockers, were superior. But at 6′ 2″ and 225 pounds, he didn't have much fight.

Every rookie has a play where he stops and thinks, "Well, I've finally made it in the NFL." Mine was unusual. We were playing the Chicago Bears in Soldier Field. Dick Butkus was their middle linebacker. It's impossible to play on a team with a guy like Butkus and not be a hitter. His ferocity is infectious. As a result, the Bears, as they are today, were one of the nastiest teams in football. Show a team like the Bears that you're afraid and you're dead meat. They'll walk all over you. So I decided I'd play it their way.

I guess I got carried away. I smashed Bobby Douglass, their quarterback, a few counts after he'd released the ball. I got called for a personal foul and I deserved it. But I was so hyped up, when I saw the flag I went crazy. I threw the ref the old double whammy: not one middle finger, but both of them. Everyone was waiting for another flag but it never came. Standing on the sideline, Butkus was in a rage.

"Everyone says the Bears are a dirty team," he roared at the ref, "but look at what Matuszak gets away with. If *we* had done that you'd have thrown another flag."

Actually, Dick's reaction wasn't that sterile. He tossed in some harsher language, just to let the official know his anger was sincere. I watched it all with fascination. Dick Butkus, *the* Monster of the Midway, had cursed me out. I knew I had arrived.

My first confrontation with O.J. Simpson did not come during my rookie year, but it was early in my career. O.J. was running one of those sweeps around the end, the kind he made famous. I knew that once you let O.J. get some room to dance, he was as good as gone. I broke through the wall of blockers and nailed him with a solid shot. As he lay there trying to gather his senses, I looked him in the eye. I conjured up my deepest, roughest, most maniacal voice. And then I yelled at him, very loudly:

"CAN I HAVE YOUR AUTOGRAPH?"

I also took my share of poundings as a rookie. The first few days in the NFL are not like the first few days at a normal job. You don't just coast along, content to locate the water fountain and the Men's Room. In the NFL the honeymoon never ends because it never starts. Particularly when you're a lineman. Every week it seemed like the offensive linemen got bigger and stronger and more surly. And they all wanted to give a big hello to the hotshot number one draft pick.

Many of my bruises came courtesy of the Pittsburgh Steelers. Those were the Steelers of Joe Green and Mel Blount and Jack Lambert, the only team in the league that was as ornery as the Raiders. The bitterness between the Raiders and the Steelers was not a bunch of hype. Both teams truly disliked each other. The games were always a war.

I could probably write a whole book just on the rivalry between the Raiders and the Steelers, but here are only some of the juicier highlights:

• In 1972, Franco Harris caught the hotly disputed Immaculate Reception, knocking the Raiders out of the Super Bowl and leaving them feeling robbed. Back then, the rules said only one offensive player could touch a pass. The Raiders felt Frenchy Fuqua had deflected the pass before Franco touched it. Tatum and Al Davis insist to this day that the refs blew the call.

• In 1974, a Raiders tight end named Bob Moore was returning to the team's hotel the night before a game in Pittsburgh. A hostile crowd of Steelers fans surrounded the hotel and the police were called. In the ensuing confusion, Moore mistakenly got smacked in the head with a nightstick. Bob suffered a concussion, couldn't play the next day and wound up suing the city. I think he eventually dropped the suit.

• In 1975, on the day of the AFC championship, Pittsburgh's artificial turf was virtually frozen. Steelers owner Dan Rooney said the tarp covering the turf had slipped off the night before. The Raiders swore it had been intentionally slashed. The icy turf negated Oakland's passing game, particularly Cliff Branch, and Pittsburgh won.

• In 1976, after Lynn Swann suffered a concussion from a George Atkinson forearm, Pittsburgh's coach Chuck Noll called Jack Tatum and George Atkinson part of the "NFL's criminal element." That was the game before the Raiders signed me, and I watched it from the stands. I think Noll is an excellent coach but I thought that was bullshit. It's true that our defensive backs didn't care for Swann. They felt he was a prima donna who liked to score touchdowns but didn't care to get hit. But no one tried to hurt him on purpose and no one felt good about it afterward. And it's not as if Pittsburgh played like sissies. Lambert and Blount used to beat up our offensive people pretty well. Those who make their living in the NFL should not throw stones.

• This final item best summarizes how the Oakland Raiders and the Pittsburgh Steelers felt about each other. Ray Mansfield, their center, once looked down at the ball during a game in Oakland and noticed that it had been written on with magic marker. FUCK YOU had been written across the laces. (I have no clue who wrote it. Seriously.)

Getting back to my rookie days, playing against Pittsburgh's offensive linemen was usually good for three or four postgame Bufferins. Per quarter. They had guys like Mike Webster and Jon Kolb, weight-lifting fanatics who would cut the sleeves off their jerseys so they could terrorize rookie linemen with their massive arms. I wasn't in awe of those guys, just a little wary.

The Steelers have run the trap play since the beginning of

man. They run it better than any team in football. Basically, the trap is where the offense lets a defensive lineman penetrate, then blows him away with a pulling guard. My first year I fell for the trap in the worst possible way. One of their tackles ran right by me like I was invisible. I edged into the backfield with a shit-eating grin on my face. This was going to be the easiest tackle of my life. BOOM—I got steamrolled by one of their trapping guards. It took me one game against the Steelers to figure out why they called it a trap.

There were more surprises my rookie year. When I came to the Oilers, they were coached by a man named Bill Peterson. Bill was one of the nicest men I ever met. But he didn't command the respect of his players. I was amazed—Bill would be speaking to the team and players would giggle when he wasn't looking. It was a strange situation, especially after playing for a hard guy like Earl Bruce. I never thought the pros would be like that.

Bill's biggest problem was the way he spoke. Things would come out differently from the way he intended.

The night before each of our games, the entire team would go and see a movie. One of the guys once asked Bill what the movie was that night.

"I think it's called Two-Eyed Jacks," Bill said in all earnestness.

"Yeah," somebody piped up, "I think I saw half of that once."

Bill used to set himself up for comments like that all the time. If we were winning, it all would have been a lot of fun. When you're winning you're allowed your eccentricities. As it was, Bill became the butt of a lot of jokes. I liked Bill a lot and it bothered me. He really cared about his players. He deserved better.

I remember a meeting we had after we lost our first four games. It was clear that we were starting to press, and Bill told us he had something to say. He told us to relax, that even though we were playing poorly, nobody's job was in jeopardy. That he couldn't speak for the future, but everyone would have a job for at least the rest of the year. Then he said to go home and tell our wives and girlfriends that everything would turn out fine. That's the kind of person Bill was.

The following week, after we lost Game Five, Bill was fired. Sid Gillman, previously our general manager, took over as head coach. That same week about eight of our players were either traded or released. The whole thing irritated the hell out of me. I felt lousy about what happened to Bill. And no matter how hard I tried, I couldn't get used to losing.

Football is a grueling game. You know that when you join the league, and you either accept it or you find another occupation. When you're winning you can live with the hurts. The victories make it all seem worth it. When you're losing you just plain hurt.

My first serious injury in the pros came in our eleventh game against Kansas City. I was running on the artificial turf when I heard an ugly popping sound. I had strained both my ankle and my knee. It wasn't severe as far as football injuries go, but it hurt like hell and I could barely walk. I remember hobbling back to my apartment that night, trying to balance myself on one leg as I fumbled through my pockets for my keys. We were one and ten at the time and I remember thinking to myself: *What the hell am I doing to my body? What did I get myself into? We're one and ten. I can barely walk and it's all for nothing.* Then I wiped the thought from my mind. I missed one game and was right back out there.

No pro team begins a season thinking it's going to lose. The first day of camp everyone's spirits are soaring. You work and you believe. You survive the two-a-days and the injuries. Because this year you're going to win. Anything is possible if you want it badly enough.

Then the games begin and you start to lose. And lose. And lose. All week you get beaten up at practice, and then on Sunday you lose. You practice each day the following week, and on Sunday you lose again. The only thing that keeps you playing hard is your own set of values. Sometimes that's tough to do.

A loser's dressing room is mostly quiet. There's no jiving or back slapping. The sounds you do hear are the sounds of failure. Moans and excuses and curses. There are grown men sitting with towels draped over their heads and faces. They don't want their teammates to see them crying. When you win you want to sit around that locker room forever, to savor your success. When you lose you want to shower and get the hell out of there. Going out in public isn't any better. Everywhere you go people want to know what's wrong with your team. Even if *you've* played great, people want to know why the team is so lousy. You run off the field each week and the people are booing. I don't care how much money an athlete makes, anyone with a sense of pride detests playing for a loser. All the money in the world can't make a loser feel good.

It's weird. Even if you've played on winners all through high school and college, you forget what it feels like to win. You're under so much pressure to win, and you want it so badly, that even when you're winning, those nagging doubts creep up. You know *something* is going to happen.

Something always used to happen to the Houston Oilers. We had a great receiver named Billy Parks. If Billy were on a good team, he would have been famous. But good players on losing teams are mostly afterthoughts. It's as if they're tainted. One game Billy jumped offside on two different touchdowns. Things like that used to happen all the time. Little mental breakdowns. We had some talent on that team, we just didn't believe we could win. Not the players, not the coaches, not the fans. And so we lost.

One of the first casualties on a losing team is unity. There was no unity on the Oilers, and it was one of the most disturbing things about my rookie year. Everyone looked out for himself, nobody really gave a damn about anyone else. That's the way it is in life sometimes, I suppose, but I wasn't ready for it yet. I was young, still somewhat innocent. I wanted more than that.

Things got worse when Gillman became head coach. Sid is one of the founding fathers of the modern passing game. His disciples include some of the sharpest minds in the NFL, including Al Davis. Sid's ideas about football have always been up to date, even ahead of his time. His ideas about dealing with players have not. Sid began coaching in the 1930s. In the old days players were treated like cattle. Do this, do that, go over here, run over there. By 1973, the NFL player had changed with the times. He asked questions and felt he was entitled to explanations. He demanded to be treated as a person. Sid could not and would not accept this. No one is all good or all bad. I'm sure Sid had his understanding side. But I don't remember seeing it.

As soon as Sid replaced Bill, he instated three- and four-hour practices. This was six games into the season and bodies were already starting to deteriorate. In the NFL this is unheard of. Practices were getting ugly. Every time a player screwed up, the coaches would jump down his throat. One of the coaches once got in the face of Tody Smith, one of our best defensive linemen. He was berating Tody and then he made the mistake of knocking into Tody's chest. Tody hauled off and punched the coach right in *his* chest. It was a terrible scene. For the second straight year the Oilers finished at one and thirteen. I was no longer a rookie. I had spent five years that season with the Houston Oilers.

———

As my second year in the NFL approached, I was looking forward to going to camp. Anything would be an improvement over the season before. No such luck. That summer the National Football League Players Association went on strike and all veterans were asked not to report to their respective camps. There were dozens of reforms wanted by the NFLPA, mostly involving things like medical and dental benefits, insurance and pensions. This was twelve years ago, when salaries were nowhere near what they are today. Issues like that were extremely important.

I supported the strike, as did about 80 percent of the members of the NFLPA. At first the Houston Oilers were also united in their stance against management. Several of the team's leaders said we had to stick together if we wanted management to realize we were serious. Elvin Bethea was the single Oiler who most eased the other players' fears. Elvin was tremendously respected by his teammates. Elvin felt the players had a legitimate reason to strike, and most of the players believed he would never steer them wrong. The veterans made a pact to stick together.

But you could never count on anything with the Houston Oilers, and the strike was no different. A few players started crossing the picket line. No one ever tried to prove anything, but we were just about certain that the Oilers had paid these guys under the table to do it. They were trying to break the union's back. Two players I thought I was close to—my roommate, Greg Bingham, and Ken Burroughs—promised me in a private conversation that they would tell me first if they decided to break the picket line. Both went in without saying a word. The striking veterans felt they'd been double crossed. The bitterness turned into open hostility.

Steve Kiner was in his first season with the Oilers that year. Before the season had begun, I met Steve when we were both visiting Tampa. He had just been traded to the Oilers from New England and was training for the upcoming season. I knew Steve was a hell of a linebacker, but I also knew his appearance wouldn't go over big with the Oilers front office. He had a full beard and long, stringy hair. I suggested to Steve that he come into camp looking more clean cut, just to avoid any potential hassles. Steve appreciated that and we became pretty good friends. While we were both in Tampa, we spent a lot of time working out together.

When camp began I was sure Steve would support the strike. He was new to the team and I was certain he would not want to alienate his future teammates. And as a veteran, he would surely sympathize with the position of the striking players. I invited Steve over to my apartment to discuss the strike. I cooked us a nice spaghetti dinner. Just as we were about to eat, Steve said he was not going to honor the strike. I snapped. I was still furious at the other guys who had broken the picket line, and I took it out on Steve. Without saying a word, I took Steve's plate, walked to the kitchen and threw his spaghetti down the disposal. Here I was in my second year and I was willing to put my ass on the line to support my teammates. It infuriated me that a veteran like Steve would not.

Finally, a compromise was made and the NFLPA instructed us to return to our camps. With the exhibition season already under way, most coaches were happy and relieved to have their veterans back. They realized the strike was a labor issue, not a football one. Not Sid Gillman. After two consecutive one and thirteen seasons, Sid had wanted to get an early start on refurbishing the franchise. The strike delayed his plans and he took it as a personal insult. Sid felt he had to punish us.

When I got back to camp, Sid seemed particularly annoyed with me. I had a good idea why. Although I fully supported the strike, I had only walked on the picket line for one afternoon. It was under a bright Texas sun. I took off my shirt and put on a pair of sunglasses. I was carrying a sign that said ON STRIKE FOR FREEDOM AND DIGNITY. One of my teammates, Al Jenkins, noticed a photographer from *Sports Illustrated*. Al told me to shoot him a power sign. So I clenched my fist and stared into the camera. It was all in fun. The next week the picture ran in *Sports Illustrated,* and I looked like some sort of revolutionary. Somehow I know Sid did not appreciate that. Nor, I'm sure, did the rest of the NFL powers that be.

I really believe that one *SI* photo was the beginning of my "bad guy" reputation. The strike was very painful and emotional, and a lot of owners never forgave the players they considered to be the ringleaders. I was anything but a strike leader, but I did look pretty radical in that photo. I think it was at that point that the league started looking at me as a malcontent, a troublemaker. In the past I had never really considered myself that much trouble. I sure as hell didn't feel like a revolutionary. Basically, I still thought of myself as a Polish Catholic kid from the Midwest who was a little immature. I was a second-year player who was simply supporting his teammates. But to the NFL, I was now John Matuszak, the radical.

Houston's training camp was held in Huntsville, Texas. Huntsville is seventy miles north of Houston, the home of Sam Houston State, which is Dan Rather's alma mater. There is a hill in Huntsville. On one side the Oilers held their training camp, on the other side was a state penitentiary. They were roughly a mile apart. While we were in camp, prisoners took over the main part of the state prison. They tried busting out of the prison by capturing hostages. Cops were stationed every-where with automatic rifles. Eventually the prisoners were either shot to death or captured. It was a hot, tense summer in Hunts-ville.

On the other side of the hill, where one of the ugliest train-ing camps in NFL history was unfolding, emotions weren't much cooler. There were players who hated the coach. There were players who hated other players. The wounds left by the strike were deeper and fresher in our camp than in any other team in the NFL. Bill Curry, our starting center, was then the president of the NFLPA. Sid had been an angry, vocal opponent of the strike, and now he was clearly ready for confrontation.

Sid didn't waste any time showing us who was boss. The first full day of camp, the striking players were made to practice on another field. Then, when we thought the day was over, Sid told the other players to go in and take their showers. He told us to run extra laps. Although many of us had been keeping in excellent shape, Sid didn't play any of the strikers in our first exhibition game after coming back. There were substantial fines for minor offenses. One meeting Sid told us that if we didn't like what he was doing, it was just too bad. He said that trying to get traded was a waste of time, because they wouldn't trade us anyway.

One day, I ran out to practice wearing a pair of red gym shorts. I have very thick legs, and with all the extra running we had to do, the tight gray shorts that the Oilers gave us were chafing my thighs. I had a nice soft pair of red ones that gave me some room when I ran. We weren't practicing with the rest of the team anyway, so I didn't think anyone would give a damn. When Sid spotted me he came storming over to our field. He made me go back into the locker room and change into my grays.

All of those incidents were annoying enough on their own. But one of Sid's acts earlier that week was totally indefensible. When it was first announced that the strike was coming to an end, veterans began migrating to Huntsville from across the country. To make up for all the lost time, they rushed there as quickly as possible. One veteran, Paul Guidry, owned a restaurant in Buffalo. Paul drove twenty-six straight hours, from Buffalo to Huntsville. Sid called a team meeting when most of the veterans had arrived. I was still in transit and didn't attend. But I heard what happened. Soon after it began, Sid reportedly dismissed himself and an aide walked in. The aide called out seven names, all veterans who had participated in the strike. He said they were cut. Just like that, they were out of football. The entire room let out a horrified gasp.

The seven veterans became known as The Huntsville Seven. One of the players was Guidry. He drove twenty-six hours to get dumped on. My buddy Al Jenkins got cut too. It was bad enough to cut those guys in front of the entire team, but Sid let them come all the way to camp before he did it. Sid later said that he didn't have any of the players' numbers. But Bethea said he had the numbers of every player on the team. All Sid had to do was ask. The cutting of The Huntsville Seven was the cruelest, most vengeful act I've ever seen in my NFL career. There was no turning back now—I decided I had had more than enough of the Houston Oilers. I began to formulate a plan. Sid had told us that trades were out of the question. I decided to call his bluff.

That spring the World Football League had been formed. NFL players now had some bargaining power in their negotiations with the NFL. If an NFL owner didn't want to pay a player what the player thought he was worth, the player could consider playing in the WFL. In the past you had to play for whatever NFL team you were drafted by. If you got shortchanged on your contract, well, there was always Canada. For athletes who wanted to stay in the United States, the WFL gave them an alternative.

The WFL had a franchise named the Houston Texans just across town. Soon after the Oilers veterans returned to camp, when the Texans got wind of my discontent, they invited me to their office. They offered me a contract to become a Houston Texan.

On the surface this would seem impossible. I had three years left on my contract with the Oilers. But I wasn't real concerned with the rights of the Oilers at that point. I saw what they did to Guidry and the others. I couldn't remember the last time Sid had looked me squarely in the eye. After a few weeks in the Oilers camp, I accepted the Texans' offer. I knew the Oilers would fight it, but I didn't care. My adviser, Gary Caposta, told me he had found a loophole in my Oilers contract. If I had to I could challenge them in court. But I never expected it to go that far. Most people think I jumped to the WFL for the money. I didn't. I jumped because I wanted to get away from the Oilers. If I didn't do something drastic, who knows?—I might have been stuck there the next several years. I figured if I could get the Oilers angry enough, maybe they'd break down and trade me. Playing for the Oilers was not what I thought the NFL should be all about.

What followed was one of the strangest chapters in Houston Oiler history. I was there, right in the middle, or I might not have believed it myself.

On a Monday night I played with the Oilers in the Astrodome in an exhibition game. After the game I walked out of the locker room with my helmet, shoulder pads and size fifteen shoes. (The Oilers would later make a big deal out of this. What they failed to mention was that, in payment for the equipment, I left with them a full week's paycheck.) After the game, I gave Greg Bingham my playbook and my dorm room key. I asked him to give them to Sid, but not until the following day at dinner time. I didn't show up at Tuesday's practice, for which I was fined. The Oilers had no idea where I was. At dinner time Greg told Sid that I had joined the WFL and then handed him my key and playbook. According to Bingham, "you needed a dustbuster to pick Sid's chin off the floor."

That night—twenty-four hours after I had played a game in the NFL, in the Astrodome—I was back in the Astrodome again. Only this time I was playing in a different league. The Texans also played home games in the Astrodome and they had a game that night against the New York Stars.

The original plan was for me to suit up but not to play. After all, I'd only been to that afternoon's practice. Early in the second quarter I was watching the game from the bench when I noticed a crowd of people approaching our sideline. What the hell were they doing on the field? The I realized they were all looking right at me. There were about twenty-five people, and at first I thought they were all policemen. *Holy shit,* I thought, *I'll never mess around with the NFL again as long as I live.*

I didn't know exactly what they wanted, but I didn't want to be there to find out. I ran over to the coach and asked him to put me into the game. He said it was fine. Although I had one eye on the sideline, I played in seven plays and I actually got a sack and a few more tackles. Then, when the Stars went to punt, I knew I had to face the music. My throat went dry as I walked toward the posse.

At least they weren't all policemen, most of the crowd were reporters. The news was bad though. Immediately after he'd heard I was going to play with the Texans, Sid had persuaded a local judge into drafting a restraining order that would keep me from playing. Sheriff John Growson had tried to serve me before the game, but he'd gotten lost in the maze of the Astrodome. As the sheriff handed me the thick stack of papers, his hand was shaking like a leaf. It looked like the real thing. After all of seven plays, my career in the WFL was temporarily on hold. I waved the document to the crowd, and the 10,000 fans started cheering.

I spent the next several weeks in limbo. I refused to report to the Oilers. The Oilers sued the Texans, the Texans sued them back. My attorney subpoenaed the entire Oilers organization. Meanwhile I was getting more and more edgy. It was my second year as a pro, I wanted to play some football. I was getting a little nervous. Maybe I hadn't been so smart after all.

The gamble worked.

In late October, seven games into the season, I got the word. Rather than risk a drawn out legal battle, the Oilers traded me to the Kansas City Chiefs for Curley Culp and a first round draft choice. I was free.

I certainly wasn't rich though. The contract I had signed with the Texans had not called for any money up front. For all the aggravation and risk, all I received from the WFL was a short trip to Hawaii and a green football with the letters WFL emblazoned across it. I was content though. Make that ecstatic.

6

THE DARK SIDE: THE PIT, VIOLENCE AND INJURIES

Welcome to The Pit. The Pit is where I used to play, where the offensive and defensive linemen play. If you're the average football fan, you don't pay much attention to The Pit when you're watching a game. You follow the ball, so you focus on the quarterback. I don't blame you. A perfectly thrown spiral to a streaking receiver is a beautiful thing to watch. But regardless of what the headlines say, the glamour positions are not where football games are won and lost. Football games are decided in The Pit. Dominate The Pit and you can do what you want all day. The Pit is the bottom line.

The Pit is a world within itself—dangerous, desperate, primitive. Its inhabitants are the biggest, strongest players in the game. Men who weigh 250, 275, even 300 pounds, collide violently on every play. Football, at any position, is a brutal game. In order to win a game, you must first win the battle of the hitting. But the hitting in The Pit is by far the most constant. Other players get moments of rest—quarterbacks hand off, receivers run decoy patterns. In the Pit the contact never stops.

You don't really play in The Pit, you survive it. The Pit is brutally isolated. The ball is often forgotten, and no one keeps score. You get stepped on, jumped on, bent, twisted and kicked. The Pit isn't like playing wide receiver. There is no room to stretch out. You're all jammed into a tightly packed area, with helmets and shoulder pads and pumping knees. When there's a pile up in The Pit, sometimes you feel like it's difficult to breathe.

The Pit is not for the weak of heart. But for all its ferocity, I found satisfaction playing there. It was all face to face, eye to eye. You were completely on your own. Nowhere to hide, no one to help you. There was no bullshit in The Pit. No lawyers. No agents. No contracts. No hypocrisy. No hype. No backstabbing. Just the *game*.

Rivalries in The Pit are the fiercest, longest running in football. In the course of a game, it's true that I would confront almost every player on the offense. But first and foremost, I would ultimately have to conquer one man—in my case, the offensive tackle. Every play, every quarter, every year. I never had to look too far—he was six inches from my face every Sunday. I could hear him breathe, I could smell his sweat, I could see his eyes. I could always measure a man by his eyes. If I saw fear or uncertainty, I knew I would have my way that day. If I detected arrogance or, worse, a sense of calm, I knew I would be in for a fight.

I played against a lot of great linemen in the course of my career. Players who'd make you hurt for the whole next week. Two of the best were Ed White, a guard for the Chargers, and Dan Dierdorf, a tackle for the St. Louis Cardinals. When I first came into the league, Dierdorf made me look like a baby. Dierdorf was the best I ever played against except for one man. Russ Washington was even better.

I played in the NFL for nine years. Except for the few times I was hurt, every year, at least twice a season, I played across from Russ Washington. He was a bulldozer of a man, 6'7" and 295 pounds, one of the few players in the NFL who was bigger than I was. Russ played for the San Diego Chargers for fifteen years and he went to the Pro Bowl five different times. Russ could play you any way he wanted. He could stomp right over you like a bull, or he could rely on his surprising quickness. But what made Russ special was his pride. His performance barely fluctuated. Every Sunday, Russ was *there*.

During the weeks when we played the Chargers, I wanted to beat Russ Washington more than anything on earth. But I could never talk myself into hating him. Some players, the dirty, career-threatening ones, I *could* hate, at least for those three hours on Sunday. But Russ and I had a mutual respect. We knew neither one of us would ever quit. We knew neither one of us would take a cheap shot. We were like heavyweight boxers who pound each other for fifteen rounds and then fall into each other's arms when the fight is over. You reserve your deepest respect for your toughest opponent. You know exactly what he's been through.

From 1970 to the fifth game of 1980, Russ played in 178 straight games. In The Pit, with players falling at your knees, that's remarkable. In Game Six of 1980, we were playing against the Chargers. Dan Fouts, their quarterback, dropped back to pass. When I was rushing the passer, there were a dozen ways I could try and beat the tackle. Speed, finesse, an assortment of inside or outside moves. This time I used brute strength. At the snap of the ball, I butted my helmet into Russ's helmet. With my legs, I kept driving him backward toward Fouts. As I was still pushing Russ back, Fouts got sacked by one of our other linemen. Fouts and the lineman fell forward, directly on the back of Russ's unprotected right leg. POP—I could hear something snap. It was a hideous sound and I knew it meant serious injury. As it turned out, Russ would be out for the rest of the season, and his knee would have to be operated on. Now he was rolling around on the ground, his face a mask of pain. I took off my helmet and I crouched by him.

"Russ, I'm so sorry," I told him. "I mean it. I'm really sorry."

He was oblivious to everything but the pain and he didn't answer. I couldn't take my eyes off his face. His eyes looked like they were rolling around in their sockets, and his teeth were gnashing violently. One of my teammates was pounding on my shoulder. Another was grabbing me by my hand to pull me away.

"Come on, John," they were saying. "Leave him alone. There's nothing you can do."

They were right, there was nothing I could do. But I didn't want to leave him lying there. I wanted to carry him to the sideline, ride with him in the ambulance. I was shattered as they carried him off the field. He was almost thirty-four years old. I feared for his career.

I walked back to the huddle but I wasn't listening to what was being said. I was still worried about Russ. So many years I had tried to beat him up physically. Now that he was actually hurt, it turned my stomach.

Russ made it back. Despite having fluid on his injured knee, he played for two more seasons. In 1983, at the Chargers summer camp, Russ was one of the final cuts.

It was strange. For nine years I battled Russ Washington. I knew his tendencies, his weaknesses, his strengths. I knew when he was tired and when he was hurt. In the week before a Charger game, I thought about Russ Washington more than I thought about myself, my girlfriend, or my family. Not just when I was studying him on film. He would creep into my mind at breakfast, be with me in my car on the way to practice, at times invade my dreams. And yet, Russ was still a stranger, I didn't really know him at all. In all those years we rarely if ever spoke. If he made a good play, I might tell him, "Nice block." If I had stopped the ballcarrier, he might say, "Nice tackle." Even then it was only once or twice a game. That was it. I don't know exactly why. Maybe we were too absorbed in our war. Maybe we were afraid we'd start liking each other.

———

To the fans, offensive linemen are the Rodney Dangerfields of professional football. It doesn't matter how good they are. The only time an offensive lineman ever gets noticed is when he screws up—when he's caught holding or when the quarterback gets sacked. Offensive linemen don't like it when the quarterback gets sacked. They get booed by the fans, reamed by the coaches at films, sometimes berated right on the field by the quarterback. As a result, trying to get by an offensive lineman to mess up his quarterback is like trying to steal food from his mother. He'd just as soon see you die first. If she were about to sack the quarterback, some offensive linemen would blindside Doris Day.

Holding was a given. And, yes, if they wanted to, the refs

could call holding on every play. Whether or not they did was another matter. It wasn't a question of how you got held, but who was doing the holding. If it was a rookie who was holding you, the refs might nail him a couple of times. If you were playing against an All-Pro, forget it. It's the same theory as in basketball. When was the last time you saw Larry Bird or Magic Johnson get called for traveling? It's the divine right of superstars and it never bothered me. All-Pros busted their ass to get there. They deserved anything they got.

Rookies also got called for holding because they didn't understand the subtleties yet. The longer an offensive lineman was in the league, the more adept he got at holding. The most popular ploy was to grab you by your jersey, fall down, and pull you to the ground. If a guy had it down to a science, that never annoyed me too much either. I could almost respect his cunning. It was the guys who would blatantly wrap their arms around your legs, flat out tackle you, that used to piss me off. Even then, though, I could sympathize with an offensive lineman who held. We were getting paid to make tackles, they were getting paid to stop us. They did what they felt they had to.

In 1978, the league changed the rules about holding. Offensive linemen no longer had to cheat—the league made it legal for them. It was no coincidence. NFL defenses were getting too good. Scoring was down, sacks were up. Six to nothing games don't sell tickets, 35–30 games do. Defense is bad for attendance, ratings and the health of famous quarterbacks. Defense is bad for business. So the league changed the rules. In the old days the blockers had to keep their elbows locked and pointed toward the sidelines, with hands pulled in to the jersey. The new rules said that a blocker could extend his arms and open his hands. With their hands now open, offensive linemen had a license to hold.

Legalized holding I could live with. Those guys were doing it anyway—why not put it out in the open? What really made me mad was when they outlawed the head slap in 1977, another effort by the league to hinder defensive linemen and jack up scoring. The head slap was simple—you swung your outstretched arm into the helmet of the opposing player. I used the head slap all the time. I would use it as a tactical device. When you see a large arm being swung at your head, your reaction is to drop you head. Or at the very least to blink. That's all I ever needed. As soon as an offensive lineman took his eyes off me, I would run right by him.

If an offensive lineman insisted on playing dirty, I also used the head slap as a weapon. You have to understand, head slaps were never delivered with just a bare arm. First I'd tape my arm from my knuckles to just below my elbow. Then I'd put a rubber pad over that. A head slap like *that*, delivered with sufficient force and speed, felt like getting hit with a baseball bat. With all the shit the offensive linemen used to pull on us, we felt we were entitled to the head slap. Now we had to learn all new moves. It was like "Okay, Picasso, paint like hell. . . . Just don't use those damn brushes."

As you might have guessed, the abolition of the head slap made the offensive lineman's job easier. It also cut down on their headaches. Not that linemen took head slaps lying down when they were legal. I've never seen it myself, but I've heard of offensive linemen sharpening the screws on the sides of their helmets. If a defender would give a head slap, he'd find himself with a gouged and bloody hand.

Offensive linemen had other means of retaliation. They would thrust the palm of a hand under your facemask and jab you in the throat. Or they'd grab your facemask and practically twist your neck off. If you were already going by them, they'd leg whip you—spin around and kick you in the back of your knees. Done hard enough it could leave you black and blue. Done with malice it could break your ankle.

The worst of the lot was Conrad Dobler. You may remember him as "the dirtiest man in football." Off the field I liked Conrad. He was witty and intelligent, and he was always friendly. On Sundays he had no conscience. I rarely went head to head against Conrad, but I'll never forget one of the times I did. Conrad was wearing a big cast on his arm and he was swinging it around at everybody like a club. One play he jumped a mile offside and smashed me with his cast beneath my chin. It hurt like hell and I was sure he did it on purpose, so I started screaming at him, calling him a dirty bastard. Conrad just stood there smiling.

Conrad had an arsenal of dirty tricks for every occasion. He'd bite you, scratch you, trip you, stick you in the eye with a finger. Conrad's career had a curious evolution. When he was young and relatively healthy, he was just good. When he was older and more banged up, he was good and dirty. Toward the end of his career, when his knees were virtually shot, he was just dirty.

Had I come in contact with Conrad more often, I might have hated him. I never did though. I didn't approve of the way he played, but I understood it. Once his knees went bad, he didn't have the physical skills to survive in the NFL. By playing dirty, Conrad extended his career. Most defensive linemen were not so sympathetic. In fact, most of them despised him. Doug Sutherland, a Minnesota Viking who played against Conrad for a lot of years, probably summed up their feelings best: "When you play against Dobler, what you really need is a string of garlic beads and a wooden stake."

I've been called a lot of things in my life, but never once a dirty football player. I prided myself on playing clean. If I had to play dirty to win, then it wasn't worth it to me. When I say playing dirty, I mean intentionally trying to hurt someone. I loved to *compete,* but I never felt the desire to injure. I also played it clean for another reason. Personal vendettas were self-defeating. If I got too absorbed in beating up on the man over me, I was likely to forget about making the tackle. My philosophy was never to mangle the man in front of me, but to get away from him.

Of course there were exceptions. And when the circumstances called for it, I had several means of retribution. I could throw my head slaps with more ferocity. I could grab a man by his jersey, pull him to me, and butt him in the facemask with my helmet. If a running back was a cheap shot, I could hold him up during a tackle while one of my teammates moved in and delivered another blow. But for the reasons stated above, I almost always stayed away from that type of thing. The only time my sense of reason went out the window was when I felt my health was being endangered, when I knew someone was deliberately trying to maim me. Like that time I punched out the milkman. Also, whenever I played against the Denver Broncos or Seattle Seahawks. Those two teams did things that could have ended my career.

Everyone talks about how wild the Raiders play. It's true, the Raiders play rough. Most of their games have more than their share of extracurricular activity. But I've never in my life seen a Raider try to end another player's career. They may push and point and provoke, and even punch. But those are not things that can end a player's career. The Broncos and the Seahawks went far beyond punching. They hurt some people badly.

Denver's favorite ploy was a variation of something called the crackback or the chop block. When a defender—usually a defensive lineman—had his back turned, an offensive player would plow into the back of his knees with a helmet or shoulder pad. A lot of teams employed the crackback, but none as dangerously as the Broncos. They would use two men—one to stand you up at the line of scrimmage, another to drill you from behind. The play would start with their tight end lined up a few yards wide of you, toward the sideline. At the snap of the ball, the offensive tackle would engage you at the line of scrimmage. While you were still tied up with the tackle, the tight end would plow into the back of your knees with his shoulder pads or helmet. On Denver, Claudie Minor was the tackle and Ron Egloff the tight end. Egloff was 6'5" and 225 pounds. When he took out my legs it was serious business.

Denver used to chop me at least a couple of times a game, more often if I was putting a lot of pressure on their quarterback. One time I decided I'd had enough. Egloff hit me from behind and my leg bent back in an awkward position. I wasn't injured, but it wasn't from their lack of effort. I was screaming and cursing at Egloff. I wanted to know why he persisted in cutting me. I told him I wanted an answer and I wanted it now. Egloff's face turned a pale white.

"My coach told me to do it," is all he said.

He didn't say which one, but I'm sure he meant their head coach, Red Miller. Nothing much happens on a football team without the man in charge knowing about it. I didn't doubt what Egloff told me. I knew there were coaches who taught that kind of thing. I was fortunate enough never to have to play for anyone who did, but I would hear talk from other players. I also knew there were very few players in the NFL who would pull something like that on their own inclination. For two reasons: One, they had too much respect for their opponents. Two, they didn't want it happening to them. In the old days, cheap-shot artists were much more prevalent. There wasn't as much at stake if someone decided to seek revenge. Today the players make too much money, there's too much to lose.

Beyond all that, I knew how Red Miller felt about the Raiders. He hated us because we always used to beat him. In the Raiders, Miller saw an obstacle that was keeping the Broncos from greatness. Miller didn't have the personnel to beat us fairly, so he would stoop to almost anything. There was no excuse for what Miller did. Nor was there an excuse for Minor and Egloff. Just because Miller told them to cut people, it didn't mean they had to comply. A lot of players refuse to do that stuff regardless of their coaches' wishes. It's beneath them.

The Seahawks weren't any better, just a little different. They would chop you with a tackle and a running back. The tackle's name was Steve August and the halfback was Dan Doornink. At the snap of the ball, Doornink would flare a few feet toward the sideline and out of my vision. August would tie me up briefly at the line of scrimmage, then allow me to slip into their backfield. Just after I got free from August, Doornink would rush from my blind side and take out the back of my knees.

In 1981, after several teams repeatedly complained about the Broncos and the Seahawks, the league took a ''stand''—you could not crackback against a man who is engaged with another blocker. I think it was too little too late. A lot of careers had already been lost. With the way our legs got ripped up, I'm amazed that defensive linemen lasted as long as they did. Even with the new rule, it's not much better today. Linemen are still getting chopped and not just by one man. Teams still pull tag teams, but it's rarely called by the refs.

———

The war on a football field is not just physical. There also exists a war of words. In a game you utilize every last resource, and for some players that includes their mouths. Some talk to intimidate, but most use words to get an opponent angry, and thus distracted. If you can stir the man across from you into a frenzy, he may forget about what he's supposed to be doing out there. The offensive linemen may jump offside or get off the ball a moment late. The defensive linemen may get wrapped up in punishment rather than tackling. Since football players have basically heard it all, you can't call someone a dummy or an asshole and expect to get any kind of a rise. The magic word seems to be "motherfucker." That almost always hits a nerve. Most of the verbal abuse goes on at the end of a play, but sometimes it continues all the way to the next snap of the ball. You can see the guys still jawing while they're getting into their stances. I was never much of a talker out there. I knew what they were after and I didn't want to get trapped in their little game, especially when we were down by the goal line. They'd call you every name in the book, hoping you'd go crazy the following play. Sure enough, while you were sticking a forearm down the tackle's throat, the halfback would go running right by you for a touchdown.

Playing against the talkers never bothered me. In fact, I liked it. There was nothing better than playing against a guy with a nonstop mouth, then seeing him get quiet when you drilled him. And you could always tell when you had a talker beat because he would suddenly shut up. He was too discouraged to keep it up. The scariest guys were the ones who never said a word. No matter how hard you hit them, they just popped back up like you were nothing. That's the way Walter Payton was. There were running backs who were faster or stronger than Walter, but no one I ever played against ever ran *harder*. Walter would amaze me—he'd get absolutely leveled, then pat the guy who did it on the butt. Sometimes he'd be smiling. Now *that* was frightening.

That August guy from Seattle had one of the bigger mouths in the league. He would curse me up and down the entire game.

We beat them in Oakland one year and August walked up to me after the game.

"Wait until next year you asshole," he yelled at me. "Then we'll see what happens. You won't have it so easy up in Seattle."

I walked away, but first I filed away his comments for the future. The next time we played the Seahawks I was pumped beyond belief. August couldn't do anything with me; I was in Seattle's backfield all day. Every time we played them I took August to school. I guess he should have kept his mouth shut.

Early in his career, Matt Millen was probably the biggest taunter on our team. When Matt first played against the Redskins, he even taunted John Riggins. If the NFL was a league of actors, this would be the equivalent of taunting Brando. After a few years in the league, Matt didn't talk so much. You live and you learn. He's still verbal out there at times, but it isn't always what it seems. In Super Bowl XVIII against the Redskins, Matt was standing across from their quarterback, Joe Theismann, and jawing at him all game long. From the stands it looked like Matt wanted to kill him. Uh-uh. Matt and Joe had run a camp for children together and Matt thought Joe had stiffed him on some minor bill. Matt was screaming at Joe, alright, but it was that Joe owed him a lunch.

When Howie Long is mad enough, he'll challenge a guy to meet him after the game in the parking lot. But then, I don't think Howie is afraid of anyone. One time the Seahawks were standing around in their huddle. Time was out and a water boy was handing them containers of water. Howie walked across the line of scrimmage, about a foot from where the Seahawks were huddling.

"Just give that water to me," Howie said. "These guys aren't doing anything anyway."

In another game against the Cincinnati Bengals, Howie was badgering their center, Dave Rimington. Dave is a weight-lifting monster, about 6'3" and 290 pounds. When the Bengals were in their huddle, Howie told Rimington he looked like a "bridge toll."

I've had players insult my heritage, my honor, even my haircut. If a player was getting older, Millen might tell him he couldn't do the job anymore. It all sounds pretty severe, but no one takes it too seriously. There's an understanding among NFL players: You can say just about whatever you want to, *when* you're on the field. A lot of it is nervous chatter—everyone knows that no one really *means* it. And a football field is a private world, whatever you say is not going any farther. What you don't do is degrade an opponent to the press, embarrassing him to the general public. Do that and you'd better watch yourself.

Talking on the field can work both ways. Some guys will brownnose you, talk real sweet, hoping you'll go a little easy on them. Whenever I was having a big game, all of a sudden everyone was my friend. Jack Rudnay was like that. But Jack was a *real* friend. He was one of my teammates when I played with the Chiefs. He was their center for thirteen years, and when people talk about "throwbacks," they are talking about players like Jack. In a game against the Chicago Bears, Jack once broke his little finger. Even though the bone was sticking out, they pushed it back into place, taped it to his next finger, and he only missed two plays. It later took eighteen stitches to close. But whenever we played the Chiefs, on the plays when I lined up over center, you'd have thought Jack was my favorite uncle. He'd always have a kind word. He'd say, "Hey, Toozie, how ya' doing?" Or "Looking good today, Toozie." Jack wasn't afraid of me, he wasn't in fear of anyone. He was trying to disarm me with his kindness.

A few players would distract you with their humor. One game we were playing against the Green Bay Packers. It was after I'd already been in *North Dallas Forty* and everyone knew I would have designs on Hollywood after I retired. The Packers had a guard named Greg Koch who was as dirty as they come— late hits, leg whips, whatever he could think of. Whenever I'd play against Koch, I would resign myself to a day of cuts and bruises. But one play he pushed me too far. It was a pass and I started to blow right by him. He lunged at me and stuck his hands right around my throat. He had thick, meaty hands and I felt like I couldn't breathe.

"Get your hands off me," I screamed at him.

Koch started grinning, which only made me more furious.

"What's the problem, Tooz?" he asked me. "I'm just trying to be a star. I'm just trying to get to Hollywood like you are."

As dirty as he was, I broke up laughing. It was hard to stay mad at a guy who was as crazy as that.

Ron Yary of the Minnesota Vikings must have liked my face as much as Koch. Because I could always find his hands there. Yary was a tremendous tackle in his prime. Near the end of his career he was still better than most, but his style had changed. Now he was an old, tricky pro who would do whatever he had to in order to finish the job. One game Yary had his hands in my face for four quarters. He was yanking my facemask around like I was one of those dolls with the bobbing heads. I didn't say anything to him that game. I respected him, for one thing, and I had a good game regardless. The next time we played the Vikings, Yary clutched by facemask on the first play from scrimmage. He was twisting it like crazy and it hurt my neck. Respect my ass, I figured I'd better draw the line.

"Put your hands in my face one more time," I began very calmly, "AND I'LL RIP YOUR FUCKING HANDS OFF."

Yary looked shocked, as if he didn't even realize what he'd been doing. Amazingly, Yary kept his hands out of my face for the rest of the night, for the rest of my career. I really don't think he realized what he was doing. Yanking my head around had become second nature.

I had another confrontation with a Houston Oilers guard named Morris Townsend. We were playing that day in the Oakland Coliseum. Two weeks earlier, I had broken my right hand in a game against New England. On the final play of the game, Sam "Bam" Cunningham dove over the goal line to beat us. I got a piece of him, but only with one hand. One of his shoulders slammed right into my outstretched hand and shattered it. I played with a broken hand for the next five games. The NFL

allowed you to play is a cast, provided you covered it with half
an inch of foam padding. That was what I was wearing when
we played the Oilers.

When a play was over—-but a guy kept hitting me because
his back was turned and he didn't know—I would tell him the
play was over and that he should hold up. No sense in either
one of us getting hurt when nothing was at stake. Townsend
was a strong, rawboned rookie—meaning he was cocky and naive enough to think he could get away with anything. On one
play Townsend kept pushing me after the play was over. I told
him to take it easy, the play was over. He kept on pushing.
Then the whistle blew. But he kept on pushing. I told him he'd
better stop, and he pushed me again. Obviously I hadn't made
my point. I wound up and hit him square in the chest with my
cast. His feet flew out from beneath him, and the first thing that
hit the ground was the back of his helmet. All at once, 50,000
Raiders fans went WOOOOH! Townsend's head wasn't hurt but
his pride sure was. It also scared the daylights out of him. As
he climbed back to his feet, the whites of his eyes looked like
big, round pancakes. Townsend minded his manners the rest of
the day.

Some of the guys just make noise out there, all kinds of
noises. Groans and snorts and hisses and sighs. We used to call
Ed Muransky, a guard for the Chargers, The Mad Growler. Every
time he'd pull out to block you, he'd be growling. John Hanna
played for the Patriots. He was one of the best, hardest-hitting
guards in history. John also played with a lot of sound effects.
Thank God for that. If he hadn't been so noisy on one particular
play, I might not be here to write this book now.

It happened on a trap play. The tackle let me slide by him
and I moved into New England's backfield. Then I saw the halfback running beneath me toward the middle of the line. Then I
heard a loud and violent scream. As I turned to see who or what
it was, I was nearly cut in half by Hanna. He hit me—right in
my facemask with his helmet—at the precise moment I turned
my body. I felt like I'd been hit in the face with a brick. I knew
I was bleeding. When the Patriots punting team came on the
field, I jogged to the sideline. I took off my helmet and I was

shocked. My entire facemask had been crushed into my face. The bridge of my nose was split wide open and blood was streaming down my face. Since I still had my wits, I kept on playing. They bandaged me up, attached a whole new face-mask, and I went back out there. It was the hardest I'd ever been hit in my life. If Hanna hadn't screamed, and I hadn't turned around, he could have broken my neck.

Professional football, obviously, is not a game to be taken lightly. When John Madden was coaching the Raiders, the Saturday before a game he would give each player an itinerary. It would list Sunday's times for things like taping, team breakfast, practice, etc. At the point on the itinerary for listing the game time, John wrote three words: GO TO WAR. Although the NFL eventually made him remove that from his itinerary—don't ask me why, I never understood it either—that's what football basically is. The consequences are rarely as final or brutal as a war, but some of the principles are the same. If you get right down to it, you are fighting for your life out there.

Today, when I watch a game, I look at football differently than I did when I was a player. When someone delivers a devastating blow—I'll wince. I think to myself, *I can't believe he's getting up. That must have hurt like hell.* I watch it more as a fan would. When I was a player, I'd occasionally have thoughts like that, but only during game films or when I was watching another team on TV. Never on a game day. When I was on the field, I never thought about getting hurt for a minute. I wouldn't allow myself. When you're on a football field, you can't be scared or have second thoughts. It's suicidal. Flinch or hold back when eleven angry men are coming at you hard, and you're setting yourself up for disaster. A football field is not a healthy place for reflection.

The same line of thinking holds true when a player gets injured. No one even wants to think about him. It's one of the most bizarre aspects of playing in the NFL. Except for your very closest teammates, it's almost as if you become invisible. Everyone else tends to freeze you out. Guys will come up and ask you how you're doing, but it's like they're not even listening.

"How ya' feeling, Tooz?"

"Not so great. My arm is broken in nineteen places and last night I found my kidneys on the side of my bed."

"Good, good. Looking forward to having you back."

It's not a matter of being insensitive, although football can certainly be a callous game. Again, it is a question of survival. You just don't want to stay too long around a player that's injured. Even when a player is lying injured on the field, you won't find many players staring. You don't want to start wondering if it can happen to you.

Football players get rewarded well for what they do. They drive nice cars, own large homes, get cheered when they do something well. On balance, I think football is the greatest job in the world. It gave me a lot more than I ever expected to have, and I feel very, very fortunate to have played it. But it still galls me when people lump football players in with other "overpaid athletes." Because football players also pay a terrible price. They pay with their bodies.

When you first join the NFL, you're full of yourself. You're strong, tireless, you can run all day. You believe you can play for ever. You can't. It doesn't matter who you are, the game will wear you down. The human body can only take so much. If you listen closely enough, your body will tell you when it's time to retire from the NFL. The sad thing is, most football players don't listen.

Jim Otto is the most dramatic example of a man who truly loved pro football, but who will pay for it the rest of his life. The first Raider in the Hall of Fame, Jim was retired before I got to the Raiders, but I've met him several times. He's just a wonderful man. On the field, Jim was one of those tougher-than-nails guys, always bleeding, always hurt, but never willing to miss so much as a play. In the course of his college and pro career, Jim suffered thirty concussions, twenty-five broken noses, 150 stitches in his face, a detached retina, and untold broken ribs. Both his kneecaps and both of his elbows have been broken, he's had his teeth kicked out and he's got two cauliflower ears from where his helmet smashed into the side of his head.

He has a metal and artificial joint beneath the skin of his left knee. Every joint in his body is arthritic and, all told, he's had fifteen football-related operations. Jim says he can barely sit or stand for any length of time. At night he can barely sleep. He can't run, can't swim, can barely bend over to pull up his socks. For any man this would be terrible. For a man who spent the better part of his life running and jumping and tossing his body around, it's unthinkable.

Jim retired in 1975. He owns several Burger King franchises in Northern California, and his life after football has been financially rewarding. But all the money in the world can't make your body stop hurting. Jim's will be a life of chronic pain.

Most players are much more fortunate than Jim. But no one plays football without forfeiting his health. You get to the point where the pain becomes all too familiar. We used to have injuries called hangnails—so minor that you don't give them a second's thought. Hangnails included bruises, cuts, groin pulls, twisted ankles, dislocated fingers, pulled hamstrings and slightly fractured bones. The injuries you tape, disinfect, ice, warm and try to forget.

I don't think most fans fully realize the sacrifices made by players in the NFL. I know I never did before I became a pro. And it's perfectly understandable. Fans never see you during the week. They only see you on Sunday, with the band, the cheerleaders, the colorful uniforms and the polished helmets. It all looks very glamorous, almost like a fantasy. But for those who play it, the game is very real. Because we're such big people, some folks think we're somehow invulnerable. We aren't even close. We bleed and break and get hurt like any other man.

There is no such thing as a healthy football player. In my entire career, I never played a single game when I was 100 percent. Not one. You see, you're hurting before you even take the field. You're hurting from practice, from the game the week before, from chronic injuries you've had for years. Most of those limbs banging off each other on Sunday are tender and sore, sometimes fractured, before the game ever starts. Imagine getting punched in an already blackened eye. I think NFL games are dynamic as they are, but if the players could somehow stay healthy, you'd see play after play that would boggle your mind. Football, as it is, becomes a war of attrition.

Battling the pain becomes a mind game. Your body hurts like hell, your mind tells you to ignore it. Amazingly, it works. When you get out there on Sunday, and your adrenaline is pumping like wild, you actually forget about the pain. It's later that night that the pain comes back to you. Monday mornings are even worse. Monday mornings are a football player's nightmare. You feel like you've been run over by a truck.

Painkillers are a way of life in the NFL. If the sight of needles makes you sick, you have to overcome it. If the pain is too great to play without them, then painkillers become a necessity. I'm only talking about local anesthetics now, but it's still a dangerous proposition. Painkillers mask the pain—letting you use the injured body part—so you're actually making yourself vulnerable to further injury. You really can't win—either you sit on the bench and risk losing your job, or you play on painkilling drugs and risk serious injury. I chose to take painkillers myself. Nobody held a gun to my head and said take this needle. The doctors and trainers, at least on all the teams I played for, never even suggested that I take a painkiller unless I asked. The coaches pressured me to play, as I'll get to shortly, but they never pushed me specifically to take a painkiller. The decision was mine. I took them because I wanted to keep my job.

In the NFL, playing with pain is not an option. If you can't play with pain, then you can't play in the NFL; you'd better find a new profession. Because if you can't play in pain, there's always someone on the bench who will. An athlete finally gets a chance to play. Then he gets hurt. If he can't make it back out there, he's in danger of losing his spot. So he takes painkillers. Being tougher than your opponent isn't enough in the NFL. You also have to be tougher than the teammate who's looking for your job.

In 1976, my first season with the Raiders, we were playing the San Diego Chargers. It was the first game I started for them, just one week after I foolishly asked John Madden to take two women with us on the team plane. My position was still very much insecure, especially with someone as talented as Charles Philyaw just waiting to take his starting spot back. Early in the game I tackled a running back. As I was bringing him down, I accidentally pulled him on top of me. I felt both of my shoulders go POP. The pain cut through me like a knife, but I didn't even leave the game. Not for a single play. When I went into the locker room at halftime, I found out that both of my shoulders were separated. For the first time in my career, I was probed and then shot with Novocain. I was shot twice in each shoulder with Novocain. I played the whole next half and twelve more games that season, right through the Super Bowl, with two separated shoulders. It hurt like hell and it was probably stupid— my shoulders ache to this day—but I did it anyway. Why? Because I didn't want to let Charles Philyaw back into the lineup. If I did, I knew I might never get my position back.

The pressure to play when you're hurt comes mostly from within. The final decision is truly up to the player. It's been suggested many times that playing hurt is mostly machismo, a way that players reaffirm their manhood. I don't buy that for a minute. If you've made it to the NFL, you may have some self-doubts, but the question of your manhood probably isn't one of them.

Yes, I prided myself on playing hurt. Yes, it made me feel good to know that I could play hurt. But not because I wondered how much of a man I was. Because I wanted my teammates to know they could count on me. Because I hated like hell to miss a game. Because I knew if I didn't I might not keep my job. Because I knew if I played hurt, Al Davis would remember it when it came time to write the checks. And because if I didn't play hurt, he'd remember that too.

However, we also got pressure from the coaches. Not all coaches, but some. When a player was injured, the question from the coaches was never "how are you feeling?" Or "are you getting proper rest?" It was "can you go this Sunday?" Coaches would say a lot of things to try and make you play. They'd tell you that you could do it, that you were better hurt than anyone they had healthy, that you had all summer to rest your body. The assholes would just tell you to get your ass out there. Please don't misconstrue this—a resounding majority of coaches are decent, responsible people. But coaches have pressure too. Pressure to win. Pressure to keep their jobs so they can feed their families. A good coach wouldn't let the pressure corrupt his sense of right and wrong, but the bad ones aren't so fussy.

We were playing the New England Patriots one year in an exhibition game. It was raining. I dove to make a tackle but the quarterback's jersey was too slippery. My fingers slid from his shoulder pads to his waist. When he jerked away I hit the ground. My arms were fully extended and I fell sharply on my elbows. CRACK—you could hear it on the sideline. My elbows stung, but it was my right shoulder that suddenly felt as if it were burning. It was separated again.

I sat out the last exhibition game, but I was back in the starting lineup the following week. It was the season opener against the Rams, and no one likes to miss an opener. The pain in my shoulder was still intense, and my range of motion was limited at best. I went into the training room before the game and was again forced to use Novocain. I stretched out on the table and clenched my teeth. The shots in themselves were very painful. A shot of Novocain was inserted into my shoulder. It burnt like hell. I was shot four more times, all in my injured right shoulder. Ten minutes later my shoulder felt numb, I could barely feel it at all. I was ready to play football.

On the first series of downs, I paid the price. It was a handoff to Cullen Bryant. Cullen was their fullback, one of the most punishing runners in the game. He was running up the middle, and I was moving laterally from my left defensive end. As I moved in to make the tackle, I wasn't even thinking about the shoulder. I wanted to run into Cullen before Cullen ran into me. I was too late, Cullen forced the impact. He lowered his head and dug his helmet into my right shoulder. It was a violent collision. Now the pain—sharp and piercing—shot all the way from my shoulder to my hand. I was scared but I tried to compose myself. I thought it would go away in a second. But it didn't. My right arm was quivering violently at my side. Maybe I was delirious, maybe I just didn't know any better. But I said to myself—*man, you've got to finish this series.* When the Rams went to punt one play later, I went running to the sideline. I couldn't lift my arm and I was afraid. I was screaming on the sideline.

"I can't lift my arm, I can't lift my arm."

One of the coaches walked up when he saw me screaming. I couldn't believe what he said to me.

"John," he told me, "we need you. You're better with one arm than anyone else we've got with two. Suck it up. You're playing."

When the defense went back on the field, I ran out there with them. When I look back at my career in football, I see things I did that I can't understand, situations that just didn't seem to be logical. This was one of those times. I could not lift my arm above my shoulder. Every move I made, I made with one arm. I was a one-armed man playing football.

Jackie Slater was playing offensive tackle that day. Jackie was a good one and usually our battles were fairly even. But at least in the opening half, Jackie was pushing me around pretty good. As the game wore on and the pain again became secondary, I developed some one-armed moves and actually wound up playing fairly well. But Jackie still got the better of me. We hadn't exchanged a word all day. In the final quarter, I spoke to him.

"Having a big day today, huh, Jackie? Well, I'll see *you* again, pal."

I was frustrated and angry at the world, not really at Jackie. He was just doing his job. I was playing and so I had to be dealt with. It wasn't his fault that I was out there.

We beat the Rams, 24–17, but I had anything on my mind but celebration. My arm felt like it was hanging by a thread, my shoulder was inflamed and burning. While the rest of the guys were jumping around in the locker room, I was sitting perfectly still in front of my locker, head bowed between my legs. On top of everything, it had been a hot and sticky night. I was hurting and I was exhausted. I had that cold, hollow feeling that players get when they know they're seriously injured. I was still sitting in a daze when one of the assistant coaches—

not the one who had sent me on the field—snapped me from my trance.

"Lift your head up, boy," he boomed. "Be proud. You look like a loser. We won today. Be proud."

I didn't smile, didn't even lift my head. I was scared for my career, and this guy wanted me to act like a winner. I glimpsed at him as he walked away. He was shaking his head and frowning.

For the next five weeks, I couldn't lift my arm. But I was back on the field three games later. I'm not boasting, just relating to you what happened. And it's not as if my threshold for pain was extraordinary. Every player in the NFL can recall a similar horror story.

———

I'll tell you one thing they could do to reduce NFL injuries. Do away with artificial surfaces. God may not have made man to play football, but he definitely didn't make him to play on artificial turf. I don't care what the league office or the people who make turf say, they never played on the stuff. I did and I can tell you that it's terrible. It's obvious why they have it: It looks nice for TV, and it's cheaper to maintain than grass. Meanwhile, players are going down like flies. Turf is bad in every way. Period. It gets too hot when it's hot out, it gets too slick when it rains. It cuts you and burns you when you fall on it. Whenever I played on turf, I'd have abrasions scattered across my body. I'd get them all over—on my back, ankles, knees, hands and elbows. Bad ones, the kind that don't heal for weeks. I'd wake up some Monday mornings and I'd be stuck to my sheets.

The worst part about turf is that it shortens players' careers by ripping up their legs. Because it's so hard, turf doesn't give when you make sudden stops. It jars the ligaments and joints, rips them to pieces if the impact is harsh enough. Football on grass is dangerous enough—on turf it's almost insane. You don't even have to play football on turf to feel its effects. Just running on it before the game made my legs and feet hurt. I've seen guys get hurt without even getting hit. They'd be running full speed and they'd get their feet caught in a seam in the turf. It happened to Matt Millen in a game in Seattle. The disturbing, tragic thing about all this is that the NFL is perfectly aware that turf is dangerous. I guess economics takes precedence over players' health.

7

WINE, WOMEN AND TROUBLES IN KANSAS CITY

Football players generally have large egos. If it doesn't come naturally, most guys will force themselves into developing one. At least from July through December, you've got to believe you're the strongest, fastest, meanest SOB in the world. Self-doubt is a football player's greatest liability—ego, one of his most vital tools. It's part of the reason he made it to the pros in the first place.

There's another reason why athletes sometimes get overinflated egos: Women swarm all over them. If an athlete believed everything he was told by his adoring female fans, he'd never be able to get his helmet on. Whether it was our celebrity, our wealth, or because they simply liked us for ourselves, women were always available if you looked for them. A lot of times they found you.

I've changed a lot of my ways over the years. When I first came into the league, I was twenty-two years old. Like a lot of men that age, the more women I would date, the more of a man I thought I was. It was important to me to be seen with a variety of beautiful women. I suppose I was trying to pump up my ego.

I don't have that need anymore. Today I'm in love with an intelligent, lovely woman named Stephanie. I'm totally monogamous. A solid relationship with Stephanie is much more satisfying to me than several superficial ones. Even if I wasn't so crazy over Steph, I still wouldn't be some kind of a swinger. It's too dangerous, for one thing. In the old days, you didn't have so many terrible diseases. If you did contract something, you could take a shot and it would be gone in a week. Those days are over; now the stakes are often life threatening. I would say the sexual habits of American athletes have mirrored those of American society on the whole—the days of casual sex are mostly gone.

Times have certainly changed. When I was a rookie with the Oilers, Houston was a single person's paradise. At that time, the city had 6,000 people under the age of twenty-five moving in every month. I had never been much of a ladies man in high school or college. I was basically shy and wrapped up in playing ball. But suddenly I was a pro and I was meeting all these exciting women. I felt like a child let loose in a candy store.

My ritual the night before a game was always the same: I'd take a couple of sandwiches, some peanut M & M's, a few magazines and retire to my room, by *myself*. When it came to having sex the night before a game, I was from the old school. I thought it would hinder my performance on the playing field, either by sapping my endurance or reducing that irritated edge I'd tried so hard all week to maintain. The last thing I needed was to be feeling happy and content out there. I needed to be feeling mean.

(If there's one player in football I don't think would be bothered by pregame sex, it has to be a quarterback. Those guys don't want to get too worked up anyway; they have to stay on an even keel. Maybe a little fooling around would actually help.)

In the 175 or so games that I played during my career, I had sex the night before maybe two or three of them. One of those exceptions came right at the beginning—in the week before my first pro game. We had just left our isolated camp in Huntsville, and by the time I got to Houston my hormones were in overdrive. I don't want to sound like Mr. Macho here, but somehow I wound up sleeping with a different woman every night that week. Including the Saturday night before the game. It certainly wasn't by design, and I've never been a believer in promiscuity, but that week it just turned out that way. It was an unusual time in my life. I suppose I was full of myself—I was the first pick in the draft, my first week in the pros, and I thought I was a big shot. And I'd never met so many fascinating women before. But on the morning of the game, my legs were curiously weak. I had a good game but I could have played better. For the rest of my career I was much more, uh, prudent.

People always ask me about groupies and athletes. I never liked that word. *Groupies.* It sounds like a school of fish. I admit it, some of the women who hung around athletes weren't looking for intellectual stimulation. With their smiles and their dress, they made their intentions perfectly clear. There were times when I'd be lying in bed in the middle of the night and I'd hear a knock at my door. It would be a woman, a perfect stranger, asking me to let her in. I don't think any of them were after my autograph.

But contrary to what some people think, they are hardly the only kind of women who like to associate with athletes. We also met a lot of bright, well-adjusted, career-minded women who were not looking for anything fleeting. They knew athletes had careers, and these were the type of men they liked. Those women were usually looking for something more permanent.

There's also a perception that all athletes—single or married—fool around when they're on the road. It isn't true. Boredom and loneliness on the road are part of being an athlete. One way to fill the void is the pursuit of female companionship. But that's mostly the guys who are single. Maybe I'm too idealistic, but if I had to make a guess, I'd say about 85 percent of the married guys are true to their wives.

It's the single guys, especially the rookies, who were preoccupied with chasing women. And when you're single and lonesome, staying in some strange hotel, sometimes you didn't discriminate a whole lot. Especially after a night when you've been drinking, you occasionally woke up the next morning with some real bloopers.

One season I shared an apartment with Teddy Hendricks. After an unusually rough evening, I staggered into the kitchen the following morning. Teddy was fiddling in the refrigerator with a pitcher of orange juice.

"Teddy," I groaned, "you will absolutely not believe the person I brought home last night."

"Tooz," he countered, "at this point, there's not a single thing you could do that would possibly surprise me."

Famous last words. Just then, as Teddy was pouring some juice from his pitcher, a 200-pound Oriental woman waddled into view. (I didn't actually weigh her, it's just an educated guess.) There she was, bigger than life and filling the entire doorway. She had looked fairly attractive the night before—ah, who am I kidding? Anyway, when Teddy looked up and saw her—CRASH—he dropped the pitcher to the floor. For a moment we all stood there like idiots, staring as the orange juice spread across the kitchen floor. Teddy explained to the girl that he'd just been startled, so there weren't any hurt feelings. After my "date" had gone, Teddy admitted he was wrong. I had clearly surpassed myself.

Some women collect autographs from their encounters with athletes, others prefer a more personal memento. The Raiders were walking off the field just after a road game against the Rams when a woman ran up to me. She said that one of her friends was a cheerleader for the Rams, and that the cheerleader would like me to call her in a couple of hours. Then she gave me a scrap of paper with her girlfriend's phone number. It sounded good to me and I called her. She said there was a party later that night at Hugh Hefner's mansion, and asked if I would like to go as her date. This sounded *real* good to me and I said I'd love to. We had a great time at the party and, well, let's just say the relationship accelerated at an extraordinary rate. We decided to go back to my hotel room. But when we walked in one of my teammates was fast asleep in his bed with his girlfriend. My date and I went into the bathroom. The festivities picked up from there and we wound up breaking the toilet seat right off the commode. When the fun was over, my date picked up the toilet seat and started walking out the door with it. I asked her what she was doing.

"If I don't take this," she explained, "no one will believe that I really met you. This will be my personal souvenir from the Tooz."

Then she walked out the door with her reminder.

That kind of stuff didn't happen between the Raiders and the Raiderettes, our cheerleaders. In fact, there wasn't any dating at all. For some reason, management had an edict that Raiders and Raiderettes were not to socialize. I believe every team has a similar rule. This is not to say we were blind to their charms. One of my teammates had the worst timing imaginable. He would wait until the national anthem was actually being played, and then he would nudge me.

"Hey, Tooz," he'd exclaim, "check out the ass on the girl who's third from the left."

I'm thinking destruction and mayhem, and this guy is talking asses.

"Are you nuts?" I'd reply. "We've got a game here in a minute. Would you leave me alone and let me play football?"

I never looked, of course . . . okay, maybe for a second.

There was one exception to the division between Raiders and Raiderettes. Mickey Marvin, an offensive guard for the Raiders and one of my closest friends, was sitting in the press box one game while recovering from an injury. Mickey was looking through a pair of binoculars when his eyes stopped on a cheerleader named Lisa Conway. Mickey was enraptured—he decided he had to meet Lisa Conway.

Mickey and I were going to speak at a luncheon, and Mickey asked a Raiders official if Lisa could be there too. Unknown to me, the whole meeting was neatly orchestrated. There was another cheerleader there named Donna. By chance, I was seated next to Lisa and Mickey, right near Donna. I was trying to get Lisa's attention. I had no idea Mickey liked her and I thought she was attractive too. Mickey would lean back to look at Lisa, I would lean back to block his vision. He'd lean forward, I would follow suit. It must have looked like a Marx Brothers routine. This went on for several moments before Mickey pulled me aside and clued me in. Six months later Mickey and Lisa were married.

Matt Millen is one Raider who gets testy around forward women. Matt is devoted to his wife and normally would not be

In 1974 I played with the World Football League.
For exactly seven plays.

I was always a Raider at heart.

You gotta love Christmas. My lady, Stephanie (right), and her cousin, Andrea, in their Bunny attire.

On our way to Hugh Hefner's Playboy Pajama Party. Am I a lucky guy, or what?

Apples of my eye: Back home with Simone, Justine and Luke, my niece and nephews.

My parents, Audrey and Marvin, before they were married. Milwaukee, 1949.

When I was fourteen months old, my parents bought me a football. Little did they know.

*First Communion,
eight years old, Milwaukee.*

*Junior Prom,
1967.*

*Track and Field sectionals, 1968, on the way
to the Wisconsin state championships. I won state
that year, in both the long shot and the discus.*

The Raiders don't hate the Broncos. Really.

At Missouri I began as a tight end, When I transferred to Tampa, I found my niche on defense.

A sack is good for the soul.

My sisters, Dawn, Karen, and Christine.
This picture was posed, the affection is real.

Family Day,
training camp in Santa Rosa.

On the Set of "A-Team" with Joe Namath, one
of the all-time greats, and a hell of a nice guy.

*Me and my paisan, Phil Villipiano, in
transit to the Italian Festival in Reno.*

*John Madden put on airs? Not once in
the time I've known him.*

John Matuszak and fiancée Stephanie Cozart.

caught dead in a singles bar. After some serious, prolonged peer-group pressure, some of the guys finally persuaded Matt to accompany them to a bar called Sausalito South in Manhattan Beach. Not a good call. Matt was in there five minutes when an unfamiliar woman started batting her eyelashes at him. Matt just turned away. But this lady was persistent. She was also blitzed. She walked up to Matt and brushed all over him.

"Do that again," Matt told her, "and I'll break your arm."

Matt didn't mean it literally, of course, he was just trying to make a point.

Matt's night wasn't over yet. A few minutes later he was confronted by another woman. Without so much as a little small talk, she asked Matt for his name and number. Matt took a napkin and obliged. With a big, friendly grin, Matt handed the woman the napkin. It said "Matt Millen, number 55." The woman looked at Matt with disgust.

"That's not what I wanted," she told him.

"I know, but that's all you're going to get."

Aggressive women are not unique to Southern California. They also reside up north in Santa Rosa. Our practice facility at training camp had two separate fields and the players would split up according to platoon. One day I saw a civilian running on the sideline of the other field. It was a woman. Since our practices were closed to the public, this caught me by surprise. When I focused a little harder, I saw that she was nude! This was back when streaking was in vogue, and it turned out that a couple of rookies had paid her on a dare. She started on her trek around the other field in a sprint. But by the time she got to us she was winded and could barely walk. As she moved ever so slowly past the defensive linemen, we all stopped to admire her, uh, sense of adventure.

While I'm on the topic of nudity, this one you may not believe. But it's true. One Saturday night the Raiders flew into San Diego before a Sunday game. As we rode a bus from the airport to our hotel, it was dark outside and everyone was settled quietly in his seat. Cliff Branch shattered the silence. He was standing in the back of the bus, jumping up and down and laughing like a maniac. When he finally regained his composure, Cliff started to scream at us.

"Get over here," he yelled, "get over here. You're not going to believe this."

Cliff was normally a quiet kind of a guy, so we knew something special was up. About twenty of us packed our way to the back of the bus, each guy fighting for access to a window. Driving in the lane next to us was a middle-aged man. In itself this was not unusual. Lots of middle-aged men transport themselves in cars. But this was not your everyday commuter. For one thing, he wasn't wearing any clothes. That's *nothing*, as in totally naked. He was also driving with only one hand. With his other hand he was masturbating. By now the back of the bus had erupted in chaos. Guys were screaming, pointing, just about in tears. Mr. Happy looked up, saw twenty Oakland Raiders, and nearly wrecked his car. He swerved to the side and sideswiped a pair of parked cars. Hell of a guy, that Mr. Happy.

I once had a short-lived relationship in Milwaukee with a girl named Donna. Social graces, I soon found out, were not her strong point. Donna drove a motorcycle. One night we had a date and I forgot completely about it. I even forgot to call. A few days later my mother had some company in her backyard. Suddenly we heard the roar of a motorcycle. It was Donna. Judging from the look on her face, she was not there to sample the jello mold. Without a word, she walked up and punched me in the nose. She had a very respectable right and you could hear the crack across the backyard. What could I do? I could already hear the newscasts: Tooz Hammers Motorcycle Queen. Film at eleven. I simply pinned her arms until she assured me she was cooled out. Then I heard a buzzing from across the yard—my mother's friends had taken in the entire scene. Uh, hi, ladies, I'd like you to meet Donna.

When the Oilers finally traded me to the Chiefs, it was eight games into the 1974 season. The Chiefs had a great group of veterans—Len Dawson, Buck Buchanan, Willie Lanier—and a terrific person and coach in Hank Stram. The organization was undoubtedly conservative, but Hank treated his players so well that no one seemed to mind. With all that talent, we could never put it all together on the field. We were five and nine my first season, and five and nine again the next. That second year I started all fourteen games and played well. And, for a change, my life had been pleasantly calm. I was looking forward to an eventful 1976. I got my wish, but not in the manner I expected.

My second year in Houston, I had been introduced to a twenty-year-old woman who we'll call Sally. It was one of those relationships that move faster than you ever plan. Sally moved with me when I got traded to the Chiefs, and at first we were very happy. Having a healthy relationship with an athlete is never an easy proposition. It takes a woman with a strong sense of self. Initially, Sally and I were perfectly compatible. Even when our relationship suffered from unusual strains, she accepted it.

Here's a pretty good example. Like all pro teams, the Chiefs used to house their players at training camp prior to the regular season. There was a rule: No women in the rooms after eleven o'clock. This was a rule that was largely ignored, particularly by me. Once the coaches had made their bed checks, at eleven, I prided myself on not wasting anytime: I could usually get Sally in there by 11:05.

A few weeks after I came to the Chiefs, I had snuck Sally in, and we were about to go to sleep, when we heard a sharp knock at my door. It was one of the assistant coaches, looking for me!

Sheets and pillows went flying. Warning Sally, in a whisper, not to say a word, I told the coach to give me a second. Damn: It was just a dorm room, with no place to hide her.

Nowhere except the closet.

I had no choice; it was either the closet or a healthy fine. Without a word of protest, Sally, half-dressed, hurried into the closet.

When Sally was stashed, I let the coach in. It was no big deal: Because I was new, he wanted to brief me on all of Stram's rules. He went up and down the line; eventually, he reached the rule about women and curfew.

"John," he said, "a lot of the guys sneak women into their

rooms. We know they do. But if anyone ever gets caught, there'll be hell to pay. I trust that's something you wouldn't do, though.''

I couldn't believe it. Was this guy pulling my leg, or what? Maybe one of the other guys had fingered me, and this was all a big joke. On the other hand, maybe it wasn't, so I wasn't about to turn myself in. I searched the coach's face for a clue, but it was expressionless. He appeared to be on the level.

"No, no," I assured him, "I'd never have a woman in my room."

The coach rambled on for another five minutes, but I didn't hear a word he said. My heart was beating like a drum. I was sure Sally was going to burst out of the closet and I would be exposed. But she never did. After the coach felt I'd been properly indoctrinated, he turned and left. Sally and I laughed about that one for weeks.

Remember that Eddie Murphy song—*My Girl Wants to Party All The Time*—which came out in the winter of 1985? They should have made that song about Sally. Only with a stronger title. Sally never met a party she didn't like, and her willingness to have fun—any time, anywhere—was a constant source of amusement to my teammates. One of our escapades made us living legends. They talk about it in Kansas City to this day.

At training camp, in a room adjoining the players' locker room, the Chiefs had what must have been the world's largest hot tub. One day, one of the coaches told us we could use it as we pleased. He said we could even invite our wives or our girl-friends. I was amazed. Maybe the Chiefs weren't so stodgy after all. Sally and I went to the hot tub one morning at ten. To get to the hot tub, you had to walk through the locker room. We looked to our right and then to our left—no one was around. We waited about a minute but, still, the coast was clear. Why not? We took off all our clothes and threw them by my locker. Then we hurried to the hot tub. We were enjoying the heat, relaxing, when a moment later one of the coaches walked by. First he took a serious double take. Then, when it registered that I was actually with a woman, his eyes nearly popped from his head.

"Who the hell is that?" he screamed.

I introduced him to Sally. Then he threw us out. Later I was reprimanded by the coaches. It seemed that they had meant what they said about the players using the hot tub, but only at certain times and only after we'd checked ahead of time. They probably figured we'd also be wearing clothes.

By now you know that Sally was never dull. But for all of her good points, Sally had a side that used to frighten me. She had absolutely no control over her temper. When something would ignite her, there wasn't a thing I could do or say to calm her down. Sally could be very, very dangerous. When her mood was at its darkest, she had one small habit I found especially disturbing: She would try and run me over in her car.

Our problems started in the summer of 1976 when she moved in with the wife of one of the other Chiefs. It was an ugly relationship. The player was sleeping with another woman. His wife was having an affair with another man. Sally had a ringside seat to the betrayal and it tore her up. Not knowing any better, Sally started to think that there wasn't an honest relationship in the entire NFL. That included ours. She started to badger me constantly, asking me if I was seeing other women. I wasn't, and I told her so, but she never believed me. Twisted by her paranoia, she became irrational. We began to have long, nasty arguments, usually over nothing.

One afternoon, I told Sally I had to go to a meeting. She started screaming at me, bellowing that I wasn't giving her the time or the consideration that she needed. She insisted I was going to see another woman. I wasn't about to take part in the same empty argument we'd had at least a dozen times before. I stormed out the door with Sally shouting at my back.

The Chiefs held their training camp at a junior college in Missouri. After the meeting there, Ed Budde, a huge offensive guard, and I were walking through the campus. We heard something loud, moving from the shadows behind us. It was Sally, rushing at us in her car. She was driving right over the lawn. It looked as if she was trying to run me over.

Whether on purpose or not, she missed me by about three feet. As she slammed on the brakes and tried to pull away, I ran over to the car. I reached in Sally's front window, grabbed the steering wheel with both hands, and bent the damn thing completely in half. Just folded it from the top to the bottom, as you would a piece of paper. Budde looked at me with total disbelief, but I was too busy gaping at Sally. There was no longer any question about it—the romance was not progressing smoothly.

Believe it or not, that little fiasco did not spell the end of our relationship. I knew Sally was mixed up and that she didn't know anyone else in Kansas City. I didn't want just to dump her. This was not a wise choice in terms of my own personal safety. I would have two more automobile incidents with Sally.

The next time was at the Marriott Hotel in Washington, D.C. Sally and I were sitting by the pool when she got up to get us a couple of drinks. When Sally came back, I was talking to a woman I had known in college. Sally didn't take this gracefully. In fact, she called me an asshole. With the entire pool now watching, I urged her to shut up. This only poured gasoline on the fire. She threw down our drinks and ran for her car. I told the woman that it was a pleasure to see her again, but if she valued her life she would get away quickly. Sally started chasing her around the parking lot in her car. Seriously. The woman finally escaped by running up the hotel stairs.

Sally snapped one more time, about a year later, in Oakland. I know you may find this hard to believe, but we had an argument. She decided to take it out on my brand new Lincoln Continental, which was parked outside. Sally jumped into her car and started nudging up against the back of my Lincoln. When I stupidly tried to reason with her, Sally responded by punching the gas and pushing the Lincoln even harder. Enough was enough. I opened my trunk and pulled out my old college helmet. I swung it at her windshield with all my might. It was a safety glass, and it shattered into a thousand little cracks. Sally wasn't through and I knew it. I took off down the road and Sally followed right behind me. Cracked windshield and all.

I finally broke up with Sally in 1978. It was painfully clear that we'd never be another Ozzie and Harriet. Besides, I knew the law of averages was working against me: And my mother didn't raise me to be a hood ornament.

Please allow me to backtrack. In the summer of 1976, as I went through summer practice with the Chiefs, our country had its 200th birthday. I felt a few years older. My battles with Sally were wearing me out. The intensity of our fights was getting higher. It got to the point where getting beaten up at practice was preferable to going home. The summer heat made everything worse. I'll never forget it. It was one of those sticky, relentless, Midwestern heat waves. The kind that makes every small hassle feel like a major trauma. Every day seemed more miserable than the one before.

A wildly jealous lover, sweltering heat and two pro football practices a day—it's a dangerous combination. My nerves were already at the breaking point when I started having problems sleeping. I would sleep for five minutes and wake up. Sleep for half an hour and wake up. This would go on all night. And the heat would not relent. I would lay in my bed and be drenched with sweat.

Then it all began to unravel—the blackest summer of my life. That July 3, I had been driving through the streets of Tampa with a friend. We were looking for another friend in an unfamiliar neighborhood. I was glancing at an address when I noticed something from the corner of my eye. It was a little girl, walking carelessly across the street. I cut my wheels, slammed on my brakes, and somehow managed to miss her. I was catching my breath when I felt the crash. My car skidded into the back of a truck that was parked near the curb. My car was totalled. The little girl glanced over her shoulder but just kept walking. Although my friend and I were both fine, I think we were more shook up than she was.

The police arrived minutes later. I explained about the girl, but they said they would have to ticket me regardless. They cited me for careless driving. They told me to leave the keys to my car, and they would later have it impounded. My friend and I jumped in a cab. When I paid the ticket a few weeks later, and settled with the owner of the truck, I considered the matter closed. I was just glad that no one had gotten hurt.

On August 16, forty-three days after the accident and about a week after Sally's first attempt to run me over, I was thumbing through a Kansas City newspaper. I turned to the sports section. I was sickened by what I read. The Tampa police were charging me with a misdemeanor for possessing a small amount of marijuana. I was livid. What the hell were they talking about? I read on. After they had towed away my car, the police had combed through its interior. The article did not say why. In an old piece of luggage in my trunk, they said they had found a plastic bag with one joint in it. I had tried marijuana when I was in school, but I didn't like what it did to me. I hadn't touched any in years. I had no idea how long it had been there or how it had gotten there. For such a small amount, it seemed crazy to press any charges. Especially since they waited forty-three days after the fact to do it.

I was distraught. After my problems in Houston, this was the last thing I needed for my career. I was so happy when I got traded to the Chiefs. I saw it as a chance to start over clean, but now I was right back in trouble. My career was turning out completely wrong, not at all the way I'd dreamed, and I felt like it was skidding crazily out of my control. To aggravate everything, I was still feuding with Sally and I still couldn't sleep. I may have been the only one who couldn't see it: I was an accident waiting to happen.

I went to practice that morning but my mind was not on football. I was confused and depressed. I was sure everybody was looking at me. Actually, there was someone watching me. It was a gorgeous woman I'd seen in the crowd at a few other practices. Every time I looked over at her she would smile. By now her interest in me was obvious to my teammates and a few of them suggested I speak with her. They said it might lift my spirits. By then I felt completely alienated from Sally. During a break, I asked the woman if she would like to get together following practice. She accepted.

She walked into my dorm room with a chilled bottle of wine. You could say there was a tremendous mutual attraction, and by the time we finished the bottle of wine we were in bed. Suddenly there was a loud pounding on my door. It was a couple of my teammates reminding me we soon had practice. I was preoccupied and didn't answer. A few minutes later there was another noise, only this time it was louder, almost like an explosion. I looked at the sheets and there were sparks licking at their ends. My teammates had slipped firecrackers under the door.

When I showed up for afternoon practice, I was feeling drowsy and high from the wine. Paul Wiggin had replaced Hank Stram that season as the Chiefs head coach. Paul had a crewcut and a rigid manner, and at first I thought he'd be Sid Gillman revisited. Paul wasn't like that at all. He was a decent man; I eventually liked him a lot.

He also wasn't stupid and he didn't want his players coming to practice tipsy. When Paul saw my condition, he didn't ask for any explanations. He ordered me off the field.

I went back to the dorm and tried to get some sleep. I was lying down when some of the guys came by my room. They had finished practice, there was a team meeting that night, and a few of them were going to a local bar in the meantime. I knew it was a mistake, but I joined them at the bar and continued to drink. At that point I was in no hurry to sober up.

By the time I got to the evening's meeting, I was drunk. I was also late. When I entered the room, everyone was already in his place. At that time I was a big fan of Boz Scaggs and I used to play his tape on one of those portable tape players. When I walked into the room with my Boz Scaggs tape still blaring, Wiggin decided he'd taken more than enough. He demanded that I leave the room.

"Your wish," I told him as I took a deep and exaggerated bow, "is my command."

That night I was supposed to meet Sally at a bar. I figured I'd go back to the dorm and get a few hours sleep first. When I got to my room, the door was locked and I realized I didn't have my keys. I kicked the door in and went inside to get some sleep. I woke up about an hour later and looked at the clock. It was time to meet Sally, but I didn't want to go. I just wanted to sleep until the morning. I called her house but she wasn't home. I figured I'd better show up. Once she arrived, I'd ask her if we could make it another night.

When I got to the bar, Sally wasn't there. I was getting impatient, I wanted to get back in my nice warm bed. I was sipping on a beer when I reached into my pocket. I pulled out two sleeping pills. They were Tuinals, and because of my size they were a powerful dose. I had taken them before, when I felt as though I couldn't get to sleep any other way, but I had always been careful about mixing them with liquor. To this day I don't know why, but I popped both of them into my mouth. It was one of the biggest mistakes of my life.

First I started feeling nauseous, then freezing, then as if I was burning up. My clothes felt too tight, as if they were cutting off my supply of air. I was hyperventilating. I literally stumbled out of the bar. I tried to walk around but my legs wouldn't work. I fell to my hands and knees and was crawling around on the sidewalk. The last thing I remember is a bunch of people standing around me laughing. It was like some terrible, grisly nightmare. Then I lost consciousness.

The next time I opened my eyes, I was staring at the somber walls of a hospital room. I was strapped to a bed. There were tubes protruding from all over my body. My God. What on earth had I done?

Coach Wiggin and another official from the Chiefs were sitting in my room. I had no idea what had happened, but I could tell by the look on Paul's face that it was something serious. I tried to tell Paul I was sorry but I couldn't choke out the words. I was crying.

Paul told me everything. Sally had arrived at the bar minutes after I had blacked out. With the help of another man, they carried me to her car. Sally drove back to camp, where she ran into Paul's office screaming hysterically. I was still unconscious.

Paul rode next to me in the ambulance on the way to the hospital. He put his head to my chest several times, and one time he didn't hear a heartbeat. The lethal combination of depressants had momentarily stopped my heart. Paul didn't panic. He beat on my chest and my heart started up again. As Paul related the story, he tried his best to be matter of fact. I'm sure he didn't want me alarmed. But I could tell he was shaken up badly. Paul had saved my life.

When I got to the hospital, Paul explained, I was still not out of danger. Now I was having convulsions. I spent that night in intensive care, fighting for my life. When the doctors told Paul I was going to live, Paul said he was shocked. He believed I was going to die.

While my teammates flew to San Francisco to play the 49ers, I spent the next four days in the hospital. Without much else to do, I did a lot of thinking. I also did a lot of feeling. I felt like a skinny little kid again, humiliated and embarrassed. I was shocked at my own stupidity. I was ashamed.

I was thankful to be alive.

Paul told me not to come to practice until I felt completely recovered. Within two weeks I was traded to the Washington Redskins.

The trade to the Redskins cut deeply. I was sick of moving around, I was beginning to feel like a nomad. I liked everything about Kansas City—the players, the coaches, the city. And I wanted so badly to get out and play football again for Paul. I owed him the ultimate debt. It was even more than that. I wanted to show him that I had made a reckless mistake, but that I was still a good football player. And that I was still a responsible person.

As bad as I felt, I wasn't angry at the Chiefs for trading me. I wasn't even surprised. I had screwed up one too many times, given them too many worrisome nights. Paul had given me more rope in the last several weeks than just about any coach in the NFL would have, probably more than I deserved. If I had been in his position, I might have traded me too.

8

OFF THE FIELD:
HIGHS AND LOWS

What upset me most about my final experience with the Chiefs was the perception that people had of John Matuszak. Jumping leagues was one thing, that was a business tactic. But this was far more serious. I could tell by the looks I got: People thought I was some kind of wild man.

The truth is, I did have a dark side, a self-destructive side, which I never clearly understood myself. All through my career, I seemed to place obstacles in my path. Just when it appeared my life was going smoothly, I would go and screw things up again. It was a side of me I didn't like, and it never surfaced when I was clean. Almost every heartache I've ever had, every time I've lost my self-control, every time I've hurt someone I cared for, it was related to foreign substances. I mean alcohol and drugs.

I don't drink at all now, not a drop. In June of 1985, I sought help, and I didn't have a drink for the next twelve months. Last summer I fell off the wagon. It was ugly and hurtful, to myself and the people close to me. I haven't had one drink since. I pray that I never will.

I believe, I hope, I'm finally on the right path. It took me much too long to see it, or maybe to admit it, but I've finally come to understand: I'm not the kind of person who can just be a social drinker. Sure, there were plenty of times when I had a few beers and called it quits. But there were other times, too many times, when the abuse didn't stop. And so now I don't even kid myself: I just abstain completely. When I was ten years old, I put away my toy soldiers, now I've put away my other toys. I'm thirty-six years old. It's time to stop playing the fool.

It wasn't that I drank every day. I didn't. But when I did drink, sometimes my self control went out the window. I've been asked: If I knew I was prone to overdrinking, why did I drink at all? Good question; I'm still trying to figure it out myself. One thing I know for sure: More than anything, I drank to fall asleep, to deaden the pain I felt in my body from playing football. As I said before, even before I became a pro I always found sleeping difficult, at best. When my body was beaten up from football, it only got harder. I came to rely on alcohol, to use it as a crutch. Nights when I really needed my sleep, and when I felt I couldn't fight it a second more, I would reach for a bottle. Some nights, it took four or five Crown Royals.

I remember the week I separated my shoulder. I got shot with anesthetics every day that week, just to get through practice. I'd numb it, practice, go through hell that night, have a bunch of drinks, finally fall asleep, wake up, shoot up for practice and start it all again. It was insane.

Deep down, I suppose I knew I was asking for trouble. But I didn't admit to myself the extent of the danger. I was young, strong, I could run all day; I told myself I couldn't be hurt. Everyone who drinks too much rationalizes. I became a master at it. You should have heard me: It doesn't matter how much I drink, I can sweat it out tomorrow on the practice field. My body's torn apart from football, what's a few cocktails? The other guys are drinking, why can't I? It's part of the camraderie; I've got to go out with the boys at least a few times a week.

It was bullshit. I sold myself a bill of goods.

At the same time, while I might have developed a problem if I were a butcher or a lawyer or an insurance salesman, I also think my profession might have had something to do with my drinking. And why other players drank to excess. Every Sunday, we polluted our body with whatever we felt was necessary. Freeze it, numb it, dull it—just get through the game. It became second nature, a part of the job. Maybe that kind of mentality contributed to players drinking. You hurt before a game, you take something to stop it. You hurt after a game, why not stop it with a drink? Once the barriers have been broken down, that drink doesn't look so lethal. When that drink leads to several, to habit, of course it's lethal. But maybe we lost sight of that, with all the other garbage we put in our bodies. I suppose, ultimately, it comes down to the individual. Everyone in the league used pain killers. But everyone in the league didn't become a problem drinker.

I can talk all day about drinking, and the million reasons I might have started. And it's a perfectly valid subject: If you know the reasons why you drink, it can make it a hell of a lot easier to stop. But the bottom line won't go away: When it came to alcohol, I should have been stronger, smarter, more of an adult. Alcohol, when abused, is poison. The stuff can kill you.

It can also destroy your reputation. When I first started dating Stephanie, people would ask her how she could go out with a guy like me. She'd tell me about it when she got home, and I'd feel miserable. Like maybe I didn't deserve her. Even today I'll do a charity affair, or meet strangers, and they'll be amazed. "You're such a nice guy," they'll say, "I can't believe all those stories I've heard about you." When I ask them what stories they mean, every damn one of them has to do with drinking.

Because of my problem, during my career, I was in and out of trouble, in and out of the newspapers. Some of the accounts were less than accurate. I'd like to set the record straight.

The first incident was in Stockton, California, in November of 1979. I was invited to a Raiders Booster Club dinner with two of my teammates. There was a lot of drinking and, foolishly, I tried to drive home. We were stopped by the local police and I was arrested for drunken driving. I spent two hours in a Stockton jail and was later convicted on the charge. Sadly, it was only the beginning.

If you've ever wondered why you never saw me in one of those TV beer commercials, here's the reason why. In February of 1981, a month after we beat the Eagles in the Super Bowl, I was getting ready to spend some time in Florida. First I was going to visit my parents in Oak Creek. The night before I left, as I drove to a party in Hayward, California, many of my belongings were already packed in my car. I was driving to the party, about to make a turn, when I had to stop. The main light, the one to go straight ahead, was green. But the arrow for turning was on red. I was waiting and waiting and then I got impatient. Finally I turned while the arrow was still on red. Just then I heard a howling siren. It was a police car pulling me over.

Why did I turn when the arrow was red? Well, the main light was still on green and I saw that there wasn't any oncoming traffic. But maybe it was more than that. Maybe I thought I was too much of a big shot. After all the publicity I got from the Super Bowl, I thought I was a real big deal. My agent, Charles Stern, had lined me up for a lucrative series of endorsements. The biggest plum of them all—a TV spot with a major beer company—was just about to be finalized. I was the Tooz, star athlete, soon-to-be star of a big-time commercial. Why should a guy like me have to wait for a light?

The policeman approaching my car brought me quickly back to earth. I'd been drinking rum before I left for the party and I was still feeling high. I asked him if he could give me a break, that I was up for several endorsements and that an arrest of any kind—with the resulting publicity—could cost me up to $100,000. I asked him if the woman sitting next to me, who was totally sober, could drive me home. The cop didn't bite.

"Why should I give you a break?" he snarled. "Just because you're a big football player?"

That was OK, maybe I had that coming. But then he started treating me like garbage, calling me boy, shit like that. I lost my temper. As he slipped the handcuffs over my wrists, I called him a prick; he immediately radioed backups to assist with the arrest. Then the trouble got worse.

While packing for my trip back east, two of the things I had placed in my car were a bayonet and a .44 magnum revolver. I know: It sounds crazy. It really wasn't. The bayonet was very old and very expensive, a beautiful antique from somewhere in

Japan. My father and I are war buffs, and I was going to give him the bayonet for his birthday. The gun also belonged to me. I've always liked guns. My grandfather taught me how to shoot a gun when I was a little boy in the fields near his home, and I've been interested in them ever since. Normally, though, I always left them at home. But I had a lot of things in my car that night—including a whole trunk full of luggage. In any case, the officer found the bayonet and the gun. I was arrested and convicted—for carrying a concealed weapon and for drunken driving.

This did not sit well with the people at the beer company. When they heard what happened, they immediately dropped me from their plans. So did several other sponsors. In that one night, with the NFL pay scale the way it was back then, I cost myself more money than I normally earned in two or three years. And I deserved exactly what I got.

(Before I go on, I think I should put this in proper perspective. Despite what you've just read, and are about to read, I have nothing against police officers. The Raiders used to play basketball games against police teams in the offseason; my grandfather was a police officer. I've met hundreds of officers who were great, I've always known how trying the job can be. Unfortunately, on a few occasions, I've met officers who were hostile the moment they saw me. Maybe they got nervous because of my size, or got off on taking a dump on a well-known athlete. Regardless, if I'd been wiser I would have kept my mouth shut. But sometimes, as prideful as I am, I couldn't help myself: Rather than a little humility, I told them where they could go. That's when my problems would begin. Those are the encounters I'm writing about here, the situations that somehow escalated. But they were isolated incidents, exceptions to the rule.)

In June of 1985, in Milwaukee, I had my last incident with drinking and driving. I'd been drinking, but despite that I went to visit one of my old friends. It was a decaying neighborhood; in my Lincoln Continental, which I kept immaculate, I suppose I looked totally out of place. I was only going about twenty-five miles per hour when I saw I was being followed by an un-marked car. After three blocks, I saw the little red light start flashing on their dashboard and I knew they were after me. I was livid when they pulled me over; not at them, but myself, for getting in another jam. I got out of my car, slammed the door violently, and the driver's side window broke, shattering into hundreds of little pieces. Up until then the officers had looked relatively calm. After that, their manner changed; they seemed like they were out for blood. (I'm sure the sight of a 295-pound man had something to do with it.)

One of the cops screamed at me to freeze. I stopped in my tracks; I asked if I could please call my attorney. He said I had to take the field sobriety test first. I asked again if I could first call my attorney. They ordered me into the back of their car. I didn't like the way things were developing; more than ever, I wanted my lawyer to be present. So I did something dumb: Seeing a phone outside a store, I started walking to it to call my attorney. Bad move. One of the cops darted behind me and grabbed my right thumb. I told him I just wanted to call my lawyer. I guess he wasn't listening: He started bending back my thumb until I was sure it was going to break. I had still made no sudden moves, no attempt whatsoever to resist him, and the SOB, I mean, the good officer, threw me down on the pave-ment. They locked me in handcuffs and leg chains. I was taken to the station, then booked and arrested on three charges: drun-ken driving, obstruction of justice and refusal to take the sobri-ety test. I was in shock; it had happened so fast and gotten so crazy.

At first I wanted to fight it. Then I changed my mind. I was so sick and tired of court, rather than spend one more minute there, I pleaded no contest to all three charges. The two other charges were dropped, but I was convicted of drunken driving. I was fined, and my license was suspended for ninety days.

That was the last time I got behind a wheel when I'd been drinking. But my dealings with the law weren't quite over; I still had some dues left to pay. In the winter of 1985, I spent three days in a Milwaukee jail. It was the culmination of another arrest, this one from June of 1984. Once again I had been charged for carrying a concealed weapon. Again, I wasn't aware it was in my car.

I was in Milwaukee. I was driving around, sober, with my brother-in-law, who'd been drinking. We were in the old neighborhood, looking for a buddy from high school. We stopped at an apartment complex, where another friend had told us he'd moved to. For no good reason, my brother-in-law started arguing with the complex manager. Once again, shattered glass did me in. On our way out, my brother-in-law slammed the manager's door. The glass broke into pieces.

My brother-in-law was acting crazy; I had to get him home before he did any more damage. I hustled him into the car and drove him directly home. There was still the manager's door to take care of. I headed back to the apartments, trying to figure out what the hell I was going to tell the guy. I decided I'd just apologize and pay him for the door. What else was there to do?

As I approached the complex, I saw a police car. With the way my life had been going, another confrontation with the police was the last thing in the world I needed. I decided to drive around the block and come back when the police had left. Then I would deal with the manager one-on-one.

It was too late: When the manager spotted my car, he started pointing and yelling to the two policemen. They jumped in their car, tailed me for a couple blocks, then pulled me over. They both got out to talk to me, a man and his female partner. The guy was polite, easygoing. The woman was rude and obnoxious. I was talking to the guy, explaining what had happened, and the woman kept bursting in. When I kept ignoring her, talking only to her partner, she got abusive. And I kept on ignoring her.

When she called me some name beneath her breath, she'd gone too far: I told her partner I wouldn't even acknowledge her, but I'd be happy to answer whatever *he* wanted to know. The fat lady cop didn't like that: That's when she started sniffing around my car, kind of like a cat looking for a place to shit. Beneath the passenger seat, she spotted the barrel of a nine millimeter pistol. I wanted to cry, faint, something, when I saw it. I was as shocked to see it as she was.

It was my other gun, but it wasn't supposed to be in my car. I found out later, not that it helped any, how it got there. Earlier that week one of my friends had driven my car for me from Oakland to Milwaukee. The gun had been locked in the trunk for the ride, but when the car had arrived in Milwaukee, I hadn't seen the gun in the trunk, and figured my friend hadn't brought it. Well, he had brought it, but when he saw it in the trunk, he moved it under the passenger seat. When I asked him why he put it there, and why he didn't bother telling me, he said he felt more secure with it up there, and he had forgot. I told him thanks a million.

That was all discovered later. At the time I told the police what I knew: Yes, I owned the gun, but that I had no idea it was in my car. It didn't matter. By then the lady cop had found her place to shit: squarely on a well-known football player's head. They booked me on three different charges: drunken driving, carrying a concealed weapon and driving with a suspended license.

This time I decided to fight it. For one thing, I wasn't even close to being drunk. For another, I had been waiting for my new license to arrive for weeks, and every time I called the DMV they told me it would arrive in the mail any day. The gun you already know about. When I went to court, I was found innocent of the drunken driving and the license charge, but guilty of carrying a concealed weapon. My lawyer immediately appealed. But in December of 1985, although the case was still in appeal, I went back home and pleaded no contest. I never wanted to see the inside of a court room again. I wanted to do my time, get it over with and move on.

I was sentenced to three days at the state House of Corrections. They put me in a cell with about thirty other men. Some of the guys looked okay, like ordinary citizens who had done something uncharacteristically stupid, and who were learning their lesson. Some of the others looked like maniacs. It smelled like a zoo in there, and the sound effects weren't much better. I tried to sleep, but with the stench and the noise and the one-inch-thick plastic mattresses, I didn't have much luck.

It's not a pretty picture, is it? Frankly, it's something I'd rather forget, a subject I don't enjoy discussing. It's certainly not the way I want to be remembered. I've done too much good in my life to have it all obscured by the times I've screwed up. It's a part of my life that shames and embarrasses me. But I have a problem, I'm doing something about it, and I think people should know it. Hopefully they can learn from my mistakes. I was incredibly fortunate: I never hurt anybody but myself when I was driving drunk. For that I thank God. But I also have to face up to it: I could have killed someone.

I've come to accept something I used to resist: I have an obsessive personality. I was 6'8" and 300 pounds, I had to do everything more than the next guy. Moreover, I was big number 72, the *Tooz*. I found myself trying to live up to that image, trying always to be the Tooz. Whatever it was, I always had to do it harder and longer than everyone else. More weights, more women, more vodka, more food. When I first started dating Stephanie, I'd order half a dozen eggs for breakfast, half a pound of bacon, four glasses of milk, two or three OJ's. Did I need that much food? Hell, no. But it was hard to be one person on the field, the Tooz, and then turn it off in my private life.

Overdoing helped me at times; in part, I believe it's why I own a pair of Super Bowl rings. But on balance, it did me much more harm than good. I still don't know what the hell I was trying to prove, but I could never seem to do anything in moderation. Sadly, at periods of my life, that included cocaine.

I used to have a cocaine problem. And if I ever use it again, I will have a problem again. But as I did with alchohol, I'm doing something about it. I sought professional help in the fall of 1986.

Using drugs started out as a social thing, and I think that's true for a lot of people from my generation. It was the whole Drop-Out mentality: We thought it was cool, romantic, to get wasted. We'd do it and not really think about the consequences. It was just another way to rebel, to say, fuck you.

Bullshit. It was just another lie; there was nothing glamorous, nothing hip, nothing remotely intelligent about cocaine. And who was I saying fuck you to if not myself? Take it from someone who has been stupid enough to be there: Cocaine is poison. It can kill you.

I'm as tired as the next person of hearing ex-users make speeches about drugs. But if it helps one person, wakes one person up, I'll stand in line. Let me put it this way: I'm 6' 8" and almost 300 pounds; I used to laugh in the faces of offensive linemen. But when I was using cocaine, just the doorbell could make me shudder with paranoia. I realize how ugly that is.

I went long periods without using any cocaine at all. During my career, I would go months, entire years, without using it. It was after I retired, when I was bored, in between acting jobs, when I had some problems. Even then, I'd go months without touching it. But I'd slip back, even for a day or so, and undo all the good I'd done. Last fall, realizing there's no worthwhile cure except a complete one, I entered a rehabilitation center. It helped set me straight, gave me a hell of a start, but in itself that wasn't enough. It's the follow-up program, what you do when you get out, that truly counts. If you don't follow up, the rehab won't mean anything. It's not an easy thing, but you have to keep fighting. You're not alone out there. There are lots of good people who want to help.

I abstain from cocaine, and any other foreign substance, entirely now. I take nothing, not even sleeping pills. I've hit damn near bottom. I don't ever want to go back.

My priorities are in their proper order. I'm on a twelve-step, follow-up program, I've got support groups to help me out. But, ultimately, it's up to me. That's the way it should be. I'm going after sobriety the way I used to go after quarterbacks, the only way you can. All out.

9

AL DAVIS: REBEL WITH A CAUSE

*If Al Davis had decided that he wanted
to become president of this country,
he could have done it. He's that brilliant.*

Edward Stanczyk
former athletic director
Adelphi College

Al Davis makes Darth Vader look like a wimp.

Hunter S. Thompson

Black, I believe, is Al Davis's favorite color. It dominates his wardrobe, it's the primary color of the team he owns. He's liked it ever since the 1940s, when Army football was in its glory years and Al was one of their fans; back then the West Point team wore black—the Black Knights of the Hudson. They looked menacing, fearless. The same way most people see Al.

An image like that might bother some people. Not Al. I think he likes it.

During my trials and tribulations my first few years in the league, I was like any other football fan: I admired Al from afar and I wondered if everything people said about him was really true. I'd heard all the stories. Davis was relentless, almost impossible to get to know, yet one of the most brilliant minds in all of sports. His nickname was The Genius. In August of 1976, I got a chance to make my own judgement.

Before I get into my first real encounter with Al, and so you'll understand why I feel about him the way I do, I should explain what happened after the Chiefs traded me to the Washington Redskins. I was traded to the Redskins just seventeen days before the first regular season game of 1976. I still hadn't lost hope and Washington seemed like a good destination. The Redskins were winners, they always seemed well prepared and their coach, George Allen, was truly committed to quality defense. I was hoping Washington would be my final stop.

At first everything went perfectly. In my first exhibition against the New York Jets, I had a sack and got good penetration. The Redskins had been worried about their pass rush. The coaches said they were happy with the way I played. It looked like I could help the team.

In the last exhibition game against the Chicago Bears, it all went sour. I made another sack on a third down play. The Bears were about to punt when Allen noticed there were only ten guys out there. I was the missing player. George had me playing on four different special teams. I was not used to playing on even one. In my excitement over my sack, I'd completely forgotten that I was on the punt return team and I ran off the field. Allen asked the other coaches who was missing. One of them yelled out, "Matuszak."

Don't ask me how, but I knew right then and there that I would be cut. After my fiasco in Kansas City, I had come to the Redskins on thin ice to begin with. Some people were surprised Allen had traded for me at all. Outside of football, Allen had few interests. His greatest passion was vanilla ice cream. He and I made the oddest of couples. Allen was also one of those coaches who was an absolute stickler for details, and this was the kind of thing he would not forget. I figured I was done for.

For the next few days, I felt like The Fugitive. I was paranoid, glancing over my shoulder, anticipating the tap on the back from The Turk. But when they handed out the game plans for the season opener against the Giants, they also gave me one. I had made it. Or so I thought.

I was standing on the practice field Monday morning when someone tapped me on the shoulder. It was you know who. "Coach Allen wants to see you," he said.

My heart just about sank to my socks. There were still a few cuts to be made, but I tried to convince myself that George wanted to see me about something else. Then I saw all the veterans pointing and staring as I walked to George's office. Just like that, I knew it was over. When I got to George's office, it *was* over.

"I'm sorry, John, but you're cut," he said.

"Why?" I wanted to know. "I've been playing well."

"I just can't fit you into our plans."

"You're making a big mistake. I'll tell you right now, I can help this team."

George looked away in dismissal. End of conversation. I left his office and went back to the team hotel. I tried to sort it all out. If Allen hadn't planned on giving me a fair shot, then why trade for me in the first place? To this day I still don't know for certain why Allen waived me, but my only guess is that he was uncomfortable with my image. He wasn't so much worried about me, but what he'd *heard* about me. After he let me go, Allen said I had been a "role model with a great attitude." Apparently this was just lip service.

I wasn't with the Redskins long enough to form much of an opinion of Allen. I knew he had molded some excellent teams. I knew he could motivate veteran players, and I knew he would also trade those veterans without much hesitation. One thing did strike me as being strange about him. Everyone used to say what a player's coach he was. I remember flying from Washington to New York for that exhibition game with the Jets. As we were walking off the plane, there was this stretch limo parked to the side of the runway. It was waiting there for Allen. Here was this so-called player's coach taking a limo while his players all crammed into a bus. I found out later that Allen traveled by limo throughout the season. If George was a player's coach, I'd hate to see a coach's coach.

I was humiliated. Getting traded from one team to another is bad enough. When a player is traded, at least when it's against his will, his pride and feelings are punctured. No matter if you've heard all the rumors, the actual trade hits you hard. I was single, that made things a little easier. Trades are much tougher on a player who has a family. His wife has to find new friends, his kids get yanked from school. I've seen it throw entire families into disarray. The alternative, the player moving for the season and the family staying behind, can be even worse. From July to Christmas, the children lose their father and the wife her husband. The longer a player is with one team, the longer the family has had to get situated, the more painful a trade is. Everyone gets torn from his roots.

There's still one bright spot. At least when you're traded, there's a sense of feeling wanted by someone else. You know your new employers feel you have something they need. Getting cut is a one-way ticket to nowhere. People look at you sideways, they wonder what's wrong with you. It's embarrassing as hell.

Players aren't the only ones who get hurt when they're traded or cut. It can be just as painful to the coach. Which is one reason why most coaches never get too friendly with their players. If a guy is going to have a hard personnel decision somewhere down the line, he doesn't want to make the wrong one because the player in question is one of his pals. When Tom Flores was the quarterback for the Raiders in the sixties, he threw a young Fred Biletnikoff his first reception. In 1979, when Tom was head coach, he had to tell Fred he was letting him go. You know Tom had to be hurt by it.

The only thing that kept me going was that I knew I would be picked up on waivers by another team. The price for a player who'd been waived was a lousy hundred bucks.

The next several days dragged on for what seemed like weeks. I flew back to Milwaukee. I told my family and friends to relax, that everything would work itself out. It was all a facade. Inside

I was a mess. The season was only a couple of days away. Teams were set, no one would be eager to make a move. Scared and depressed, I felt as if I could barely move, almost as if I were paralyzed. I didn't even want to leave the house. When you've been playing football since you were a teenager, the prospect of suddenly giving it up is terrifying.

I kept walking by the phone. I would stop and I would stare at it, as if my will could somehow make it ring. But it didn't. I couldn't believe it.

Over the years, I've been asked by reporters if I felt I had been blackballed by the NFL. I can't answer that. For one thing, blackball is a term that's tough to define. I don't think there was a "let's get Matuszak" conspiracy. I don't think twenty-six general managers sat around a conference table and plotted on how to end my career. I do know that NFL executives are a closeknit fraternity and word travels fast. I was twenty-five years old, healthy and still had my strength and speed. Three years before, I'd been the number one pick in the college draft. Now, I could be had for a hundred bucks. There must have been people in the NFL who knew I could help their teams. Still, not a single team tried to pick me up. It became painfully clear to me—to the franchise owners of the NFL, the name Matuszak meant trouble. I feared for my career.

Later that week I got an offer. But it came from another country. I was offered a job with the Edmonton Eskimos of the Canadian Football League. The coach was the guy who'd been my tight end coach at the University of Missouri. The coach who had demoted me to the second team. Wonderful. Here I was a veteran in the NFL, and I would be going back to play for a guy I didn't even like in college. I didn't know what to do. There's nothing wrong with the Canadian Football League. It's a hell of a lot better than the Egyptian Football League. But ever since I'd been in high school I'd dreamed of playing in the NFL. Going to Canada would have been the end of my dream. I mean, who rushes to the paper to find out how the Edmonton Eskimos did the night before? Still, it was a job. And it wasn't like I had a lot of options.

I told them I'd think about it and call them back. A short

time later I decided to go. Canadian football was better than no football. But before I called them back, a day later, the phone rang again. It was the Raiders, one of their front office people! Al Davis wanted me to fly to Oakland to see him! He was interested in signing me with the Raiders, but first he wanted to meet me in person. With all the crap Al had probably heard about me, I'm sure he wanted to see if I had three eyes and a pair of heads. His assistant said there would be tickets waiting for me at the Milwaukee airport. Could I see my way to make it?

I'd heard simple questions before but this was ridiculous. I said, yes, I would be happy to fly to Oakland to see Mr. Davis.

My heart was beating like a drum. Not only did I still have a shot in the NFL, but with the Oakland Raiders. *The Oakland Raiders.* I must have said it out loud a dozen times. I was dancing around the room like a kid. I nearly broke my mother's back with a bearhug. *The Oakland Raiders.*

I didn't really know Al Davis. I'd spoken with him only one time before, when I was a Chief. I was saying hello to some of the Raiders in their locker room after the game. I was wearing a pair of silver socks, the silver of the Raiders. Al told me he liked my socks. Not a real deep conversation. Other than that, Al knew me only as an opponent. I never particularly cared for the Raiders before I played for them. For one thing, they used to kick my team's ass all the time, both in Kansas City and in Houston. But I had always played well against them, so I knew I had that in my favor. I had also bloodied one of their quarterbacks and cursed at their sideline.

Both encounters happened when I was with the Chiefs. The Chiefs and the Raiders can't stand each other. The rivalry goes back to the old American Football League and it's just as heated today, with both teams in the AFC West. The games were like alley fights and both sides went wild any time they felt they'd been burned on a call. One game I tackled Clarence Davis just as he was about to run out of bounds. It was a hairline call that could have gone either way. But John Madden went haywire. He started screaming at the refs, demanding that they call a penalty. If the hit had been obvious, I would have minded my own business. But I didn't think John had reasonable grounds for arguing so wildly on such a borderline call. And our games with the Raiders were never well mannered anyway. I started jawing with the Raiders sideline, and they responded with a few obscene replies. Then I gave the "we're number one" sign to no one in particular. In the heat of the action, I must have used the wrong finger.

My other run-in with the Raiders came on the final day of a regular season. The Raiders had clinched a spot in the playoffs and had us beat too, so they took out Kenny Stabler and put in George Blanda. George was at the end of his career. He was forty-eight years old and his mobility was just about gone. His protection broke down and I busted through for a sack. The shot was clean—helmet to helmet—but George went down as if he'd been shot by a cannon. There was blood running down his face and he had to be helped off the field. I didn't know how Al would take that. The Raiders loved George and I had messed him up.

———

As I prepared to enter the office of Al Davis, owner and managing general partner of the Oakland Raiders, my stomach was doing flipflops. I dressed that day in a three-piece black suit with a silver shirt. It was my favorite outfit but I also had another reason. Those were the colors of the Raiders and I wanted Al to know how much that meeting meant to me. My NFL career was on the line.

After a few moments in the Raiders lobby, I was led by an assistant into Al's office. Seated behind his large black desk, Al looked as if he'd just stepped out of the Fifties. His hair was slicked back in a pompadour, a ducktail creeping down his neck. His business suit was black and conservative. I was a little startled by his office. It was quintessential Raider: *Everything* was done in silver and black. Black walls, black couch, black telephone. Silver drapes, silver carpet, silver chairs. Al was a man who obviously knew what he liked.

Before we got down to business, I was hoping we'd begin

with the usual idle chatter. I wanted a few moments to steal some glances, to study him, to see if the legend fit the man. But Al didn't fly me cross-country for small talk. He went directly to the point.

He said that whatever problems I'd had in the past didn't mean a damn thing as far as he was concerned. He knew I could play in this league and that's all that really mattered. He couldn't use me in that week's opener against the Pittsburgh Steelers, but he would definitely find me a spot on his team. He shook my hand and said he was glad to have me as a Raider.

I was flabbergasted, close to tears. I probably would have hugged him, but I didn't want to get fired before I was hired. I think he could tell I was tremendously grateful. It was written all over my face. To this day, I can't say enough for the way I feel about Al Davis. I love the guy. When most of the NFL thought I was nothing but a pain in the ass, Al didn't care. He gave me the chance I needed. He helped save my career.

We did have one difference of opinion. Al had heard about my escapades with Sally. He gently suggested that I not bring her with me to Oakland. This was a serious dilemma. Here was a man who was keeping me in the NFL, not to mention the United States. On the other hand, I was still in love. What was I supposed to do? Call her and say, *"Listen, I'm crazy about you but my boss says we have to break up. Maybe if I get traded again we can get back together."* I took a deep breath, cleared my throat and told Al no. I said she was very important to me and I couldn't just give her up like that. Although he wasn't pleased, Al dropped the conversation. The night after the Steelers game I was given a contract.

I was thrilled to be working for Al. The other owners I'd played for, Lamar Hunt at Kansas City and Bud Adams at Houston, were nice enough people. But their knowledge of the game didn't even approach Al's. Along with Paul Brown of the Bengals, Al is the only owner in the NFL who was once a head coach. Al does things the other owners wouldn't dream of. He studies film, scouts players himself, constantly works the phone in search of a trade. Al would always come to both full-contact practices, Wednesday and Thursday, and sometimes the practice before a game. He'd keep his profile fairly low, standing alone on the distant sideline or underneath the goalposts. But you always knew he was there. One thing about Al used to amaze me: Even during training camp, when there were dozens of rookies and free agents, he knew every last player by name.

Believe me, this is the exception to the rule. On some teams you might see the owner three or four times all year. On some teams that's three or four times too many. Most owners have their roots in another business and have to rely on others when they're faced with a football decision. They don't know Red Grange from red wine. They think Bronco Nagurski is a tropical disease. Some owners buy teams purely for their egos, just one more expensive toy. Mostly it makes them famous, something their other endeavors, no matter how successful, probably couldn't do.

It's no great secret why so many players want to play for the Raiders—Al feels that it's the *players* who are the game. They're the ones risking their bodies out there and Al knows it. Most players look at practice as something to tolerate, if not despise. Football practice isn't like other sports. Football practice hurts. When you get hurt in a game, you can rationalize to yourself that it's worth it. You feel like some kind of hero out there with the crowd cheering for you. Getting hurt at practice is just annoying. And painful. But some teams still have full-contact practices almost every day of the week. It's self-destructive. The Raiders go full speed Wednesday and Thursday and that's it. They let you save your body for the games.

Al looked out for us in other ways. The year we defeated the Eagles in the Super Bowl, we first had to beat the Cleveland Browns in the second round of the playoffs. It was one of the coldest game days in NFL history, a famous game you may remember. With the Raiders winning, 14–12, forty-nine seconds left—and the Browns with the ball at our thirteen yard line—we expected Cleveland to run the ball once and kick the game-winning fieldgoal. Everyone thought so. But Brian Sipe threw a pass, Mike Davis intercepted and the Raiders won the game. Browns fans have never forgotten.

Playing in bitterly cold weather is always miserable. Every

collision, every cut or bruise, feels like the end of the world. Arms and legs get frostbite, turn blue. When Dan Reeves, now the coach of the Broncos, was a player with the Cowboys, his two front teeth got knocked through his lip. His face was so numb, the wound didn't even bleed until Dan ran into the locker room at halftime.

The Browns game was exceptionally brutal. The temperature in Cleveland was one degree below zero, almost 40 below with the freezing winds blowing in off Lake Erie. I'll never forget walking out of the tunnel that morning. The wind was whipping through the earholes in my helmet, stinging the hell out of my ears. I also had the sniffles; and as I tried to dry the constant drip from my nose, it would freeze right on my face. As bad as it was that day, it would have been worse if not for Al.

When we had arrived in Cleveland on Saturday, Al called the Browns to confirm that they'd ordered special benches, the kind that generate heat and help keep the players warm. They hadn't and they had no intention to. Al was irate but hardly surprised. All week the Browns had been telling the press that the frigid weather gave them a decided advantage, that a bunch of guys from Northern California couldn't possibly play well in all that cold. Al figured the Browns were still following that script, so he ordered the benches himself. Since the NFL has a rule that neither team can have an unfair advantage, he also ordered benches for the Browns. It cost Al about $4,000 out of his own pocket. He knew we could beat the Browns with or without the benches. He just didn't want his people to suffer any more than they had to.

(One other thing about that game: The Browns were ass-to-ass on those warmed-up benches they supposedly didn't need. We all had a good laugh about that.)

Besides his family, Al's greatest love is the Raiders. The only time Al has ever been removed from the day-to-day doings of the team was in 1979, when his wife, Carol, suffered a near-fatal heart attack and lapsed into a coma. Al moved into the hospital, sleeping on a cot, in a makeshift room that was sectioned off. He never left Carol's side. As she slept, he would sit there and quietly talk to her. He telephoned doctors across the country, flying the best of them to Oakland. After two and a half weeks, Carol came out of it. After extensive rehabilitation, today Carol's virtually as well as she ever was. It remained unspoken, but we were all touched by Al's devotion.

I know more about Al than most people. I know he bites his fingernails when he's nervous. I know he's partially color blind and has a crooked nose from a high school football injury. I know he doesn't smoke or drink. I know when he was born: July 4, 1929. I know he always wears tinted, steel-rimmed glasses, and trenchcoats when it's chilly. I know he loves to read about military history. I know he loves his team.

But for everything I know *about* Al, I can't say I really know *him*. I don't know what moves him, what his fears are. Al is a fiercely private man, and he likes to keep his distance. When the Raiders fought the NFL over their move to Los Angeles, Al's name was in print almost every day. I think Al found that more distasteful than anything else. He is the rare owner who shuns publicity. Al enjoys his shroud of mystery.

This has made him somewhat of a loner among his fellow owners. They don't know him either. For one thing, the Raiders are the only team in the NFL that doesn't belong to a scouting combine. Al and the other coaches will scout players themselves. If Al needs additional information on a player, all he has to do is call one of his sources. Al supposedly has willing sources in every NFL city. This has consumed some of his opponents with paranoia.

One of the classic Al Davis stories involves Harland Svare, then the coach of the San Diego Chargers. In the old days, one of the rumors you heard about Al was that he would bug the other team's locker room when they came to the Oakland Coliseum. Svare was so spooked by this that he talked himself into believing it. Before a game in Oakland, as his players looked on in disbelief, Svare started cursing out the light fixture.

"Damn you, Al Davis," Svare screamed at the fixture, "I know you're up there. Damn you."

When the incident was related to Al, he wouldn't even deny it.

"I can tell you one thing," Al said with a shrug, "the damn thing wasn't in the fixture."

In a story for *Sports Illustrated*, Paul Zimmerman wrote about the time Weeb Ewbank, then the coach of the New York Jets, noticed a Raiders scout casually sitting at the back of the Jets' team bus. Shocked and enraged, Ewbank ordered the driver to stop the bus. The unwanted intruder was ejected in the middle of the highway.

Before the Super Bowl with the Eagles, Al played James Dean to Dick Vermeil's Dudley Do-Right. Al didn't shave for two weeks, he looked scruffy and foreboding. One of Al's heroes was Rocky Marciano, and several writers noted that the Rock used to do the same thing before a big fight. It's great copy for the fans. It also adds fuel to the Al Davis image. As his players, we used to hear all *kinds* of things about Al. Two were most prevalent: that he used to pump the football up with added helium for our punter Ray Guy, and that he'd water our field extra heavily the night before games against high-powered offenses.

The Guy thing is a bunch of crap. Ray was a phenomenon. He was the first college punter ever to be drafted in the opening round. For his first four years, he never had a punt blocked. He went to the Pro Bowl seven times and three times led the NFL in punting. No one had ever seen anybody punt like him before, nobody could explain his skills, so they looked for silly explanations. During one of his finest years, the whole asinine idea got planted by one of our rivals. One clue only: They play in Mile High Stadium.

As for watering the fields, maybe Al did let the hoses run a tad longer than usual some Saturday nights. When the fields were nice and wet on Sunday mornings, a team like the Chargers weren't quite as speedy. Keep in mind that this is hardly uncommon in any sport. When Lou Brock was terrorizing opposing catchers with his speed, the Cardinals would arrive at Chicago's Wrigley Field to find an infield that was sopping wet. The same thing happened to Maury Wills and the Dodgers when they went on the road. It's that good old home-field advantage.

Al is certainly not perfect. As a high-powered businessman

who has never learned to like losing, I'm sure he does things that drive his adversaries crazy. I doubt if he'll ever be Man of the Year in Denver or Seattle. One thing he is, though, is generous with his players. Al is one of the few owners in *any* league who will initiate the renegotiation or upgrading of a player's contract. If a player is performing well, Al has been known to call him into his office and tear up his contract. After my first year with the Raiders, I went in and told Al I was a little short of money. Since I didn't have much bargaining position, the Raiders had acquired me relatively cheaply. I made about $35,000 that season, not counting playoff money, back when playoff money was half of what it is today. After taxes, I didn't do that well. Most owners would rather stick needles in their eyes than give a player a bonus, so I was doubtful. Al wanted to know what I wanted.

"How about fifteen thousand?" I asked.

"Ten thousand would be fine," Al said.

"How about twelve thousand, five hundred?"

"Eleven thousand."

"Twelve thousand?" I persisted.

"Eleven thousand, five hundred," Al shot back.

"Deal," I said.

That's the way Al was. If you were loyal to him and you gave him 100 percent every Sunday, he would take care of you. Al would never admit it, but he's not as hard as he'd like you to believe. He helps players with financial problems, even some who have already left the game. He pumps money into charities. The day he traded Dave Casper, a longtime favorite, Al looked like he'd lost his closest friend.

I never met Vince Lombardi. But from what I've heard and read, he had something in common with Al: His players loved him, but also feared him. His authority was rarely if ever defied. The only time I ever saw a player challenge Al was in 1980, the year we beat the Eagles in the Super Bowl. Late in the season one of our starters on offense went down with an injury. When he was just about healed, he told Al he wanted to get back into the starting lineup. Al said no. We had been winning with the lineup we had, and Al had no desire to break up the combination. A few days later we were boarding a plane for a road game. The Raiders had a rule that you couldn't drink on flights to games. This guy was in no mood for rules, not even one of Al's. He had smuggled a bottle of tequila onto the plane and was knocking it off like it was tap water. When the plane landed, he staggered up to Al and said something to the effect of "play me or trade me." When Al didn't reply, the player started cursing him out. Right in front of Mrs. Davis. Everyone was horrified. We'd never seen Al confronted that way. At first we tried dragging our teammate away, but once he started cursing, everyone just backed off. No one wanted even to be near him when he was talking to Al like that. Al never said a word. Not one. He just shot the guy this look, a look I call the "look of goodbye." We knew that guy was through as a Raider. He never played another down for us that season. The next year he was released.

Al understands that people get angry, that wasn't the problem. This guy was just too rude and belligerent. Otherwise, I think Al actually *likes* a player with a chip on his shoulder. Those are the players who are likely to take their hostilities out on the other team. Unlike a George Steinbrenner, Al gets the results he wants without making his players look like fools in the process. Steinbrenner rips a great player like Dave Winfield to the press, humiliates him, hoping that Winfield's anger will be directed at the pitcher. Davis is too smart and too sensitive to his players to pull that type of crap. Davis signs the guys who are already pissed off, gives them some cash, then turns them loose on the rest of the league.

It's no surprise that Al understands athletes. He's been around them for a lot of years. Born in Brockton, Massachusetts, raised in Brooklyn, Al graduated from Syracuse University and later took coaching jobs with Adelphi College, the Army, the Baltimore Colts, The Citadel, USC and the San Diego Chargers. In 1963, Al became head coach of the Raiders, a franchise in shambles. Playing in the old American Football League, in their first three years before Al, the Raiders had lost three head coaches and thirty-three of forty-two games. They even lost a name. When the Raiders were formed, the original owners held a contest to name the team. The winner was the "Señors." A short time later it was mercifully changed to the Raiders. The early Raiders did not even have a home—they wandered from stadium to stadium around the Bay area.

In Al's first year he signed nineteen new players and the Raiders went ten and four. The winning has never stopped. Under Al, the Raiders have been the winningest team not just in the NFL, but in all of pro sports. The Montreal Canadians, Boston Celtics and Baltimore Orioles come next. The Raiders have won three Super Bowls. Only the Pittsburgh Steelers have won four.

In all that time, Al has only left the Raiders once—in 1966 to become commissioner of the AFL. By now it's common knowledge that Al and Pete Rozelle, the NFL commissioner, are not overly fond of each other. What some people don't realize is that their feud didn't begin when Al moved the Raiders to Los Angeles. It started back in those AFL days.

The AFL was born in 1960. For the next six years, they waged war against the older league, trying to force a merger, but the NFL wouldn't hear of it. In 1966, the AFL owners turned to Al. They wanted someone who would go right for the NFL's jugular. They made him commissioner. Al didn't waste any time. He immediately executed a plan that called for the top AFL teams to steal the star quarterbacks of the NFL. The plan was working. Roman Gabriel had already signed with the Raiders, John Brodie was prepared to join Houston and several other top quarterbacks were on their way. Only two months later, the NFL had met its match. A merger was negotiated. But with Al kept mostly out of the picture, Rozelle was named the new commissioner. I'm sure everyone knew that Al had five times the qualifications Rozelle did. They must have chosen Rozelle because he was slicker, a real smooth PR type. They also knew Al would never be a yes man.

The acrimony escalated in 1978, when Rozelle removed Davis from the NFL Competition Committee. Formed in 1970, the committee was composed of Al, Tex Schramm, Paul Brown and the late Vince Lombardi. It was responsible for all major rule changes. In other words, the entire direction of the game. Rozelle never gave much of a reason for dumping Al and a lot of owners were dumbstruck. Even Schramm, who's very tight with Rozelle, said it was a "disservice to the league."

Al never talked to us about his differences with Rozelle. He might have said something vague once or twice. Like "this guy in New York is giving us a hard time." But he never mentioned Rozelle by name, and he never badmouthed him. But we all knew perfectly well how the league office felt about the Raiders. And we were all affected by the consequences.

I'm talking about the referees, who are employees, of course, of the NFL. As an Oakland Raider, you resigned yourself to a simple fact: Unless a call was *clearly* for the Raiders, unless there was not a *shadow of a doubt,* the refs would rule for the other team. I always felt we had to win every game by at least eight to ten points, just to make up for the lousy calls we'd get from the refs. If a game was on the line, I'd say the other team would get ninety-eight out of 100 calls. I know that sounds dramatic, but that's the way I felt.

The worst shafts used to come when we were playing Denver. Maybe that was coincidence, but I doubt it. There was always a lot at stake when we played the Broncos. They were the one team in our division who could keep us from getting to the Super Bowl. Either by winning our division outright, which made our path to the Super Bowl more difficult, or by beating us in a playoff game. And if there was one thing the league office didn't want to see, it was for the Raiders to go to the Super Bowl. I had more problems with the refs in the games against the Broncos than any other team in the league. In nine years of playing pro football, I was cited for four personal fouls. Two of those came within three plays of each other. In a game against the Broncos.

It was the first game of 1977. A year earlier, the Broncos had beaten us in the AFC championship to keep us out of the Super Bowl. That was the game in which I sleepwalked. You can imagine our emotion in the rematch. We hated the Broncos anyway, and not just because we played in the same division. They had some dirty players and at least one unethical coach. They also had a linebacker named Tom Jackson. Off the field

I'm sure he was a wonderful family man and a loving husband. On Sundays he was a flaming idiot. Jackson would run by our sideline and make obscene remarks to Coach Madden, but only when they were winning. If you're beating someone, shut your mouth and don't rub it in. Maybe that's why Jackson's never owned a Super Bowl ring.

Now that I've ingratiated myself with all the Broncos fans, let me get back to that game. We were stuffing their offense in the second half when Rick Upchurch came around on an end reverse. I slammed him to the ground. As I was getting up, I pushed off on him. For a defensive player, it's one of the oldest tricks in the books. I learned it back in college. Whenever you climb off a player, push down on him. By the end of the game, especially with a guy my size, it will take its toll. Even though he'd probably seen it a hundred times, Upchurch jumped up as if it were new to him. He took a swing at me. When I raised my arm to push him away—TWEET—it was fifteen yards against Matuszak.

Two plays later Craig Morton was fading back to pass. Just as he released the ball I went diving through the air at him. I went flying right by him, but I never even grazed him. Morton collapsed as if I'd broken every bone in his body. It was like those punters that go down in a heap if you so much as breathe on them. They got me for another fifteen yards. It was a good bit of acting by Morton, a lousy call by the refs. Madden pulled me out after that play and he was livid. He wanted to know what the hell I was doing out there. I wanted to explain what really happened, but it was too late anyway. I just told him I didn't know. We went on to lose that game, 14–6, and I was miserable. I felt a little better when John apologized to me after watching the game films. He didn't have to do that, and a lot of coaches wouldn't have.

There wasn't much you could say when you were burned by the refs. If you got too abusive, you wound up hurting only yourself. Yes, NFL refs do hold grudges. I've seen refs make calls for one reason only—because they were angry at something you said. As for the anti-Raider calls, I don't think every ref got a memo reading "Screw the Raiders." I think it was more of an unwritten rule. And it wasn't all the refs; there were definitely exceptions. I do know we used to get burned on a regular basis. I never let it bother me though. To play for Al, it was a small price to pay.

10

IT'S A FUNNY GAME

To put it mildly, Al Davis has never shied away from signing football players with colorful personalities. I don't think Al simply has a weakness for characters—he's too much of a pragmatist. I think Al likes hiring people who dare to be unique, who will take the occasional gamble. He feels this kind of person helps him win, because those who are unpredictable in their everyday lives tend to be just as hard to figure out when they get on a football field. I always thought our individuality as people was one of our strengths when we came together as a team. You never knew where the Raiders were coming from, on the field or off it.

Charles Philyaw was a sideshow by himself. The guys used to tell a lot of Charles Philyaw stories, and I'll recount some of them here because they were funny. But I want to make it clear that I'm not trying to poke fun at Charles. Charles was one of the nicest people I ever met and I always considered him a friend. And believe me, Charles could play football. When he set his mind to it, I really believe he was Pro Bowl caliber. But even if Charles hadn't been as good as he was, I'm not sure the coaches wouldn't have kept him around anyway. His unusual way of doing things kept everyone smiling.

Charles was always having trouble finding the proper pair of shoes. Probably because he wore a size seventeen. Before one exhibition game in Arizona, Charles realized he had forgotten his shoes in Santa Rosa. If this had happened to anyone else, it wouldn't have been a big deal. He could have borrowed a pair from one of the guys who never played. But since Charles wore seventeens, he seemed to be out of luck. Charles had no choice—he had to borrow a size fifteen from one of the backup linemen. Charles played the entire game with a pair of shoes that were two sizes two small. If you've never seen a 300-pound man running around yelling "ooh, ooh, ooh" all night, you're missing something.

As big as he was, Charles was eternally in search of food. His stomach had no sense of decorum. He would get hungry any time or place. One day Charles was complaining during practice that he was starving. Fred Biletnikoff heard him moaning and generously directed him toward George Blanda. This was near the end of George's career and he wasn't getting much playing time at games or in practice. Fred told Charles that George's sole function at practice was to take food orders for the rest of the guys. Charles walked up to George and put in an order for a hamburger. George nearly killed him.

During games, Phil Villapiano would look out for Charles, help him whenever he saw he was having problems. In one game, Charles was unexpectedly inserted into the lineup against the Steelers. As always, he was more than willing, but they ran a lot of traps and misdirection plays, and their offense could be confusing if you weren't familiar with it. Charles was falling for too many fakes. Like Teddy Hendricks, Phil used to have an uncanny knack for guessing the other team's plays. Right before each play he began to whisper to Charles what he thought was coming. Phil was often right and Charles had a great game. The next week Charles was back in the starting lineup. Before the first defensive play, Phil noticed that Charles was staring at him as they waited for the offense to break its huddle. When the offense got to the line of scrimmage, Charles was still staring. Phil didn't know what Charles was up to, but he had no time to worry about it. He had a play to stop. Finally, just before the ball was snapped, Charles cupped his hands over his mouth and whispered to him.

"Hey Phil, aren't you going to tell me what to do this week?"

One time Charles told John Madden that he wanted his entire name, first and last, inscribed on the back of his game jersey. Madden told Charles that this was not allowed by the league unless there were two players on one team with identical names.

"That's not true," Charles protested. "We've got a guy who's got both his names on the back of his jersey."

"Who's that?" Madden wanted to know.

"Van Eeghen."

Charles thought Mark Van Eeghen's first name was Van.

When a player gets a minor injury, he's instructed to come and watch the other guys practice. Injured players always feel awkward and insecure, and they usually don't like to call much attention to themselves. Most guys dress accordingly, in some basic shorts or sweats, certainly nothing flamboyant. Charles sprained an ankle one day and came by practice to watch. He had on skintight shorts with his car keys dangling from a belt. He was wearing a tennis shirt, a hat and a pair of sunglasses. Over two different color socks, he had a regular shoe on his good foot and a sandal on his bad one. He was also sipping on a coke. Other than that, Charles blended right in.

The only thing Matt Millen has in common with Charles is that they both do things their own way. Millen's not too difficult to spot when he's on the field—he's the linebacker who's trying to tear the running back's head off. Millen is one of those classic Jekyll and Hyde types. Off the field he is basically softspoken. Put a helmet on his head and he's scary.

After the Raiders were eliminated by the Patriots in last season's playoffs, Matt saw Howie Long, surrounded by a crowd of people, getting accosted by someone Matt thought was some crazy fan. Matt swung his helmet at the intruder and clipped him in the head. It turned out to be Pat Sullivan, the son of the Patriots owner and the team's general manager. Sullivan had been taunting Howie all game from the sidelines, and they started arguing as they walked off the field after the game. After he found out who he'd swung at, Matt showed characteristic remorse. He said it was a good idea.

When a college coach really wants to land a high school

athlete, he'll often send one of the school's well-known alumni to help recruit him. In Matt's case it didn't work according to plan. In 1976, the University of Maryland flew Randy White to Millen's high school in Pennsylvania. Randy had just played in the Super Bowl with the Dallas Cowboys, and he was already becoming one of the most respected players in the NFL.

As they discussed the merits of Maryland, White and Millen went through a workout in the high school weight room. They each did a few sets on the bench. For some reason Millen then challenged White to an arm wrestling match. Just when Millen thought he had White beat, White got serious and nearly tore Millen's arm off. Millen got mad and tried to go after Randy for real. White picked him up in the air until Millen had eased back down.

"Well," Randy said, "you probably won't go to Maryland now. But I'll see you in a few years, and when I do we'll play for real."

As you can see, Millen was never a big fan of convention. That went double when it came to conventional medicine. In high school, Millen once hurt his elbow on a quarterback's helmet. His arm became so hardened by calcium deposits that it bent into a right angle. Matt says he walked around his high school looking like Napoleon, with his arm hidden inside his jacket. Rather than go to a doctor, Matt tried to fix things himself. First he tied weights to his arm and held it in a scalding whirlpool. Then he and a buddy went down to the metal shop and tried to straighten out his arm by sticking it in a vice. That didn't work either. Finally he relented and saw a doctor, but he wasn't happy with what he heard. The doctors warned him not to lift weights. Naturally he went to the weight room the following day. While he was lifting, his arm kind of snapped and a piece of calcium broke loose. His arm has been fine ever since.

Rather than Maryland, Millen wound up at Penn State, where he didn't always see eye to eye with his coach, Joe Paterno. One day during practice, Penn State's defense ran the same play over and over. Millen couldn't get it right and his frustration was boiling over. What's more, the same offensive player was trying to knock the crap out of him each time they ran the play.

Millen started a fight with the guy and the Penn State linebacker coach told him to get off the field. Millen said no. The coach pushed Millen and Millen pushed him back. Finally an enraged Paterno stepped in and ordered Millen off the field. Again Matt refused. Valuable practice time had already been lost, and still Millen wouldn't move. So as Millen stood rooted in place, Paterno moved the entire practice to an adjoining field.

Pound for pound, Matt is probably one of the strongest players on the current Raiders. George Buehler, an offensive guard when I was playing, was one of the strongest football players I've ever seen. At 6'2" and 270 pounds, George was *really* built like a refrigerator. He was solid muscle, and if George ever wanted to hurt someone it would not have been pretty. Luckily, his temper was almost nonexistent. The only time anyone ever saw George get mad was in a game against the Chiefs. Jim Kearney had leveled Mark Van Eeghen after the play was over. Buehler rushed over to Kearney, grabbed him by the front of his jersey and lifted him into the air. He looked like he was going to throw him through a cloud.

"You, you, you . . . you dirty player, you."

George was also one of our true eccentrics. He graduated from Stanford and he comes from a family full of doctors. Although he was very bright, George had a habit of drifting into his own impenetrable world. Naturally, we called him The Fog.

Even in the heat of a game, George would sometimes check into his private bubble. He was fascinated by airplanes, and it didn't matter much when or where he saw them. George and the other players on offense would all be in the huddle. The other players would be just about foaming at the mouth, blood in their eyes, and George would be looking skyward, watching planes cruise over the stadium.

George didn't just love airplanes, he even owned a few. Only his were the remote control kind. One day George started flying his plane around the practice field while everyone else, fully uniformed, was getting stretched. The plane started dipping and diving like it was going to crash. George was hammering at the controls like a madman. When it finally slammed into the goalpost, everyone was aghast. George was never the last of the big-time spenders and he had annihilated an expensive toy. But, as usual, George was unperturbed.

"I lost radio contact," he explained without expression.

When George's fog got especially deep, someone like Gene Upshaw would shake him violently and remind him where he was. In one game, Kenny Stabler was driving the offense down the field for the go-ahead touchdown. It was the moment of truth, and with Kenny about to call the next play, the huddle was deadly quiet. All you could hear was heavy breathing. Then George broke in.

"Hey, Pete," he said to our fullback, Pete Banaszak, "where did you get those shoes? I really like the fancy design. I've been thinking about making a change myself."

According to the NFL rule book, no player can smear "foreign substances" on his jersey. The rule was created because offensive linemen used to rub products like Vaseline on their jerseys during games. This made it difficult for the defense to grab the offensive linemen and toss them around. There were other "no-grab" methods. Offensive linemen would use two-sided tape to stick their jerseys tightly to their shoulder pads. Or they'd try and squeeze into jerseys that would be a better fit for little kids. After one game against the Steelers, a few of their defensive linemen complained that some of our offensive linemen were all greased up. George was one of the players they fingered. The following week George admonished our trainer.

"You know the rule about foreign substances," George told him. "Next time make sure that Vaseline is made in the United States."

One other thing about George—we all felt he blocked Joe Greene better than any other guard in the league.

Jeff Barnes, a Raiders linebacker, is a lot of fun too. Jeff was a track star in high school but he doesn't play football anything like a track person. He has a mean streak—he's been known to drill a guy and then ask him how he liked it. Off the field, Jeff is one of those people who constantly has a smile on his face. He also has an original way with words, and some of the things he used to say would crack everybody up. Jeff liked to make us laugh and he always got the desired result.

There was a joke circulating among the Raiders one day at practice: What do you see when you look down a mole hole? The answer is molasses, as in mole asses. For about five minutes Chris Bahr, the kicker, tried explaining to Jeff that it was a play on words. Jeff didn't seem to see the humor. Chris explained it again. Finally Jeff said that he got it.

Chris saw Jeff the next day at practice.

"J.B.," Chris greeted him, "what do you see when you look down a mole hole?"

"Mole assholes," Jeff replied.

Chris thought Jeff was kidding. Jeff wasn't.

"J.B.," Chris said, "it's mole asses. Molasses. It's a play on words. We just went through this yesterday."

More silence.

"Listen," Jeff finally said, "you see what you see when you look down a mole hole, and I'll see what I see."

There was once a power shortage after one of our practices at the Oakland Coliseum. The entire stadium went black, including the players' locker room. Everyone was bumping and fumbling around the locker room when a voice came out of the darkness. It was Jeff's.

"Shoot," he said, "I wonder if the lights on my car are out."

One more J.B. story. On a flight to a road game, our plane had just landed on the runway when it was approached by a man driving one of those luggage trucks. This guy was coming at one of the wings awfully fast, but we all figured he would brake in time. He didn't. He ran right into the tip of the wing. One of the guys spoke with the pilot a few weeks later and the pilot said the driver had caused something like $75,000 worth of damage. He was also fired from his job. Just after the incident, Jeff put it all in his own unique perspective.

"Boy," he exclaimed, "it's a good thing we weren't in the air when that truck hit us."

Defensive players like Jeff are not the only ones who can hand out punishment. Marv Hubbard was a good example. Marv was a linebacker at heart, trapped inside a fullback's body. He was one of those blood-and-guts kind of guys, one of the few running backs I've ever seen I could have sworn went out of his way to run people over. Where Marv grew up, in a small town outside of Buffalo, they beat each other up just to stay in shape.

One Raiders official tells about the time Marv and a few other Raiders wandered into a Santa Rosa bar. According to him, here's how the story goes: Marv, who is basically old-fashioned, got a little antsy when he spotted two men dancing with each other on the dance floor. Noting this, his teammates told Marv to behave himself. From his seat at the bar, Marv promised that he would. Marv was doing fine—until the two men starting kissing each other on the mouth. Then Marv got wild. First he ran over to the jukebox and threw it on its side. Then he jumped on top of a table and ordered everybody out of the bar.

"Let's go," Marv screamed, "clear it out. I'm from the ABC."

As the startled crowd was hurrying out of the bar, the irate owner stormed up to Marv.

"Who the hell are you?" he demanded. "And what the hell do you mean, the ABC?"

Marv meant to say the Department of Alcoholic Beverage Control, but in all the excitement his memory failed him. Finally he spat something out.

"I'm from the American Bowling Commission."

Marv had to pay for the damages.

That was obviously a crazy night. As for myself, some of the strangest encounters I ever had as a football player came from dealing with the fans. Most of the fans I met were perfectly normal. Others were not playing with all their cards.

One time my mom drove up to Green Bay to watch us play against the Packers. But she couldn't enjoy the game. Seated in the row behind her was a guy with a mouth like a sewer. For some reason, most of his venom was directed toward me. For about a quarter, my mom just tried to tune him out, but then she couldn't stand it anymore. She told him that she was my mother and could he please refrain from all the obscenities. That was all this moron needed to hear. Once he found out who my mom was, he got more obnoxious and profane than ever. Then he started jabbing her in the ribs, like "oh, so you're Matu-szak's mom." My mother doesn't get mad easily, but when she does she's got a pretty good temper. After a few more pokes to her ribs, my mother turned and spit right in his face. That seemed to quiet him down. Now here's the incredible part: The guy waited for me after the game in the parking lot. Then he asked me for my autograph.

Rod Martin, the Raiders linebacker, is not the kind of person you want to mess around with. He's the kind of guy who would be strong if he never lifted a weight in his life. Rod's father was a coalminer in West Virginia. When Rod was young, his dad would come home periodically and dump two tons of coal next to their home at the top of a hill. They would use it to warm the house. But in the winter their truck couldn't make it up the hill. So Mr. Martin would leave the coal at the bottom. Rod, his brother and his father would carry the coal up the hill in buckets and wheelbarrels. All day long, until every last piece was at the top of the hill. That's how strong Rod is.

Rod was in the parking lot a couple of years ago after a game with the Seahawks. He was signing autographs and chatting with the fans. Suddenly he felt someone's fingers in his back pocket. When he whirled around, some little thief was trying to pick his pocket. This guy was either stupid or drunk as a skunk, probably both. Rod was so shocked he just stood there as the guy ran away.

The amazing thing is, incidents like that aren't all that rare. As I was saying before, it's as if some people want to see how far they can push you. One night I was sitting in the Bamboo Room with Dave Dalby and Teddy. Seated at a table, I suppose we looked like average-sized human beings. We were shooting the breeze when some guy I'd never seen before walked up to the table and interrupted our conversation. He was looking at me.

"What's your name, Fatso?" he asked me.

I didn't respond.

"I said," he repeated, "what's your name, Fatso?"

I unfolded myself from the table and stood straight up. The guy didn't look quite as cocky then.

"How would you like to eat this table," I asked the wise guy, "whole or in splinters?"

Sometimes you have to speak to people in a language they understand.

Dave Pear got the ultimate fan letter. Dave was a talented Raiders noseguard before a neck injury cut his career short. Running off the artificial turf one game in Seattle, Dave tripped on a seam and fell on his face. When the crowd started jeering and laughing at him, Dave responded with an obscene gesture. A week later Dave got a letter that was postmarked from Seattle. Dave thought it was great and he read it aloud in the locker room. It was only one line long.

"Dear Dave," it read, "fuck you and the horse you rode in on."

I admit it, there were times when we also had some fun with the fans. I'm not part of this next story but it's a Raiders classic. There was a young couple we'd always see at the Bamboo Room. They were obviously in love and we'd ask them how the relationship was going, how they managed to keep it fresh, things like that. One day they announced that they wanted to get married. One of the Raiders told them they were in luck, that we just so happened to have a reverend on our team who would be more than happy to marry them. A few nights later the couple said they'd like to go ahead and tie the knot. The following night several of the Raiders joined the young couple at the Bamboo. First they set the mood with lighted candles. Then, with Pat Toomay posing as minister, Teddy as the best man, and several other Raiders singing in the choir, the happy couple exchanged their vows. Finally the Bamboo groom kissed the Bamboo bride.

———

Football is a funny game, all right, and one thing I always found amusing was the superstition. I didn't have many myself. I liked to put my pads on in the same order each week, and that was about it. But I was in the minority. Some players clung to their superstitions like they were matters of life and death. And the more those rituals met with success, the more they got reinforced. If a player did something a certain way and his team went on to win, he usually did it that way forever. Or at least until a loss.

John Madden was not alone—several of the Raiders were superstitious. Mark Van Eeghen might have had the strangest routine of all. When we were on the road, Mark would climb on top of his TV set, then dive off it onto his bed. If he didn't do that, he couldn't fall asleep. Mark started doing it when he was in college, and he didn't want to jinx himself once he got to the pros. Speaking of habits, Mark had another distinctive one. He and Dave Casper would get back to back, drop their pants, lock their elbows together, and lift each other off the ground. You won't find it in many astronomy books, but it was the rarely cited double moon.

Lester Hayes is superstitious to the same extent that Arnold Schwarzenegger is muscular. Lester has seen the movies from the Star Wars series over seventy times, and he truly believes he's a Jedi Knight. Whenever someone was getting frustrated or depressed because we were losing, Lester would tell him everything would turn out fine. The Force, he would explain, was with the silver and black; therefore, the Raiders were destined for greatness. It always sounded logical to me.

Lester wears the same chin strap he bought in junior high school for a dollar. He used to wear a towel hanging from his uniform belt, and he'd always have to have it taped exactly seven times. He and an assistant trainer would sit there and count it out. If it wasn't taped seven times, Lester felt naked out there. After every coin toss, Lester would touch the helmets of one of the veterans, usually Hendricks or Upshaw. Since they had been through the wars so many times, Lester wanted to soak up some of their aura.

The year we beat the Eagles in the Super Bowl, Lester had a dream season. He had thirteen interceptions in the regular season—one fewer than Night Train Lane's all-time record—and four more were called back because of penalties. In the playoffs he had five more interceptions, for a total of eighteen. A lot of cornerbacks don't have that many during a whole career.

But when Lester was a rookie his hands were suspect. One

game he had an easy interception but the ball bounced right from his fingers. As Lester was moaning on the sideline, Fred Biletnikoff walked up. At first he didn't say anything, just took Lester's hand and stuck it into a jar of sticky, resinated goo. He told Lester that he was too good a ballplayer to drop easy balls, and that the glop had always worked for him. Lester became addicted. He even gave it a name: stickum.

Lester attacked stickum with the same restraint he did his other routines—none whatsoever. He would spread his stickum everywhere. And I mean everywhere. On his hands, his pants, his jersey—probably styled his hair with it. Lester was the only player in the league who could run back an interception for a touchdown and not get hugged—or even touched—in congratulations by a single one of his teammates. No one wanted to get slimed. One time a ball was flying past Lester when it stuck to the inside of his arm. Just stuck there and didn't move. The next year stickum was outlawed.

Biletnikoff was also wildly superstitious. He'd wear the same pair of socks every game and chew the same number of pieces of gum. Before every game Fred would tie and untie his shoe-laces about fifty times. Then he would lie on his back on the locker room floor, tossing a football to himself over and over and over. When it came to stickum, Fred used twice as much as Lester ever did. Fred had a routine: He would come back to the huddle and go right to John Vella. John would literally pry Fred's fingers apart, or tear off the grass that was stuck to the palms of his hands. Fred was an official's nightmare. Every time he made a reception, the officials had to remove the ball from the game and clean it with a special solution. Fred was the only player I've ever seen who never used his hands when he got off the ground after a play. He'd kind of pop back up, only using his legs. He was afraid he might stick to the field.

11

KENNY STABLER AND SOME OTHER QUARTERBACKS

During my first few seasons with the Raiders, I wasn't close to Kenny Stabler. I admired him as a person and a quarterback, and I was happy as hell to have him on my side. But off the field we went our separate ways. It was not until the training camp of 1979 that Kenny and I became tight.

For Kenny, 1978 had been a rude awakening. He was still better than most quarterbacks that season, but his left arm was his meal ticket and it wouldn't function as spectacularly as usual. His left elbow was jammed and his left ring finger had a split tendon. To compound the problem, our offensive line had a rare off year and Kenny spent a lot of time running for his life. He wound up with sixteen touchdowns and thirty interceptions, the first disappointing season in a celebrated career. The Raiders finished nine and seven and missed the playoffs for the first time since 1971.

That off-season, Al Davis publicly laid much of the blame for the Raiders' problems on Kenny. He said if you had to blame anyone, blame Kenny because he was the one who got paid the most, and he was the one who got paid to take that kind of pressure. Al is much too smart to believe that any one player can make or break a team's season, and he admitted later that he was just trying to get Kenny fired up for the following year. But Kenny was stung. Al and Kenny had never been very close in the first place. Their relationship was based more on mutual respect than on any kind of warmth. Now Kenny started asking Al to trade him.

Kenny liked to have his fun away from the field. He never denied that for a minute. He said he liked to read the game plan by the light of the jukebox. But when it came to loyalty, Kenny was very much a company man. He rarely if ever sulked or complained, not even early in his career when he felt he should be the team's starting quarterback. Kenny's loyalty was one of the reasons his teammates liked him so much. By singling Kenny out, Kenny felt Al had betrayed that loyalty.

A trade was never made and when Kenny showed up at camp in 1979, his spirits soon got worse. Fred Biletnikoff and Pete Banaszak, his two closest friends, had both been released. John Madden had just retired. Kenny and John were allies, and their individual success in the NFL had depended in part on that alliance. Kenny always knew John would back him in a pinch. With John, Fred and Pete all gone, Kenny felt lonely.

After our first day of practice, Villapiano and I were going out for dinner. We knew Kenny was down and we wanted to remind him that he still had friends. We asked Kenny to join us for dinner and his face brightened on the spot. Kenny was used to hanging out with Fred and Pete, both offensive guys, and I think he was tickled that a couple of characters from the defense wanted to befriend him. Kenny and I got closer every day. A few weeks later, Kenny asked me if I wanted to share his apartment with him that season. I accepted.

When I told some of the writers that I was moving in with Kenny, several of them laughed. They probably figured we'd go wild. On the contrary, living with Kenny had a calming influence on me. He's only a few years older than I, but I looked up to him. Kenny thought before he spoke or acted, something at which I was not always so adept. I used to feel smothered when people would swarm around me, but Kenny always handled it well. He would disarm people with his sense of humor. I'd watch him work a crowd and I would file it all away.

Living with Kenny I also got a different type of education. I had never been more than acquaintances with a quarterback before. Professionally, I knew you had to have a good one to win. But I felt a quarterback's performance often overshadowed the talents of other people. Especially the offensive linemen. Without a good offensive line, a quarterback would be lucky just to survive. I thought playing quarterback was a two-sided proposition. When a team won, their quarterback got too much credit. When it lost he got too much blame. And with all the money most quarterbacks made, I never sympathized with them for any punishment they took. I figured that's what they got paid for.

I had hit opposing quarterbacks before—hit them hard—and seen them bounce back up. I respected that. But I had never thought of them as being unusually tough. Linemen were tough, linebackers were tough, blocking backs were tough, special team guys were tough. Etcetera. Quarterbacks were skillful, smart, cunning.

My thinking changed one Sunday night at our apartment. That day against the Chargers, Kenny's protection was uncharacteristically porous. He had gotten hit on almost every pass. That night I walked to Kenny's room to see if he was in the mood to talk. When I peered into his room, I stopped before I entered. Kenny was sitting at the edge of his bed, struggling to peel off his jersey. His face was contorted by pain. When he finally got his jersey over his head, Kenny's upper body was a hideous sight. He had ugly blue welts all across his chest and shoulders. There were about ten of them, each roughly the size of a man's closed fist. Kenny hadn't seen me, so I turned and went back to my room. I had a feeling he preferred to be alone.

As long as I'd been in the league, it was not until that moment that I truly appreciated how tough you have to be to play quarterback in the NFL. All of us took a beating out there. Courage is one commodity the NFL isn't short on. But quarterbacks, any time they threw a pass, were vulnerable to the most dangerous of hits. That was the blindside shot, the one hit any player fears most.

Quarterbacks get blindsided more than any other position in football. It's a risk they take on every pass. There's no way to lessen the blow, no bracing for the impact. They have to stand there—stretched out and exposed, often with their back to a rushing defender—and hope they don't get brutalized. The things they can see coming aren't much more pleasant. It takes an awful lot of guts to stand there and hold the football when a 270-pound defensive lineman is rushing at your face. Quarterbacks, at least the good ones, earn every penny they make.

Kenny was a midnight rambler, a free-spirited Southerner who loved fast boats and expensive whiskey. With his beard and silver hair, Kenny looked more like a country western singer than a traditional jock. Because of all that, some people never realized how good an athlete Kenny was. In his prime he had all the physical tools. His passes arrived on a line, he was quick enough to avoid the rush, he was strong enough to absorb the punishment. Kenny got his nickname "The Snake" in high school, after he zigged and zagged and snaked up the field for a seventy-yard touchdown on a punt return. He could also play baseball. The Houston Astros drafted him out of college as a pitcher.

But the one thing that set Kenny apart from all other quarterbacks was his cool under pressure. Some quarterbacks freeze up when a game is on the line. They miss wide open receivers. They unload the ball before their receivers have worked their way open. Especially in the frenzied environment of a road game, with a hostile crowd going nuts, they just can't handle the pressure.

Kenny was just the opposite. He was the calm in the midst of chaos. You could not shake the man. When it came to rallying a team from behind, I believe Kenny was the best of all time. Those are the times that separate the men from the boys. In the closing minutes of a game, when your team has one last chance to win, you can take your computerized printouts and your game plans and flush them down the toilet. The quarterbacks who win those games are the ones with guts.

A quarterback has also got to inspire confidence in the people who share his huddle. A quarterback who looks scared or nervous is going to make his teammates start thinking that he can't do the job. And doubt is just as infectious as confidence. Kenny was unflappable. Late in one game Kenny had his face sliced open by a nasty sack. His beard was smeared with blood, and some of the offensive linemen thought he should at least call time-out. Kenny said no.

"This feels like an awfully bad hangover, fellas," he told the huddle. "Luckily I can handle it. Now let's go."

In 1977, we played the Baltimore Colts in an AFC playoff game. It was an amazing game, one of the best I ever played in. As we moved into the second overtime, the game was still tied 31–31. We had the ball on the Colts' thirteen yard line, and 60,000 Colts fans were screaming their lungs out. Kenny walked to the sidelines to confer with Madden. Kenny used to call his own plays, but John had input too. Madden was spitting out ideas when he noticed that his prized quarterback was gazing into the stands.

"You know something, John?" Kenny said. "These people are really getting their money's worth today."

Madden's jaw nearly fell to the ground. On the next play, Kenny hit Dave Casper for the game-winning touchdown. Madden still can't believe it today.

Sometimes Kenny's devices were less conventional.

We were playing San Diego in 1978. With ten seconds left, the Chargers led, 20–14. We had the ball on their fourteen yard line, but it was fourth down and we had no time-outs remaining. Woody Lowe, one of their linebackers, broke through and rapped his arms around Kenny. It looked like the Chargers had us beat. That's the way it looked. As Woody spun Kenny toward the ground, Kenny fumbled the ball forward to the ten yard line. From there Pete Banaszak batted the ball to the three, where Dave Casper swatted it into the endzone and fell on top of it. The clock had expired and the game was ours, 21–20. The Chargers were frozen in disbelief, but we felt pretty good about it. We never liked them anyway.

I rate Kenny as the finest quarterback I've ever played with or against. He was also right up there when it came to enjoying himself. In fact, one time Kenny and I had more fun than the Raiders would have liked.

Our only day off used to be on Tuesdays. Since Lake Tahoe was such a great place to unwind, and such a short drive from

Oakland, a lot of our players would drive there right after Monday's practice. We didn't have to be back until Wednesday at noon for Defense Day. One Monday night Kenny and I zipped up to Tahoe in his Porsche. We stayed in adjoining rooms at one of the nice hotels. It was one of the best times I've ever had, and I've had some good ones. I won't get into details, but let's just say we had enough fun for an offense, a defense and maybe a couple of special teams.

Originally we had planned on returning Tuesday night. But when Tuesday night came around that didn't seem like such a great idea anymore. I looked at Kenny and he looked back at me. We each had the same thing on our minds—neither one of us was ready to leave. We considered our situation. I was playing that season with a torn rotator cuff, and the extra rest would probably do me a lot of good. And Wednesday being Defense Day, Kenny would only be needed for about five to ten minutes anyway. To us, those were perfectly good reasons to stick around, at least for another day or so. We also knew the Raiders wouldn't see it quite that way. I have to confess: We called the Raiders and said that Kenny's Porsche had broken down, and we'd be back as soon as it got repaired. They said to hurry up, and we got back to our party. Thursday morning we figured it was time to get back. We were good and rested and we did have a game that week. We jumped in Kenny's Porsche and arrived at practice fifteen minutes late. To our amazement, the coaches didn't seem all that upset. We later found out that they also hadn't forgotten. Later that season they changed our day off to *Monday*. I don't think it was only because of me and Kenny, but it may have had something to do with it. Players used to come back late from Tahoe all the time, but no one ever came back quite as late as we did.

Today Kenny is happily married. In the old days he was something of a ladies man. Walking into a party with Kenny was like walking into a nail factory with a giant magnet. Women seemed to adore him. On the other hand, it wasn't just women who liked to be around Kenny. Men would run up to him and want to talk about football. He was such a gentleman, so calm and unhurried, people just felt at ease around him.

Kenny had a hot tub in his apartment. We used to spend a lot of time there nursing our aches and pains. Sometimes Kenny invited friends over to join us. You could fit about six people in Kenny's hot tub without anyone getting cramped. I can't imagine who did Kenny's guest lists, but there was usually the kind of ratio I liked. Rub a dub dub, there were always four girls in a tub. It was all very civilized, but it sure beat hot tubbing with the other players.

In the spring of 1980, our good times ended. Kenny got traded. Although he had bounced back to have an excellent 1979, Al felt Kenny's ability to throw the long ball had deteriorated. Up until this very last season, when the Raiders changed to a ball control attack, Al had always liked to strike quickly and deep. In a rare trade of starting quarterbacks, Al traded Kenny to the Houston Oilers for Dan Pastorini.

I was shocked and hurt when I heard the news. Kenny and I had grown very close and I thought it was a friendship that would get nothing but better. It's hard to make friends in a profession as fleeting as football, and when you make a good one you want to stick with him. When Kenny left the Raiders, I felt like a part of me went with him.

Since Kenny went back to Alabama after every season, and the trade was made in the off-season, I didn't even get to talk to him about it. I knew Kenny would be stunned by the trade. Yes, he had asked Al to trade him the season before. But when everything was seemingly resolved, I knew Kenny planned on ending his career as a Raider.

When I tried to call his home, I got no answer. And for reasons we've never discussed, Kenny never called me. I had heard the old saying a hundred times: Every time you made a good friend either you or he got traded. Now I understood all too clearly. Kenny's trade taught me an even harsher lesson about football. It doesn't matter who you are or what you've done. Once you're considered replaceable, you're as good as gone.

Kenny was too tough to let it destroy him, and as usual he landed on his feet. Teaming up with Bum Phillips, Kenny helped take the Oilers to the playoffs that season. That was 1980, the year we would go on to beat the Eagles in the Super Bowl. Our first-round opponent was the Houston Oilers.

It was an odd, emotional week prior to the game. Besides Kenny, Al had also traded Jack Tatum and Dave Casper to Houston. Dave's departure was particularly awkward. Dave had been traded to the Oilers after the fifth game of that season. We were two and three and Gene Upshaw had called a players-only meeting. Gene made what I thought was a pretty good speech about the merits of team play, saying that we all had to sacrifice if we wanted to turn the season around. Dave got up and said that if everyone looked out for himself, then everything would work itself out. Precisely the opposite of what Gene had just said. When Upshaw and Art Shell told him to cool it, Dave started calling them assholes. Dave had always been one of Al's favorites, a smart, sure-handed tight end who was also an excellent blocker. He and Kenny had teamed up on dozens of game-winning passes. But Al traded Dave a week after his outburst. Dave's poor practice habits that season, and the three draft choices Houston was offering for him, was too much to overlook.

I always liked Dave. He was like Teddy—he kept people laughing. Sometimes he would come to practice with his helmet all taped up like a conehead. One day, the locker room was unusually sedate and Dave felt he should liven things up. He walked over to a wall and smashed his helmet right through it. It made a big hole but no one saw the need to fix it right away. First we put a dartboard over it, then a picture. Every time I'd walk by that picture I'd think of Dave. When Dave got to Houston, we heard that his sense of the absurd wasn't as appreciated as it had been by us. One day at practice Dave had his helmet off and he was told by one of the Oilers coaches that he was to wear his helmet at all times. Dave took this literally. That day at lunch, Dave ate his entire meal with his helmet on. Right through his facemask.

I was sorry to see someone like that get traded. But the week before our playoff game with Houston, Dave said some things he shouldn't have. Apparently he still had an ax to grind with Upshaw. He made some disparaging remarks to the press, calling Gene an underachiever.

"He's the Michelin Man in his white suit," Dave was quoted. "He never falls down and never gets his uniform dirty."

This was nonsense, Upshaw was a dynamic blocker, and it just made the whole week seem stranger. It's always a little disturbing playing against former teammates. Especially people like Casper and Tatum, both of whom I liked. It was even weirder getting ready to face Kenny, who just last season had been my roommate. In noncontact sports, those situations are no big deal. Football's different. In football, it's a given that you have to whip people physically in order to beat them. The prospect of hurting one of my friends—even accidentally—was not a pleasing one. But I couldn't think about that. For that week Kenny was the enemy.

Enemy or not, on Sunday morning I found myself wanting to say hello to Kenny. We hadn't talked much since his move to Houston and I wondered how he liked the city and the team. I wanted to see if he liked Houston any more than I had. I played with the thought in my mind. Why the hell not? I would go see Kenny in the Oilers locker room. At the least I would wish him good luck.

I walked into Houston's locker room. Kenny was sitting in front of his locker, pulling on a cigarette, staring vacantly into space. He was lost in concentration, readying himself for the game. I had to smile—some things would never change. As I was about to say hello, Kenny glanced up and saw me. A look came over his face I'd never seen before. It was a cold stare that I didn't think I liked.

"I'm going to spit in your eye," he said. Then he looked away, as if to say get lost.

I stood there for a moment in shock. Then I realized he was only screwing around. I waited for him to laugh and pound me on the back. But he never looked back at me, just sat there puffing on his cigarette. He was serious. Now I got pissed. I felt like ripping the door off their stupid locker room, but I didn't want to make a scene. I just turned and stalked away.

By the time I got to our locker room, I had walked off my anger. But I still wondered what Kenny's problem was. Then it hit me.

I knew how intensely Kenny hated to lose. And if Kenny was going to beat us, the last thoughts he would want on his mind were those of friendship. For the next three hours our past would be on hold. For now I would be nothing more to Kenny than some dangerous lineman trying to take money out of his pocket. Or worse, a lineman who could separate him from his senses. In that light, Kenny's remark didn't seem so cold. He was trying to win.

Kenny never had a chance. We sacked him seven times and beat the Oilers, 27–7.

I played an inspired game. On Houston's first play from scrimmage, I caused Earl Campbell to fumble. We recovered and parlayed it into a field goal. Later in the game I blocked a field goal attempt. I had one regret—I never quite got to Kenny. At least not legally. One play I jumped completely offside and knocked him on his ass before I could stop my momentum. As he was lying on the ground, Kenny looked up at me with a smile.

"Tooz," he said, "I believe you're offside."

"Partner," I replied, "I believe you're right."

I saw Kenny after the game. We had a few laughs, everything was fine. Neither one of us mentioned his pregame comment. We didn't have to.

———

As a teammate, a quarterback, Kenny was the best. As an author, he needs some work.

I'm referring to *Snake,* the book Kenny wrote last year. I don't want to make too big a deal out of this, because I like Kenny a lot, and it isn't worth ruining a hell of a friendship. But I have to confess, Kenny's book seriously annoyed me. I felt some of the things Kenny said about his former teammates were in poor taste. You want to be forthright about your own sins, put yourself in hot water, that's one thing. But don't drag your friends down with you. Kenny told stories about teammates who were married, who are married, that could do a lot of damage. I'm sure it helped sell books and I hope Kenny uses the money wisely. Kenny, I love you, but it was kind of a horseshit thing to do.

Something else about Kenny's book bothered me: too many inaccuracies, especially about yours truly. Again, I'd like to set the record straight.

Kenny wrote that I willfully poisoned, and killed, two of my wife's dogs when they wouldn't stop barking. Total, unadulterated fiction. Never happened. First of all, I was never married. Secondly, I used to own a pair of Samoyans who accidentally got ahold of some sleeping pills that had fallen on my rug and got very, very sick. But I took them to the vet, and afterward they were fine. End of story.

I love dogs and that story made me furious. In fact, Kenny was on one of those call-in radio shows in San Francisco last year, promoting his book, and the DJ called me to see if I was interested in offering my comments. I was still angry about Kenny's carelessness, and I said I would be happy to. They called me and put me on hold, while Kenny spoke with some callers. Then the DJ asked Kenny what he thought the reactions of his teammates might be to the book. Kenny said everything was the truth, that we were all young and crazy back then, and it was all the way it happened. The DJ broke in: "Kenny, we just so happen to have one of those former Raiders on the line. Say hello to John Matuszak."

"Hey," I said, "what's cookin', good-lookin'?"

Kenny cleared his throat. "Uh, Tooz, how you doin' buddy?"

"Fine, Snake. Look, did you straighten out all those good people in San Francisco about how John Matuszak really feels about animals?"

Kenny cleared his throat again. "Uh, John is referring to a story, a hearsay story, that got put in the book, and it shouldn't have been there. It just wasn't true, but it got put in there anyway."

Kenny explained a little of the story, repeated that it was false, and we hung up. San Francisco down, the rest of the country to go.

As long as we're on the subject:

Kenny said he was with me one day and spotted this collection of all my crazy hats. I owned one hat, a Cowboy hat, the whole time Kenny knew me. It was Teddy Hendricks, not me, who had the crazy hat collection.

Kenny said I relied solely on my natural ability, that I "never picked up a weight." I've lifted weights, diligently, since I was twelve years old. If it's humanly possible, I make it a priority, always have, not to miss my workouts. If anything, my biggest problem was that I tended to overtrain.

About the 1977 AFC championship, Kenny took what amounted to a cheap shot. That was the game when I took sleeping medication the night before, and with the Denver altitude, felt like I was in slow motion the entire first half. It was something I still feel terrible about, and always will. But I came around in the second half, was alert, and kicked some ass. Kenny wrote that we were losing 20–17 with three minutes left, but the problem was that we never got the ball back. He said the Broncos ran out the clock, over me.

For the last eight plays of that game, we were in a defense called a Red Dog Pinch. In a 3–4 Red Dog Pinch, both defensive ends step in, toward the middle of the line. On the plays that the Broncos did run to my side, in a Red Dog Pinch, there wasn't much I could do. I thought about saying, the hell with this defense, but then I'd just be screwing up the linebackers. Kenny failed to mention it, but my hands were pretty much tied.

———————

Kenny was a big favorite in Oakland, and the fans were irate that Al had let him go. As a result, Dan Pastorini was never given much of a chance when he came to the Raiders. No matter what Dan did in a game, even if he threw three touchdown passes, the fans felt Kenny would have thrown four. In Game Five of that 1980 season, Dan broke his leg when a 265-pound lineman fell on it. I'll never forget that moment. As Dan was writhing around on the ground, obviously in excruciating pain, the fans at the Oakland Coliseum started cheering. I always thought the fans were one of the nicest parts of playing in Oakland. They really loved the Raiders. But that day they sickened every one of us.

I had mixed emotions when Pastorini came to Oakland. He had been the starting quarterback when I came up with the Oilers. He was young and attractive, Houston's darling. Dan seemed terribly cocky, always driving the fastest cars and dating the most gorgeous women. He went out regularly with a British actress named June Wilkinson, his future wife and one of the most beautiful women I'd ever laid eyes on. She was also a very sweet woman. June was about ten years older than Dan, back when men dating older women was a rarity. For a twenty-one-year-old rookie like me, Dan and June were glamour personified.

During one of my first days of camp, Dan challenged me to a forty-yard dash. I was in my stance, about to run, when he walked over and said he could beat me. I was flabbergasted. Why a veteran quarterback was challenging a rookie to a race was beyond me. Maybe he didn't care for all the press I was getting and he wanted to keep me in my place. I wasn't real worried about it. I told him let's go. We had the race and I beat him. I have to admit I enjoyed the sour look on his face as he walked away. At that time I thought Dan was just a big hot dog.

A few weeks after he became a Raider, my feelings toward Dan changed drastically. He was no longer arrogant and brash. All those years playing for a team as bad as Houston had taken a toll, physically and mentally. Simply speaking, Dan got his ass kicked. Not even his harshest critics had ever accused Dan of lacking courage. Reportedly, he once took twenty-four shots of Novocain in the course of a single game—twelve before, twelve at halftime—to try and kill the pain of his broken ribs. When Dan became a Raider, he had something he never seemed to have when I was in Houston—a sense of humility. He had been forced to accept his own mortality. Now, all he wanted was to end his career as a winner.

I really felt for Dan after he broke his leg. He was used to being the star, and now he was reduced to charting plays. When Plunkett played so well in our drive to the Super Bowl, Dan was released by the Raiders the following year. He was picked up by the Rams but was soon released there too. His body just couldn't stand the grind anymore. Today Dan's a professional race car driver and he's good at it. He's like a lot of former players in the NFL—he still needs to be tested.

Joe Namath was another quarterback who used to play hurt. With all the hype about his partying, his image as Broadway Joe, his incredible confidence, even the revolutionary white spikes, people saw the style instead of the substance. Joe played with brutally battered knees and he never whined after you hit him. He was tough.

I played against Joe when I was a rookie, but it was an exhibition game and I didn't see much of him. Later, when I was with the Chiefs, Joe played against us the entire game. I'll never forget that game. Joe was never terribly mobile to begin with, not with those knees of his, but now his career was ending and he was fair game for anyone who could beat his blocker. One of Joe's linemen was also nearing retirement, and I just beat the hell out of him that day. No matter what he tried to do, I was always right by him and into Joe's face. I must have hit Joe six or seven times and I never heard him say one word to that offensive lineman. Joe knew he was outmatched and didn't want to make him feel any worse. I respected Joe for that.

Despite his lack of mobility, Joe was almost impossible to sack. Some quarterbacks were hard to sack because they threw the ball up for grabs before you got there. Joe wasn't like that. Joe had no fear, or if he did he never showed it. He would stand there until the last possible moment and take his beatings. You couldn't sack Joe for another reason—because of his release. Even if you were absolutely certain you had a sack, he would release the ball *just* before you got him. Joe had the quickest release of any quarterback in history.

After Kenny, I rate Joe as the next best quarterback I ever played with or against. Next, in order, come Dan Fouts, Terry Bradshaw, Bob Griese and Roger Staubach. I'd also say that those six were among the best of all time.

Like most other businesses, teams in the NFL steal ideas from their competitors. When something works for one team, everyone else jumps on the bandwagon. When Terry Bradshaw was at his peak, he revolutionized the physical requirements for a quarterback. Suddenly everybody wanted a big, strong, powerful quarterback. At times Terry was astounding. He could complete a pass with a defensive lineman hanging on his legs, or he could run people over like a fullback. Terry's got four Super Bowl rings, more than any quarterback in NFL history.

The only thing I never liked about Terry was his unnecessary flair for theatrics. He was one of those guys who would play his injuries for every last ounce. Especially during games in Pittsburgh. Terry would get hit. Then I would see Terry get carried off the field by a pair of teammates, his body seemingly mangled, his afternoon assuredly over. A backup quarterback would run on the field as the Pittsburgh fans cursed their misfortune. A few plays later, amazingly, Terry would sprint from the sideline to the Steeler's huddle. Meanwhile, the Steelers fans would be exploding with adoring applause. Come on, nobody gets better *that* quickly. Terry was just playing the crowd.

Bert Jones was another great actor. If Bert was as convincing on film as he was on grass, he'd be another Robert DeNiro. When Bert was in his prime with the Colts, he had a great arm and was almost impossible to ruffle. He also had the ugly habit of berating his receivers when they would drop a pass. When you screw up in a stadium full of rabid fans, you feel humiliated enough. I don't care how big you are, you feel very, very small. The last thing his receivers needed was for Bert to make them feel even smaller. That was the difference between a person like Namath and a person like Bert. Joe had a lot more class.

When it came to manipulating the refs, acting, Bert had no shame. You could brush his helmet and he'd react like you'd broken his neck. One game I swatted Bert's facemask with my hand as I went running by. He fell to the ground, screaming and gyrating, and the ref called a flag. I guess the ref admired a good performance.

Dan Fouts I always had a lot of respect for. He was another guy who would rather take his lumps then release the ball before he was ready. Because he's so low-key, and the Chargers never go too far because of their lack of defense, I think Fouts has never gotten the recognition he's deserved. Except for the fact that he played for the Chargers, I might have even invited Fouts to my house for dinner. Fouts was about the only player on the Chargers who didn't manufacture excuses every time the Raiders beat them. Next to Namath, Fouts had the quickest release I've ever seen.

When you sacked most quarterbacks, you could look forward to some interesting cursing. Not with Roger Staubach. I recall one game against the Cowboys where I put Roger down rather roughly. Not only that, but my sack forced the Cowboys to punt. It was the only time I ever heard Roger make an exclamation of any kind—good, bad or indifferent. He climbed on his feet and said, "Heck."

In terms of leadership, I rank Roger on the same level as Stabler or Namath. Of course, Roger had served in Vietnam when he was in the Navy. When you've been through something like that, you're not going to get rattled over a safety blitz. A lot of people wonder why the Cowboys are no longer as dominant as they once were. Part of it is age—a lot of their quality players got a little too old all at once. I'd say Roger's retirement in 1979 had even more to do with it. In the seventies, the Cowboys represented the NFC in the Super Bowl five times. They only won two, but the three games they lost were by a total of only eleven points. One year they went to the Super Bowl in what was supposed to be a rebuilding season. In the eighties, since Roger left, they haven't gone once. I don't think it's coincidence.

(While I'm on the topic of the Cowboys, I'd like to clarify something. Much has been said about the bad blood between the Raiders and the Cowboys. Even though they rarely play each other, a lot of Raiders have gone on record as saying that they despise the Cowboys. It's true, many of us thought that "America's Team" garbage was a bit of a joke. Actually, we used to feel that the Raiders or Steelers were more representative of America. Hard working, no-frill tough guys. But, any animosity on the part of the Raiders was never directed at the Cowboys *players*. Because we knew the players had nothing to do with that public relations stuff. It all came from the Cowboys front office. Contrary to popular belief, the players on the Cowboys aren't all wallflowers. Dallas will never be like the Raiders, but they occasionally sign a character or two. I've never asked any Cowboys about it, but if I had to guess, I'd say they all wished they'd never even heard the expression "America's Team." Who needs that kind of pressure?)

Getting back to Roger, he always used to scramble, and that's one thing I can never forgive him for. If I were the commissioner of football, I would make scrambling quarterbacks illegal. John Elway, Joe Montana and Jim McMahon would all be banished from the league. Or at least made to play in one-legged pants. Fighting past a humongous offensive lineman is hard enough. After you do, you expect to get your reward. Scramblers were ruthless. They'd look like they were going to let you have a sack—then they'd slither away from your grasp at the moment of truth. It was like seeing your girlfriend across the bedroom in a beautiful nightgown. Then having her pass out before anything could happen.

Sacks are a defensive lineman's dividend, his payoff. But I never got hung up on sacks. Playing on a three-man line through most of my career, I never got a lot of opportunities for sacks. My top priority was to stand my ground, bottle up as many of the other team's blockers as possible, and let the linebackers move in for the kill. Playing on a three-man line is hardly glamorous, and I think it was one of the reasons I never made All-Pro. It's better now, but when I played that type of honor traditionally went to the defensive linemen with the big statistics.

Frankly, I think I should have been named All-Pro in 1980. That was the season when the Raiders voted me as the team's outstanding lineman. I don't want to take anything away from the guys who did win it that year, because they were all good ballplayers, but I didn't see anyone in the league who was playing better than I was. I wasn't alone—a lot of people felt that way. On the other hand, when I left the game I did have two Super Bowl rings. And for those I wouldn't have traded twenty All-Pro honors.

There's a lot of talk these days about linemen who get so consumed by sacks that they neglect the run. This does happen, but there's a point a lot of people forget. Some linemen are so dominant against the pass, nobody expects or cares much if they play the run. It would be like asking Babe Ruth to bunt. Everyone knows Mark Gastineau of the Jets is great at getting sacks. Much has also been made about his inability to play the run. I think it's partly political. If Gastineau were more popular among his peers, you wouldn't hear so much criticism. No one ever asked Deacon Jones to play the run much, yet Deacon never got half the grief Gastineau does.

Stats are misleading anyway. Look at Howie Long. There are a lot of players with more sacks and tackles. Yet Howie is generally considered by his peers to be the best defensive lineman in the NFL. That's because he gets double- or triple-teamed on almost every play and still makes a tremendous impact. If a team ever tried using just one blocker against Howie, he would devastate their offense. Howie probably draws more holding penalties than any defensive lineman in the league. Nobody keeps stats like that, but it tells you a lot about Howie's game.

That last remark I made about Gastineau will not go over well with the current Raiders. Along with Tom Jackson of the Broncos and Lynn Swann of the Steelers, Gastineau is not a popular figure among the Raiders. Personally, I admire the way Gastineau plays. He's a tremendous athlete. But I thought his sack dance—which has since been outlawed—was totally out of line. After he'd sack the quarterback, he would stand above him dancing and waving his arms in celebration. That was bush league to begin with. But the worst thing was, he would do it even when his team was getting destroyed. What's worth celebrating then? You never saw any offensive linemen celebrating after a play when they'd stuffed Gastineau. I recall one game when Henry Lawrence, one of our offensive tackles, dominated Gastineau on almost every play. Gastineau got to the quarterback a couple of times and went into his sack dance. As if he'd been beating Henry all day long.

After I sacked a quarterback, I rarely if ever felt the need to taunt him. When I threw him to the ground, that was statement enough. One thing I never tried to do was knock a quarterback out for the entire season. If I could hit him hard but cleanly—and maybe shake him up enough to knock him out for the game—you're damn right I would. We had a lot better chance to win against a second-string quarterback.

Perhaps it's a contradiction, but at the same time I always loved playing against the Namaths and the Staubachs and the Bradshaws. Those were the games you live for. One of the greatest rewards I found in the NFL was the challenge, the pressure, the test. I can guarantee you, no one was ever thinking about contracts or money when he was out on that field. You were playing for pride. You were pitting your body, your brains and your nerve against the finest football players in the world. It was an incredible feeling to come out on top.

12

YOU GOTTA LOVE LINEBACKERS

Football has gone New Wave. Tradition has been trampled by the age of specialization, even at a meat and potatoes position like linebacker.

Today you have inside linebackers and outside linebackers. Linebackers who play only against the run or the pass. Linebackers who are great on Monday Night Football, but only so-so on Thursday Night Special Editions. They used to have linebackers named Butkus and Nitschke, vicious headhunters who would clear your sinuses free of charge. Dynamite football players, but not overly fast or athletic. Now linebackers are all 6′ 3″ and 250 pounds. They're incredible athletes. They can run like Carl Lewis, jump like Dr. J. If he chose to, a guy like Lawrence Taylor could play quarterback. Who would want to tackle him?

One thing hasn't changed though—linebackers are still as nasty as ever. But sometimes their image gets overblown. People think they're the same way when they leave the field. Since two of my closest friends used to be linebackers, I feel it's my duty to set the record straight.

Linebackers do not all have wives named Rocko. They do not brush their teeth with Black and Decker power tools. Some have been known to own, and resist kicking, puppies. A few, although you'd never know it on Sundays, even possess a heart.

Phil Villapiano was all heart. At 6′ 2″ and 220 pounds, today Phil would look like a cornerback. A very large, get-the-hell-away-from-me-sized cornerback. But a cornerback. Phil was a Pro Bowl linebacker in the seventies for two good reasons: He was a brutal hitter and he'd never stop battling. Phil's approach to the game was pure: It's me and you and let's see who's standing at the end.

Phil grew up in New Jersey, or as he used to pronounce it, New *Joisey*. Although he went to college at Bowling Green, not known for cranking out future pros, Phil was ready when he got to the NFL. Bowling Green plays in a conference called the Mid-American. Back then, just about every play was a run. It was unpolished, hardnosed football. It taught Phil how to hit.

Phil played left linebacker, I played left defensive end. We felt that the left side of the field was our domain. Our turf. Enter at your own discretion. Play football next to a man for four years and you get to know him. You can anticipate each other's moves. Phil and I could communicate on the field without even talking. If the offensive shifted at the line of scrimmage, I would nod at Phil and he would know what I wanted to do. We were a team within a team. We watched each other's backs.

Over on the right side, Teddy Hendricks and Otis Sistrunk felt the same. When we'd all be out for dinner or at a movie, sometimes we'd argue over which side had played better that week. Phil would yell out "left side" and Otis would yell out "right side." Pretty soon we'd all be screaming like maniacs. Sometimes we would do it in the huddle, but only if we had a big lead.

The quicker I got off the ball, the more havoc I created in the opponent's backfield, the easier it was for Phil to move in and make the tackle. Needless to say, Phil loved to get me fired up out there. Phil was all guts and emotion and he felt I should play that way too. Playing with Phil, I had no choice. If I'd just made a big tackle and was feeling pretty good about myself, he would run up and crack me in my facemask. Phil liked to keep me irritated.

In his efforts to pump me up, Phil would utilize his imagination. He'd pull me to the side. Then he'd look me straight in the eye.

"Tooz," he'd say in all earnestness, "I was talking to that bleeping quarterback the other day. You know what he said? He said you weren't worth shit. That's exactly what he told me."

I knew, of course, that this was nonsense. No quarterback who hadn't had a frontal lobotomy would say something like that to one of my closest friends. But I would play right along with it. *This guy thinks I'm shit, huh? We'll just see about that.*

One game we both got carried away. We were playing against the Pittsburgh Steelers and Dave Brown was the tackle across from me. With the Steelers' high-powered weight training program, Brown would later bulk up and become an excellent tackle. At that time he had just been moved from tight end and was still struggling with the adjustment. Early in the game, Phil intercepted me on the way to the line.

"John," he said, "the man playing across from you may look like an offensive tackle. He's not. He's a tight end. Are you telling me that a tight end is going to get the better of you?"

This may not rank with Knute Rockne's best stuff, but in the heat of a game with the Steelers these were very powerful words. I dug into my stance. I was going to take this converted tight end and knock him into Cleveland. At the quarterback's first sound, I exploded up and hammered Brown with a forearm. There was one hitch. The ball was hiked on the second sound. I was blatantly offside. As I walked back to the huddle feeling like forty-five cents, Phil had this real innocent look on his face.

Phil was a world-class prankster. On the Raiders, he had plenty of company. Playing in the NFL is like an extension of your childhood. That's part of the reason the players don't want to give it up. The cruelest thing that can happen to an athlete is that he suddenly becomes too old to compete. Some guys figure that if they act young, maybe it will *keep* them young. We're also playing a kid's game, but the pressures are very adult. Pressure from management, pressure from the fans, pressure from the press. Pressure from within. Screwing around relieves some of that pressure.

Now that I've done my disclaimer, I can tell you about one of the Raiders' favorite pranks.

Its beauty was in its simplicity. We would casually approach one of our teammates and engage him in some meaning-less conversation. When he was good and preoccupied, we'd grab his T-shirt by the front of the collar. Then, we'd rip it right down the middle. Totally blow the shirt. The size of the victim was never a consideration. One night in the Bamboo Room, we got Steve Sylvester and totally misused him. First, we tore his shirt off, but that only whetted our appetites. We ripped off his sweat shorts. A bunch of us started spinning him around like a top. Steve is 6' 4" and 260 pounds.

If you're ever in Santa Rosa, check out the Bamboo Room. Just don't order a Piña Colada or look for the Village People on the jukebox. The Bamboo Room has no trendy theme. It's a bar bar.

After summer practice each day, most of us would shower, change and stop by the Bamboo. One sweltering afternoon, Phil and I were badly dehydrated. We walked right from the practice field to the Bamboo. We were fully dressed—cleats, pads, jerseys, everything but our helmets. We told the patrons we wanted to be just like any other working class person—right from the job to the tavern. Phil was in the middle of a story and it was loud in there. He felt he was having some trouble getting his point across. So he stood up on a table. Phil is Italian and likes to speak with his hands. He was on the table, swinging his hands around, when his metal cleats began to slide from beneath him. He fell with a crash. Drinks and pretzels flew across the room. Phil banged up his elbow. His point was even misplaced amidst the confusion. I think there's a lesson here that we can all apply to our daily lives: Never let a 220-pound Italian line-backer climb up on a table with his cleats on . . . in Santa Rosa . . . when it's hot out.

As I said, Phil could be mischievous. He, Art Thoms and I used to play on a Raiders basketball team in the off-season. I missed a game one night, and I suppose they felt it was their duty to avenge my negligence. When I walked into my apart-ment later that night, I was horrified. Someone had ransacked my house. When I made a closer inspection, I realized it couldn't have been a burglar. Burglars aren't that crazy. Someone had taken all the furniture out of the kitchen and put it in the living room, all the stuff out of the bathroom and put it in the den. And on and on and on, all the way through the house. The same person had taken every one of my record albums—several hundred—and lined them up on their sides across every wall in the house. After I got over my shock, it took me all of twenty seconds to realize it was Phil. Phil still loves to tell that story, adding that he came back two weeks later and the house looked exactly the same. This is total fabrication. It was more like ten days.

Most pranks are reserved for rookies. It's a form of indoctrination. Like giving elevator passes to freshmen in high school. It's tough to sting a veteran anyway. They've been burned before and protect themselves, especially a player like Jim Otto. Jim was indestructible. He played with the type of injuries that would put most people in the hospital. He was beloved by his teammates, marveled at by the opposition. Jim is a Hall of Famer, the only Raider center for the first fifteen years of the franchise. We thought he had seen it all. We were wrong.

One Thanksgiving, Phil told some rookies about a local meat market that was giving free turkeys away to all the Raiders. Phil laid it on thick—these guys really loved the Raiders and if the rookies didn't go and get some turkeys, we'd probably lose some extremely devoted fans. This was an old Raiders routine. Rookies being rookies, these guys bought it completely. Unbelievably, so did Otto. He overheard Phil and figured it was a pretty good deal. Even though he'd already ordered his own turkey for the holiday, Jim canceled it to get the free one. It gets worse. Phil had found a meat market in one of the seediest, most dangerous sections of Oakland. You wouldn't go there on a dare. I can imagine the look on Jim's face as he drove there. When Jim walked in and asked for his complimentary turkey, the employees thought he was nuts. They shooed him away like they would any other freeloader. Phil thought he was done for. Because he is a peaceable man, Jim decided to spare Phil his life.

Along with Teddy, Jack Tatum and a retired Kansas City linebacker named Jim Kearney, Phil was one of the biggest hitters I've ever seen play. The most *important* hit I ever saw him make was in the 1976 Super Bowl against Minnesota Vikings.

It was scoreless in the opening quarter when Ray Guy had the first punt of his career blocked. When they recovered all the way back at our three, it looked as if the Vikings would take the early lead. Chuck Foreman ran the next play down to the two. Then the Vikings tipped their hand. They inserted Ron Yary, normally a guard, as an extra tight end. Phil knew the next play was coming his way. Slipping beneath Yary's block, Phil stuck his helmet directly in the vicinity of Brent Mc-Clanahan's heart. McClanahan fumbled and we recovered. The offense drove to the other end of the field for a field goal. The momentum of the game swung to the Raiders and we beat the Vikings, 32–14. Phil considers it one of his proudest moments.

Like any other player who's willing to mix it up, Phil took some punishment in return. The worst shot Phil ever took was from San Francisco's Ted Kwalik, a tight end who later played for the Raiders. Tight ends and linebackers never care for each other anyway. When a tight end goes out for a pass, it's the linebacker's duty to bottle him up at the line of scrimmage. This leads to encounters you'd normally find in professional wrestling. Ted and Phil's dislike for each other went beyond this. They would go looking for each other.

It was one of those shots you never see coming. It came on a reverse. Phil had changed directions and was running full speed in pursuit of the wide receiver. Running from the blind side, Kwalik struck Phil's helmet with his own. Phil was a bloody mess, his forehead cracked down the middle. John Madden had to run on the field and literally pull Phil to the sidelines. Phil could care less about all the blood. He just wanted to discuss the matter with Mr. Kwalik.

Teddy Hendricks used to kid that even though I was younger, Phil used to think of me like an older brother—always getting into trouble because he knew I'd come running to his rescue. One game his joke came true. We used to have a cornerback named George Atkinson who hit like a train. In his overexuberance one play, George gave a vicious blow to the head of Kansas City's Ed Podolak. They rolled through Kansas City's sideline. When one of the Chiefs came rushing at Atkinson's blind side, Phil had no choice but to take him out with a flying block. The opposition's sideline is the one place you *don't* want to be at a football game. Phil somehow wound up beneath the Chiefs bench, where the Chiefs were kicking his ass. Literally. I ran over to their bench and threw three or four guys out of the way. Then I picked Phil off the ground and carried him back to the playing field. Aw shucks. What are buddies for?

Phil scared the hell out of me one night. He was at a party in Santa Rosa when a couple of guys kept calling on the phone and cursing everyone out. Phil took the phone and told them to go to hell. Some time later two bikers burst in the party. They asked who they had talked to on the phone. Phil unwisely admitted it was he. They jumped him before he knew what was happening. They beat him with hammers, brutalized him. About three in the morning, I heard someone at my door. It was Phil and for a minute I thought I was having a nightmare. It took the doctors forty stitches to clean him up. A few of the guys wanted to form a search party, but Phil said no. He said he'd messed with the wrong guys and there was no sense in taking it any further.

Santa Rosa has its hard guys, but it's nothing like Oakland. Oakland is a rough-edged town. Hard workers, hard drinkers, hard streets. I had an incident there one night that could have ended in tragedy.

I was with a couple of the Raiders and we walked into a bar that was normally popular. That night, the place was nearly empty. We were standing around when I looked at the bartender and made a silly joke.

"Hey, this place is really jumping tonight, isn't it?"

Not hysterically funny, but a harmless little statement, right? This guy thought not. He reached behind the bar and pulled out a nine millimeter pistol. He aimed the damn thing about twelve inches from my head. He looked crazy enough to shoot me.

"There isn't a judge in the world who would convict me for blowing away an asshole like you."

I started to sweat. The last place I wanted to die was some bar in Oakland. Just as quickly as he'd blown up, the maniac suddenly cooled down. When he lowered the gun, we turned and walked straight out the door. This guy gave new meaning to the word *overreaction*.

————

For all of his accomplishments on a football field, Phil may be best remembered by history as the creator of the Oakland Raiders Air Hockey Tournament. It was the annual highlight of training camp. Ask any player in the NFL what he likes least about pro football and he'll say it's summer training camp. For roughly five weeks, you're separated from your family or girlfriend. You look at mountains of film and sit through endless meetings. That's just the mental aspect. For the first few weeks, you practice in the morning, then practice again in the afternoon. About four or five hours a day of football. This may not sound like much. But with twenty pounds of football pads, often under a blistering sun, it can wear you down. The thought of "one more year at camp" has driven a lot of older players into retirement.

The worst part was the boredom. In our quest to beat it, adhering to the Raiders' rules was never a major consideration. The coaches didn't lose any sleep over it either. When the coaches *were* concerned enough to catch us, it would lead to fines. I don't recall exactly what rules I thrashed, but I once received a one-week paycheck for exactly $3.75. The other $396.25 was taken out in fines. The check wasn't wasted though. James Logan Smith, the former mayor of Santa Rosa, bought it from me for a couple pitchers of beer. Today, it's framed on the wall of a Santa Rosa restaurant. That same week, Lester Hayes took home $3.74. Neither one of us holds the record though. Arthur Whittington once got a check for a quarter.

As I was saying, there was always the good old Air Hockey Tournament. The tournament got started in 1974 when Phil somehow talked a factory rep out of a miniature air hockey table. They still hold the tournament today. When it first got started, the tournament was held in Phil's room. He'd put up signs in his window saying THE ICE IS OPEN and THE ICE IS CLOSED, SO the guys would know when it was an appropriate time to practice. The tournament had four major rules:

1. Cheating is encouraged.
2. Verbal abuse is encouraged.
3. Drinking is encouraged.
4. Physical abuse is not allowed.

There were also some peripheral rules that were born along the way. One year, a woman named Carol Doda presided over the tournament. Carol was a brilliantly endowed, legendary San Francisco stripper who claimed to have a pair of Colt .44s. Carol made a speech to begin the games one year. We also let her play the first game. After, of course, some of the guys had persuaded her to take off her top. Every time Carol bent over, there was this natural barrier, and no one could score any goals. Thus, the Carol Doda rule: no blocking the puck with your breasts. Another rule is that rookies are not allowed to win under any circumstances, even if they should somehow win.

Once cheating became mandatory, the guys would rack their brains trying to invent new methods. One of the most ingenious cheats was John Vella, "The Happy Fella." Even if it was 95 degrees outside, Vella would show up for the tournament wearing a long-sleeve coat. He looked like he'd caught too much sun, but it was a strong move. Long sleeves are excellent for blocking shots. When their opponents had the puck, some guys would put the table up on their feet. The other team would then be shooting uphill.

Perhaps the greatest moment in cheating sprang from the devious minds of Biletnikoff and assistant coach Bob Zieman. Zieman would make some kind of ruckus. While everyone was watching him, his teammate Biletnikoff would slip a clear piece of plastic over the mouth of the goal. One game Monte Jackson was awarded a penalty shot. Monte got off a perfect shot. But when the puck reached the goal, it hit the plastic and flew right over the end of the table. The room went absolutely silent.

In 1984, Marcus Allen reached new heights of cheating. He

refused to pay his entry fee. That same year David Humm held an unusual distinction. Dave's team won the tournament. The bad news is that he was cut the same day.

Some of the guys think today's tournament has lost its luster. Todd Christensen, a Mormon and nondrinker, won the tournament three years in a row. But Todd didn't want his name inscribed on the winner's plaque because he didn't want anyone to know he'd been in a bar.

It was during one such tournament that Phil supposedly got the nickname "Foo." I say supposedly because there are two different versions. In one, Duane Benson, a linebacker, got so smashed at the tournament that he couldn't pronounce Phil's name. He kept trying to say Phil, but all that ever came out was "Foo." The other story is that Phil's eyes used to get squinty whenever he had a couple of beers. He looked almost Oriental, and someone decided to call him "Foo." Another unsolved mystery of the NFL.

Each year's winner of the tournament would get to ride in the front vehicle of the Rookie Parade. The Rookie Parade signaled the end of camp. It was a single-file procession of all the Raiders' cars, usually about thirty or forty. We would decorate the cars with balloons and streamers and shaving cream, and then make a cruise through the streets of Santa Rosa. We would always nominate a Queen to preside over the parade. Putting it mildly, looks were never a top priority. A sense of humor, however, was mandatory. In return for their presence, we would pay for the Queens to get their hair done. It seemed like a reasonable trade-off. Usually the Queens would dig out an old prom dress. We'd make them a throne of old crates in the back of someone's pickup. As the procession would wind through the streets, we'd throw candy to the people of Santa Rosa. It was a very major gig.

One year, the parade got sidetracked. The procession was moving along nicely when one of the guys in a truck felt the need to get some air. He took an unconventional route—he stuck his bare ass out the sun roof. A Santa Rosa squad car was driving by and the policemen flashed their lights for the truck to pull over. Of course, the entire caravan also pulled to the side of the road. When everyone piled out of their vehicles, there were about forty Oakland Raiders standing in front of two policemen. They immediately called for backups. When the backups arrived, one of the late arrivals weighed the situation. Then he made his decision.

"I don't want any part of this," he said.

When the backups got back in their cars and pulled away, the first two cops were again on their own. After we promised to keep our behinds in our seats, they let us go back to our parade.

Through all the craziness, Phil and I had become more than just teammates. We used to hang out together, listen to each other's problems. After playing in eighty-two straight Raiders games, one season Phil was sidelined by a knee injury. Phil was the kind of person who couldn't sit back and accept adversity. Never a "go with the flow" type, he was a fighter. The very night of the operation, he climbed over the bars of his hospital bed and began getting dressed. When his wife was awakened by the noise, Phil mumbled that he had to fly with the team to Cleveland. He wanted to be with the guys. Patti finally managed to put him back to bed.

Every Monday that season, I'd pick Phil up and we'd run and lift weights like maniacs. I drove him until he was ready to drop. I knew that was what he needed. Frankly, the last thing I wanted to do on Monday was to push my body. I was always feeling battered and it was our only day off of the week. But if there's one time that an athlete needs a friend, it's when he's coming back from an injury.

In April of 1980, Phil got traded. He was sent to the Buffalo Bills for Bobby Chandler, a quality wide receiver. I was in shock. Seeing one of your friends traded is one of the rotten parts of being an athlete. There's never any warning. You read about it in the morning newspaper. That afternoon his locker's getting emptied. A day or so later he's been replaced by someone new. Move 'em in, move 'em out. It's a reality of the profession, but I never got used to it. It sounds cold, but that's why some players never get too close to one another. It's like the old saying about the Army—no one wants to make a good friend and then have to lose him.

When it comes to discarding a player, some teams can be just about heartless. For several years, Gregg Pruitt had been the offensive workhorse for the Cleveland Browns, an undersized halfback who took a lot of punishment. In 1983, his last year with Cleveland, Gregg was on a committee for the city's public school system. He would go around to schools and talk to the kids about sticking with their education. One day, Gregg says he got a message while he was speaking to a class. There was an important phone call in the principal's office. Gregg excused himself and went to the office. The call was from the Browns. Gregg had been traded to the Raiders. Hell of a way to let him know.

Al would never pull something like that. But I was still stunned when I heard about Phil. He'd always been so close to Al. And he was so much a Raider. To me, Phil epitomized the Raiders: tough, hard working, unpretentious. I caught up with him before he left. We talked about the trade. We tried to look at it analytically, strictly as a business move. But we were kidding ourselves. We both started getting emotional. Phil told me not to worry, that everything would turn out OK.

"Johnny," he said, "I'm going back East where all my family and friends are. I'll be fine."

But I could see in his eyes that he was crushed. Phil figured he'd be a Raider forever.

It was one of the few times in my life I was upset with Al, primarily because he'd traded one of my buddies, and partly because I thought he had let a single play influence his decision to trade Phil.

That kind of stuff really does happen, and it's usually to veterans. A guy will make one lousy play at a critical moment, and it can snowball into the end of his career. Let me clarify something: It's not that one play *literally* ends a guy's career. It's the memory of the play. It stays frozen in everyone's mind, starts to change everyone's perception of the player's abilities. For example, if a receiver misses a pass in a crucial game, he may be written off as not having the "soft hands" anymore. Or if a cornerback gets outrun by a receiver, his quickness has presumably disappeared. Stigmas die hard in the NFL. No matter what you've done in the past, that one play seems to wipe it all out. It's a wonderful game, but it can be a real cold business.

I think Phil's downfall began in the 1978 season against New England. The Patriots were driving for a score and Phil's responsibility was to keep an eye on Steve Grogan, in case he tried a bootleg. That's exactly what Grogan did but Phil missed the play. Grogan ran the ball about 30 yards to our four yard line. They scored and we lost by a touchdown. It was hardly the only time Phil had screwed up, but it was a glaring mistake in a game we really wanted. I don't know if Al and the coaches thought Phil had somehow lost his speed or what, but the next season they tried converting Phil into an inside linebacker. The experiment never really worked and the following season he was traded.

Phil's trade hurt. I learned a lot from him. It was Phil who helped me see how important it was to give something back to the community. For all of his aggression on the field, Phil was soft when it came to children. We used to go and visit Oakland's School for the Deaf. The kids were always so sweet and excited to see us. I don't know who enjoyed it more, we or the children.

As usual, Al's trade turned out pretty well. We missed Phil at linebacker, but Chandler became the possession receiver we'd missed ever since Biletnikoff had retired. One thing for sure, there wasn't a player on our team who forgot about Phil. Phil wouldn't let us. Every year before the tournament, he would call and remind us to cheat.

When Phil went East, the Raiders moved Teddy Hendricks over to my side. For Teddy, the act of moving, any kind of moving, was not unfamiliar. Teddy Hendricks was a man in perpetual motion, a world traveler who felt as comfortable in downtown Oakland as in some primitive village in Hawaii. When God made Teddy, the button got stuck on fast forward.

It's probably because of his roots. A Texan, Teddy's father was a mechanic for an airline and he married a woman from

Guatemala. Although he was born in Guatemala, Teddy grew up in Miami. Teddy was an All-American defensive end at the University of Miami, but NFL coaches were leery because they felt he was too skinny at 6' 7" and 215 pounds. Don Shula, then coaching the Colts, picked Teddy in 1969 and put him at outside linebacker. Teddy went on to become the measuring stick for outside linebackers. He went to the Pro Bowl eight times, and his four safeties and twenty-five blocked kicks are NFL records. And Teddy played hurt. Before he tore a stomach muscle in his final season, Teddy had played in 215 straight games.

Like me, Teddy was labeled a troublemaker before he came to the Raiders. There's a disturbing custom in the NFL. Any time a player refuses to be pushed around by management, he's automatically branded as a malcontent. Regardless of the circumstances. If you take a good look, some of these players are about as rebellious as a golf ball. When Mike Haynes came to the Raiders in 1984, he got ripped in certain quarters because he couldn't come to terms with the New England Patriots. Mike is one of the nicest, most inoffensive people you'll ever meet. All he did was stand up for himself.

Of course, behavior like this usually gets you traded. In 1970, Teddy's Colts beat Dallas in the Super Bowl, but by 1973, the team had been dismantled. The Colts were terrible and most of Teddy's friends had been traded. Shula had left for the Dolphins and Joe Thomas, not the most reasonable man in the world, was the new general manager for the Colts. Teddy felt lost in Baltimore and asked Thomas if he'd trade him too. Thomas told him to think about it for a week and come back if he hadn't changed his mind. When Teddy returned and said he'd still like to leave, Thomas said he'd give him a choice—play in Baltimore or retire. Teddy played that season, but in 1974 he announced that he was playing out his option with the Colts and would sign with the World Football League in 1975. A week later, Thomas traded Teddy to Green Bay. I've got nothing against Green Bay, but it seems as if NFL owners have two golden rules when they trade a player they deem troublesome:

1. Trade him out of the division.
2. Trade him somewhere cold.

After one All-Pro year in Green Bay, Teddy found himself in an enviable position—as a free agent in the NFL. The WFL team had missed its first payment, voiding the contract Teddy had signed with it. Teddy was willing to play in Green Bay again, but only if the Packers would offer him a guaranteed contract. The Packers refused and Teddy began talking to other teams. Then he got a call from Al Davis. Whatever Teddy had been offered, Al said, the Raiders would top it. Teddy became a Raider.

When Teddy and his agent first met with Al, the word was that Al was concerned about Teddy's physique and immediately started talking about a weight program.

"Al," Teddy said, "when I grab 'em they're grabbed. I don't need weights."

How did Teddy survive for fifteen years without pumping a little iron? The truth of the matter is, Teddy did lift weights and eventually bulked up to 235. He just hated to admit it. One year, he brought to camp this phony weight lifting set that he had built in college. He called it the Hurricane Machine, after the Miami Hurricanes. It was a regular bar, but the drums fastened to either end were completely empty. It looked like he was tossing around huge amounts of weight. There was also a built-in holder for Teddy's beer. After practice, Teddy would work out like crazy for twenty minutes, while the local tourists would peer through a fence admiring his work ethic. Instead of a traditional bench, Teddy made a hammock out of strands of barbed wire. He vowed that it would "toughen us up."

Before it was outlawed, Teddy was a master at the clothesline tackle. One time Joe Kapp was running a naked bootleg when he encountered Teddy in the open field. Kapp tried to juke him but Teddy wouldn't bite. The clothesline went out and Kapp nearly lost his head. Kapp just looked up at him and said, "Nice hit, kid." Then he stumbled back to the huddle shaking his head. Teddy took pride in his clothesline. The NFL sent every team its "Uniform and Mandatory Equipment Code," a diagrammed poster of a player with all of his football pads in the proper place. Teddy took ours and added an outline of a player wearing number 83—Teddy's number. Number 83 was clotheslining the player in the pads.

All those blocked kicks and safeties were no coincidence. Plays like that are mostly timing and instinct. Teddy's instincts on a football field were uncanny, impossible to explain. He always surfaced around the ball, as if he could somehow read the minds of the other team's quarterbacks. Teddy rarely missed a trick. And I mean rarely. When the Raiders played the New York Jets in a 1982 playoff game, Lyle Alzado thought Chris Ward was getting away with murder, holding him on almost every play. Lyle's temper isn't small to begin with. Finally he blew up. Lyle tore Ward's helmet off his head, then was kind enough to return it to him. Through the air. At fifty miles per hour. Lyle's fastball was low and away and Ward wasn't hit. The referee called unsportsmanlike conduct and Teddy demanded an explanation.

"What's the penalty?" Teddy asked the ref.

"Your teammate threw a helmet."

"There's no rule that says you can't throw a helmet."

"Yeah, but it was the opposing player's helmet."

"There's still no rule that says you can't throw the opposing player's helmet."

"Hendricks," the ref roared, "I called the penalty, now get out of here."

The penalty stood, of course, but it was a darn good try. By the way, there is now a rule that you cannot throw a helmet at an opposing player.

Teddy's knowledge of the game drove opposing coaches crazy. You couldn't suck him into anything. Teddy tells a story about a game against the Dolphins when little Nat Moore, a wide receiver, lined up over Teddy as a tight end. His old coach, Don Shula, was then coaching the Dolphins. Shula is one of the craftiest coaches in the NFL. You never know what to expect from him.

"This is a terrible insult," Teddy yelled to Shula on the sideline. "You know this man can't block me. And we both know the play's not coming this way."

Teddy was right, the play went the other way. When he looked back at Shula, Don was standing on the sideline cracking up.

In college, Ted was called "The Mad Stork" because of his angularity. Since Teddy hated this nickname, the Raiders wanted to find something new. Teddy solved the problem one afternoon at practice. It was a running play up the middle. As Teddy went flying over the pile, he accidentally kicked Marv Hubbard in the head. Marv was out like a light. Teddy had his new nickname— "Kick-em-in-the-head Ted." It was later shortened to Kick-em.

When it came to irreverence, Teddy had no peers. Any time, anywhere, even during such sacred institutions as the Monday Night Football Game. Monday Night Football is a very big deal to players in the NFL. Since all the other teams have already played on Sunday, you know your peers will be watching you from their televisions at home. Everyone looks forward to it and wants to look good that night. If a player notices he's on camera, he'll almost always say hello to his mom. Then there's Teddy. One Monday night, Teddy sneaked one of those Harlequin monster masks onto the field. I think he had it stuffed in his pants. When Teddy saw one of the ABC cameramen coming his way, he yanked out the mask and stuck it on his head. As the cameras panned the sideline, there was Teddy with this big, ugly mask on, jauntily flashing the peace sign.

At Thanksgiving time, Teddy once came out on the practice field wearing a pumpkin on his head. It was carved in the shape of a helmet. It had a facemask and Teddy's number—83—drawn across the side. He and our trainer, Dick Romanski, had done an artful job.

"If you can't cover," Teddy yelled to the safeties, "then pumpkin head will."

Teddy would go to amazing lengths for a prank. Santa Rosa gets miserably humid in the summer. You can break a sweat changing TV channels. One August morning, everyone was bitching about having to practice, collectively dragging their ass. When the guys finally carried themselves over to the practice field, Teddy was sprawled out on the fifty yard line. On a lounge chair. Under an umbrella. Sipping on a lemonade.

Every team has a guy who loves to drive the coach crazy. It's ritual in almost every sport. Guess who it was on the Raiders? When he was coach, John Madden never let on that Teddy had him rattled. It became a little game. Teddy would do something crazy, John would stand there and yawn. Teddy could have come to practice dressed in rubber boots and an Easter bonnet, and John would have asked him about the weather.

One time I was sure Teddy had him. Everyone was sitting around our Santa Rosa practice field getting stretched. John walked up and yelled for us all to get up. John would do this every day. It meant that practice was about to begin. As we gathered around John, suddenly a gate flew open. It was Teddy, riding across the field on a horse. He was in full uniform, waving a traffic cone as his lance. He looked like some crazed Don Quixote. A little girl had been riding her horse behind the field, and Teddy had talked her into borrowing it for a minute. When Teddy raced up on the horse, everyone else nearly wet their pants. But John didn't flinch.

"That's great," John told him. "Now get rid of the horse."

Younger players tend to look at older players, especially the stars, with something close to awe. That was definitely the case with Teddy. It was a two-way thing though. Teddy would also look out for the younger guys. One of his favorites was Howie Long. Howie got hammered one play against the Denver Broncos. Howie was out on his feet, stumbling around the sideline, literally admiring the Denver skyline. Meanwhile, the Raiders' offense had gotten the ball back and then punted. When the defense ran back on the field, Howie was still on Queer Street. Since no one had replaced him, the Raiders only had ten defenders. They were up by a couple of touchdowns, it was late in the final quarter and the Broncos were about to snap the ball. So they decided to play that down with ten. Just as the ball was about to be snapped, Teddy jumped out of his stance and called time out. Time outs are sacred. You want to make everyone count.

"Where's Howie," Teddy demanded.

"He's out, he's on the side."

"Well, I miss Howie. And I'm *not* playing without him."

It was only after the guys convinced Teddy that Howie would be fine—and only then—that Teddy agreed to play the next play.

What drove Teddy to all this so-called madness? Nothing

special, he just liked to make his teammates smile. In all the years I've known him, I've only heard of Teddy losing his temper once. For a linebacker, that's a statistic that borders on unbelievable.

It happened several years ago. A bunch of Raiders were riding a bus to a golf tournament in the California desert. It was hot and dusty and everyone wanted a drink. When the guys asked the busdriver to stop at a roadside store, he kept on driving as though he never heard them. They asked again and this time he refused. This guy was either incredibly nervy, late for the hottest date of his life or demented from the heat. Teddy didn't appreciate his lack of concern.

"You stop this bus right now," he screamed. "Or *I'll* stop it. Because *I'll* be the one who's driving it."

When the driver stopped, Teddy took orders for everyone.

13

THE LAST WALTZ

For the Oakland Raiders, a team known for its work ethic, 1981 was a disaster. We finished seven and nine, our first losing season in seventeen years. At times we were embarrassing. During a three-game stretch in the middle of the season, we didn't score a single point. When the offense rallied toward the end of the season, then the defense sprung holes. At least there wasn't any finger pointing. We all fell on our faces together.

On paper, our collapse was hard to figure. The year before, as a wildcard team entering the playoffs, we had scratched and fought for everything we got, eventually beating the Eagles in the Super Bowl. Now we couldn't even make the playoffs with the same cast of players. Yes, we had some damaging injuries. But I think we also lost our fire, became too pleased with ourselves. Maybe we read too many stories about how great we were.

In 1982, we all arrived at camp like a bunch of hopeful rookies. The arrogance was gone, now we had something to prove again. I was especially determined. Since coming to the Raiders in 1976, I felt I had played solid football. But 1981 had been the exception. I had some minor hurts but nothing that I couldn't overcome. Maybe I was just complacent. All I know is that I did not play the way I was capable of playing.

When camp began I decided not to dwell on the past. I was

only thirty-two years old and I felt healthy and strong. I was ready to make amends.

In the first week of summer camp, we were scrimmaging against the offense. Everyone was thrilled over our number one draft pick, Marcus Allen from USC. Even then, you could see that Marcus was special. At USC he had won the Heisman Trophy as a senior tailback, gaining 2,342 yards. As a junior he had played fullback, and his blocking helped Charles White win that year's Heisman. Marcus was a rarity—a superstar who didn't mind the dirty work. I got a good look at Marcus that day, better than I wanted to.

Marcus took a handoff and burst through the middle of the line. I always prided myself on my ability to pursue downfield, and I took off after him. Marcus had zigged and zagged, and twenty-five yards downfield I was closing in. He was about two yards ahead of me and a yard to my right. Just then Marcus cut directly into my path. I was going full speed, and if it had been a game I would have buried him. But I didn't want to crush our prized new rookie. I pulled up suddenly. But the field, moist and slippery from the morning dew, was not conducive to sudden stops. My upper body kept going forward as my heel slipped violently from beneath me. Pain ripped through my lower back. I had never felt anything like it before. It was like a hundred hot needles had been jabbed into my lower back. The more I carried on, the sharper the pain got. After I caught my breath, I walked slowly to the sideline. Coach Leggett asked me if I was okay. I wasn't but I said I was. I figured the pain would subside in a moment. Even if it didn't, playing hurt was something I'd grown accustomed to.

"Yeah, coach, I'm fine, I think. Just give me a second."

A few plays later I ran out and finished the practice. That night my back stiffened up and I could barely bend over. I thought about telling the coaches and decided against it. It was only training camp and I knew I could work things out. I always had in the past.

I played in the next seventeen practices. Every night the pain and my fears intensified. I began to have excruciating back spasms. Everywhere I went, they were there: on the field, at night as I tried to sleep, even sitting at the dinner table. When they were at their worst, it felt like someone was stabbing me in my lower back. My palms would get cold and clammy, but the rest of my body would be sweating profusely. Back spasms are like having insomnia. The more you fight and get tense, the worse the consequences. Eventually I learned just to try and relax, think about anything in the world but my back, and simply wait for the pain to ease.

I still didn't know if I should tell the coaches. We had some good young defensive linemen in camp. I was projected as the starter, of course, but an injury could change those plans in a moment. I decided to keep my problem to myself. I didn't want the coaches to think that I might not be ready. I was also afraid to confront my injury myself. I knew that once you had back problems you usually had them for life. I didn't even want to consider that. I kept on playing and my back kept getting worse. I felt, frankly, as if I had a stick up my ass.

I played in the opening exhibition game against the 49ers. I was sore and stiff but I somehow recovered a fumble and made a few tackles. Maybe I could keep playing after all. I was wrong. At the start of the second quarter, I lunged for a ballcarrier and my back felt like it was on fire again. I had trouble just climbing off the pile, and I was relieved when the coaches pulled the entire first team a few series later. I couldn't kid myself any longer, I had a serious problem. I needed to enter a hospital.

The coaches agreed. That week I was admitted to Cedars-Sinai Hospital in Los Angeles. The doctors took a CAT scan of my back and the news was positive. It looked like a muscular problem, perhaps a pulled or ruptured muscle in my lower back. Painful, but nothing requiring surgery. Nothing that couldn't be treated with proper rest and physical therapy, and nothing that could keep me out for the season. My joy was tempered, however, because I knew CAT scans could be misleading. Like traditional X-rays, they only show bone. If I had something more serious—like nerve damage or a herniated disc—a CAT scan would never indicate it. So while I still had my doubts, the doctors seemed optimistic. If my back responded well to therapy, they said I could probably play that season. I wanted desperately to believe them. I told myself over and over that I would still play football that season.

To dull the pain in my back, the doctors had been injecting me daily with painkillers. This eased my discomfort so drastically, that it got to the point where I was worried that I was liking the painkillers too much. I told the doctors I didn't want to grow dependent on them, so they reduced the number of injections. Then my mind was at peace, but, again, my back wouldn't give me any rest.

Meanwhile, my back was not responding the way the doctors hoped. I still couldn't make anything resembling a sudden move without severe pain. Back surgery was discussed—which would have ended my season. Thank God, the doctors weren't trigger happy. They said they didn't want to put me under the knife unless it was an absolute last resort. Still, a muscular problem now seemed unlikely. My prospects looked bleak.

The doctors said they needed a better look at my spine. They decided to give me a milogram, which is similar to a spinal tap. A milogram shows more than bone, it shows blood supply and potential damage to the nerve or spinal cord. In my case, the milogram involved two injections into the damaged area. First they removed spinal fluid from my back to examine it. Then they injected my spine with a special dye. The dye shows up on a certain kind of X-ray and makes diagnosis more certain. The doctors said they would have my results in the morning.

When the doctor entered my room the following morning, he didn't have to speak. His expression told the story. He said I had a herniated disc in my lower spine. All along the spinal cord, in between each bone, there are soft, cushy discs. They separate the bones from each other and allow people to bend and turn and move freely. When a disc gets herniated, part of it protrudes from its normal position. If the rupture is bad enough, it can result in bone rubbing bone. My situation wasn't that severe, but it was extremely serious. People with herniated discs suffer intense discomfort whenever they bend or push or lift. People with herniated discs don't play football.

I was horrified. The doctors had no long-term prognosis,

but I would not be playing football in the immediate future. My career was in jeopardy.

After the doctors put me in traction, the next ten days were a blur of fear and depression. I lay there on my back, immobilized, for fourteen hours a day. The strain on my back was alleviated, but the pressure building inside my head was getting worse. When you're trapped like an animal in traction, sedated by potent painkillers, your mind can do funny things to you. My moods would shift dramatically from moment to moment. One minute I'd convince myself I was fine, the next minute I'd be certain my career was over. I was a mess.

My mood turned its darkest on September 14. That was the date of our regular season opener. The first game of any season is always a special occasion, but this one was more magical than usual. Not only were we playing the 49ers, who were the defending Super Bowl champs, but it was our first game as the Los Angeles Raiders. We had just moved down from Oakland. I could see from the newspapers that the town was buzzing. I could see it right at the hospital. That was all the doctors and nurses seemed to want to talk about. They all asked me who I thought was going to win and I would smile and say the Raiders. Inside I felt devastated. In four years in high school, four in college, and nine years in the pros, I had never missed an opening game. I had started the last forty-three consecutive games for the Raiders. But that night I lay in a hospital bed, in traction, listening to the season opener on the radio. I felt miserable, lonely, as though no one knew who the fuck I was or even cared. We beat the 49ers, 23–17, and I was happy for my teammates. But I still felt pretty rotten.

The Raiders placed me on injured reserve and I missed the entire season. It was a very uneasy and emotional time for me. For one thing, I was living that year in the Oakland Hyatt. Nice place, but there's something about living in a hotel room that makes whatever troubles you've got seem a hell of a lot worse. I went to a couple of practices a week, but I didn't like hanging around the other guys. The games were even worse. I never planned on going, but Al called me up and requested that I go.

Al said he wanted me on the sideline, it would help inspire the guys. I went to the games but I hated every minute of it. It was all so strange. Guys would run off the field bleeding and hurt, and I was standing next to them in street clothes, with my hair not even messed. I felt like a total intruder, as if I had no business being there. I remember watching Todd Christensen jumping for joy after we scored a touchdown, and me thinking that I'd give anything to be able to do the same. Standing there on the sideline, I felt the same way I did when my family first moved to Oak Creek, as if there were a big, wonderful secret— and I was the only one who didn't know it.

That was a peculiar year for all the Raiders. Although our move to L.A. had been upheld in a federal court that April, the NFL had filed an appeal that was not yet resolved by the time the season began. Since nobody had homes in L.A. yet, and the entire move was still in question, the guys would practice in Oakland and fly down to "home" games in Los Angeles. In effect, the Raiders were on the road for every game of the season. (I was flying down to L.A. for "home" games too, but I was flying by myself. That was my decision. Again, I felt odd around the other players.)

Meanwhile, in Oakland, where the fans had embraced the team so warmly for so many years, it was an ugly time to be a Raider. People wore T-shirts that said FUCK THE RAIDERS and OAKLAND TRAITORS. The bolder ones shouted obscenities at us when they saw us on the street. Oakland fans turned on the Raiders and I don't blame them. They had been the greatest fans in the world, and now they felt like their team was getting stolen from them. The players were caught right in the middle.

I'm sure there were players who were upset about leaving Oakland. We had sold out every home game for something like ten years running. More importantly, the players and their wives had homes there, off-season jobs, children in school. As Raiders, we had always prided ourselves on our no-nonsense, blue-collar appeal. I'm sure there were some who were not looking forward to the glitter of L.A. But even if there was private grumbling—and I don't honestly know because I kept largely to myself that year—not one player complained in print. Too many players owed Al to start betraying him then.

I'm not going to get into a lengthy dissertation on the Raiders' move from Oakland, but my impression of the situation was this: Al wanted to build luxury boxes in the Oakland Coliseum. This would have given the Raiders a large influx of money, money that Al could use to keep his team at the top of the NFL. When Al and city officials began serious talks about luxury boxes, Al's contract with the Oakland Coliseum was already completed. If Al was going to sign a new lease, he insisted on having the luxury boxes. The city officials finally agreed to give Al a tax-free loan to build those boxes. At that point, Al fully intended to remain in Oakland. But when other peripheral parties got involved, the city officials reneged on their agreement. Al felt as if he deserved better from a city he'd done so much for. Meanwhile, the Los Angeles Coliseum was now available. The Rams had vacated it in 1980 when they moved to Anaheim. When the city of Oakland reneged on its loan, Al moved the Raiders to L.A. and its Coliseum.

Personally, I felt bad for the fans in Oakland. But I truly believe Al wanted to stay in Oakland and—if not for the inflexibility of the city—would be there today.

Today I live in Los Angeles and I like it. I like the feeling of tolerance, that it's acceptable to be a little different. The scenery and climate are pretty nice too. But mostly I'm here for professional reasons. As an actor, it's the best place to be, along with New York. I've come full circle—at first I couldn't stand Los Angeles. Too much smog, traffic and population. I missed the people and clean air of Oakland. But I never once felt resentful toward Al. After all he had done for me, how could I turn against him?

To this day, that season still amazes me. Talk about distractions; for a team with less talent or pride, the chaos of the move would have been a nice, comfortable reason to fall apart. The only effect it had on my teammates was to draw them closer. Playing in the strike-shortened season, the guys went eight and one. If not for a bitter, 17–14 loss to the Jets in the second round of the playoffs, we would have met the Dolphins in the

AFC championship game. As it was, the Dolphins beat the Jets, then lost to the Redskins in the Super Bowl.

During the 1982 season, I was forced into traction several more times. Once they put me in for three straight weeks. I had absolutely no plans to retire though. I was only thirty-two, it wasn't my time yet. There was so much more I wanted to accomplish as an athlete. I had learned a lot my first few years in the league. But in some ways those years had also been hurtful: playing for a team as bad as Houston, sitting out half a season when I jumped leagues, bringing on my own problems in Kansas City. There was too much energy expended on matters other than football. I used to fantasize about how different things might have been had I come directly from college to the Raiders. True, I achieved a nice measure of success once I got to the Raiders. But I had played with them for just six seasons, and it all seemed to go so fast. It took me a long time to find a team where I felt wanted. I wasn't ready to give that up yet.

That winter and spring I made like Rocky. I started training like a madman. I was living in Los Angeles. Early every morning I would run, early afternoons I lifted weights. Then I would stretch and run some more before dinner. I was eating well, really taking care of my body. I don't think I had more than a dozen beers in all that time. Slowly, steadily, I started regaining my speed and strength. I was lifting a lot of weight, moving fast. My back still had twinges but never anything disabling. I couldn't conceal my excitement. I was ready to go back to work.

In early May, I got hurt again. It was like an instant replay of the Marcus Allen episode, only this time it was with an animal. I was running on the beach, working on my legs at a pretty good pace. I had my head up, looking straight ahead, when a little puppy ran right in front of me. I leaped out of the way so I wouldn't crush it. Breaking my stride so suddenly, when my foot hit the ground my back went completely out. I fell hard on the sand and I could barely get up. The pain was brutal, worse than it had been in months, and I knew I was right back to square one. I disgustedly wiped the sand off my body and walked slowly back to my car. I was so depressed I drove about ten miles an hour back to my place. For the next several nights I agonized. Training camp was only two months off and my back was as bad as ever. Maybe it really was time to say goodbye. One day it hit me hard—if I got hurt just running on the beach, how the hell was I going to keep playing professional football? There was no good answer, not even a half-decent rationalization.

There were other considerations I couldn't avoid. Even if my back felt better by the start of camp, there was an excellent chance I would reinjure it in the course of the season. Then I would be collecting paychecks while I stood around and played cheerleader. That's not the way I wanted to earn my money. What if I came back and my performance was disappointing? Would the Raiders trade me? I saw Phil and Kenny get traded at the twilight of their careers and I knew it tore them up. I didn't want that happening to me. My pride was also at stake. I had seen too many players keep hanging on long after their skills had betrayed them. I promised myself I would never do that. I wanted the fans to remember me throwing people around, not getting pushed around by players younger and quicker than I was. And I never forgot something that had happened to me when I was in Kansas City.

We were at practice one morning when a long line of expensive cars rolled up in our parking lot. Our entire team stopped to stare. About twenty well-dressed black men climbed out. Then a gorgeous, exquisitely dressed young black woman. Then Muhammad Ali got out. I was ecstatic. I had been a fan of Ali's ever since I was small, and now he was less than 100 feet away. He had just beaten George Foreman in Zaire and he had come to say hello to Hank Stram. Apparently he and Hank were old buddies. I couldn't take my eyes off Ali. He had on a beautiful suit and the diamonds from his rings were sparkling in the midday sun. But it wasn't his attire that kept me transfixed. It was his face. Just a week after such a big fight, he looked as though he'd never been hit in his life. No scars, no cauliflower ears, no flattened nose. He looked as if he were ageless. A champion at the top of the world.

Several years later I saw Ali on TV. He looked like another man. He was bloated in the stomach and face. His words were slurred and almost inaudible, and he was changing streams of thought every few seconds. Like anyone else who had ever loved Ali, I was terribly shaken up. I didn't want to remember him that way. But it was too late. He had stayed around the ring for too many years, absorbed too many dangerous blows. I used to learn a lot from watching other athletes and I learned something that day from Ali. I promised myself I would quit the NFL before I embarrassed myself or my teammates.

Now, with my back still screaming at me, I thought about that promise I had made to myself. Along with everything else, the case for quitting was just too strong. On May 10, 1983, I decided to leave pro football.

The first person I called was Al. He had kept me in the league, he should be the first to know I was leaving it. I didn't tap dance around it, I told him straight out I was through. He didn't say anything for a moment. I think he was shocked. Finally he said he was very sorry to hear that I had already made up my mind. He said that if I changed it, all I had to do was call him. I thanked him for everything he had ever done for me. Then I hung up.

I called my mother next and told her I was retiring. As usual, she was totally supportive. I could tell by her voice she was also relieved. I guess she'd seen me hurt too many times in the past. Then I called several reporters and told them the news. Like Al, they also sounded surprised. But my decision was final. I was through with my career in football.

At least that's what I thought.

That night, hours after I retired, I wanted to think, to be alone. But I couldn't—I was appearing in a film called *Ice Pirates* and I had to be on the set. We wound up working until four in the morning. It was a long, exhausting night, and when I woke up the following morning my back was killing me. That afternoon I had agreed to do a radio interview in Pasadena. It was the last thing I felt like doing, but it was a reporter I liked and I didn't want to disappoint her. So I drove out to Pasadena. By the time the interview ended, I was spent. I was driving home through Studio City, my mind drifting along, when I heard a horn. I looked up and saw a car rushing right at me. I jerked my wheels violently and slammed my Cadillac into a telephone pole. It was a terrible collision, the telephone pole went halfway through my hood. My face was thrust into the steering wheel— later they would find its implant in what was left of the steering wheel. For a moment I must have lost consciousness. When I opened my eyes, some scumbag was snapping photographs in my face. The next thing I remember is waking up in the hospital. I was looking up at a doctor, my agent and his secretary. I could hear my agent talking.

"Can plastic surgery repair the damage?" he was asking the doctor.

Hell of a way to wake up. It turned out I was basically okay. The doctors initially thought my heart was bruised, but I escaped with a concussion and a severely bruised chest. I know what you're thinking but, no, I hadn't been drinking. The police suspected the same and checked my blood. I tested out fine.

A few weeks later I was sitting in my house, groping for something, anything, to cheer me up, when I got a call from Al. His message was still the same: When I felt better, if I changed my mind, he would still be glad to have me back. I gave it a little thought. I had to admit, so far my retirement wasn't going quite the way I wanted it to. But I waited about a month before I began to consider Al's offer more seriously. By then my back was feeling pretty good, but I still couldn't make up my mind. It was against all those promises I'd made myself, and the thought of quitting and then coming back made me feel uneasy. Logic said no, my heart said yes. But the pull was too great—I couldn't let go of the game.

On July 12, a week before camp, I called Al and told him I was coming back. I said I'd give it one more shot, and if things didn't work out I'd be gone for good. Al didn't seem very surprised. Hell, he probably expected it. He did seem pleased though. He even gave me a $7,500 signing bonus. If I made it through the end of camp, he said he would match it. That made me feel a whole lot better. Al still had some faith in me.

Camp began and the guys seemed thrilled to have me. One, because they liked me. Two, because I think every athlete likes to see one of his peers come back from a serious injury. It gives him hope in case it should ever happen to him. The first few days of camp went well. I was pushing people around, I felt quick. On the second day of two-a-days, we had a pass rushing drill. I made a nice move on the tackle in front of me. As the quarterback raised his arm to throw, I jumped through the air at him. I got about three inches off the ground. Three damn inches. It felt like someone was pulling down on me from my lower back. At that precise moment, my career in pro football ended. I never played another play.

After practice that day I walked out of camp, didn't even say goodbye to anyone. I drove to San Francisco, where I stayed with a friend. I needed to be alone, to decide if this time I was truly sure. I considered my dilemma. The season I hurt my shoulders, I could still move quickly and get to the spot. Now I couldn't *even* get there. It was as simple and final as that. My decision took only two days. This time there was no great deliberation. I had been that route before. Now there was more at stake than my pride. Now there was the remainder of my life to consider. I knew I would always have pain, but I didn't want to spend it in a wheelchair.

I drove back to camp and looked for Al. He wasn't around so I went to Coach Flores's office. I told him I was through, that I couldn't play football. I walked out of his office and over to my car. I didn't want to say goodbye to any of my teammates. They had enough to worry about, and I didn't want to lay my grief on anybody else. I started driving toward the coast. I drove slowly along the water, my mind drifting back to a million different places. But it kept coming back to a football field. I saw myself as a kid in high school, back in college, finally as a Raider. I drove and I drove and I drove. I had no good reason to stop.

———

Before I retired from pro football, well before I ever considered it, I knew how cold the end could be. We all did. I knew the average NFL career was just over four years. I knew a career never ended the way you expected it to. It could be a total accident, or it could be an act of revenge. When it ended in violent injury, it happened in the course of seconds. *Seconds,* for a sport you've trained for since you were a child. Of course that was a risk you assumed when you joined the league. It was no one's fault. Still, it didn't seem right.

A lot of things about the end didn't seem right. Especially when players were told to leave before they were ready. Coaches are always telling players to play with "reckless abandon," to give up their bodies, to play when they're hurt. All for the sake of winning. And, as I've said, we did all that even when we weren't asked. We liked winning more than anyone. But in return for that kind of devotion, it would be nice to get some loyalty in return, especially at the end. I can only speak for myself: Throughout my career I felt I received tremendous loyalty from Al Davis. But for most players it doesn't work that way. Once you've given up your body a few too many times, and you can't do the job anymore, you're discarded. If the machine isn't working properly, replace it. If you're no longer valuable, then you're no longer wanted. It's goodbye, take a walk, end of story. Get the hell out of the way—we've got championships to win. And don't let the door hit you in the ass on the way out.

I saw it happen to so many great players. I saw John Riggins lead the Washington Redskins to so many glory years. When they traded for George Rogers two years ago, I saw the Redskins telling John Riggins it was time for him to get out. I saw the Rams trade Hacksaw Reynolds because they said he wanted too much money, when his demands were totally reasonable. When he got to the 49ers, I saw them ask him to become a coach when he still wanted to play. You won't meet a guy more devoted to football than Hacksaw Reynolds is. I saw one of the leading pass catchers in history, Fred Biletnikoff, get cut from the Raiders when most of us thought he still had a few good years left.

I think Fred's case was the single-play syndrome, the same thing that happened to Phil and to me when I was cut by Washington. In our AFC Championship Game in 1977, a loss to the Broncos, Fred injured his shoulder. But he was back in the starting lineup for the '78 regular season opener, also against the Broncos. We were driving in the second half when Fred had an important pass thrown to him. Fred bobbled it and the Broncos intercepted. Our momentum was killed on the spot. The Broncos went on to score and we lost, 14–6. Fred was benched the next game in favor of Morris Bradshaw and didn't start again the rest of the season. That off-season he was cut. And Fred was still good.

Before I retired, I knew all that. I knew it and I tried to prepare for it. I told myself to be ready for the end. You don't leave football, I used to say, football leaves you. You have to move on, keep your head up, get on with the rest of your life. I told myself all of that a hundred times. But when the end really came I wasn't ready. I wasn't even close. The year I retired from football was the worst year of my life.

How did I feel? You name it: anxious, depressed, frustrated, afraid. For the first time in many years I felt totally alone. I remember when people who didn't follow the game very closely would see me and ask me how my season was going. I would wince and explain that I just retired. They would drop their eyes in embarrassment. It wasn't their fault, they were just being nice. I was overly sensitive to everything. I felt like an open wound.

I spent a lot of time traveling that year, saw a lot of old friends. But no matter where I went, I could never really get comfortable. I felt as if I was always looking for something, but I was never quite sure what it was. It was strange: Except for my back, I still felt like a stud, as if I could climb into my uniform and still kick some ass. I had all this nervous energy but I had no way to release it. In the old days, I could vent my frustrations on the field. Now they just ate at me.

Life after football was a whole new world. The Real World. Professional football, on the other hand, has got to be one of the most unnatural professions on earth. A great way to make a living? No question about it, at least as far as I'm concerned. A *normal* way to make a living? Absolutely not. Mostly, I suppose, it's the nature of the game itself: The human body is not made to be hurtled at other human bodies. But it was more than that. No matter how you look at it—the highs or the lows, the rewards or the punishment—it is just not a normal occupation.

I'll never forget the interview session after our Super Bowl win against the Eagles. There was a giant press tent and several of the Raiders were asked to come to it. When we arrived, we were greeted by literally hundreds of reporters. That part was fine. Something else was bizarre. When I talk to a writer, I like to look him in the eye. He's a person, I'm a person. But that day it was impossible. The players were all seated up on a stage, about five feet above the pack of reporters. As we sat above them, they shouted questions up to us. They were also assaulting us with cameras, and in the glare of their flash I was virtually blinded. What was odd was that I couldn't even *see* who I was speaking to—all I heard were these faceless voices. Yet they could see my every movement. I looked at the other players on the stage and they were all doing the same thing I was: talking to no one, blinking from the flashes, straining to hear the questions because they couldn't see any faces. Then I was struck by a very strange thought: It was almost like we weren't real people, but some sort of curious exhibits. The reporters were the real people. We were objects, on a stage, to be viewed and scrutinized and dissected. Maybe I was half delirious from the excitement of the game, but at the time it all seemed so unreal.

The Real World presents another major problem to retiring athletes. Many have no plan of attack, no real outline for the rest of their lives. Today's athlete is much better prepared for his retirement; he lines up future opportunities even while his career is still young. He's much better versed in economics. By the time I left the game, I got used to hearing my teammates talking about things like tax shelters and development properties. My first few years in the league it was never like that. Too many players lived solely for the moment, because football was basically all they knew. Their careers would end suddenly and they'd find themselves with nothing to turn to, particularly when it came to money. Once you establish a lifestyle, it's hard to tone it down overnight. So their mortgages and car payments would be as high as ever, but now their incomes were drastically cut. When you hear about former athletes with drinking or drug problems, I believe that kind of thing has a lot to do with it.

I was fortunate. At the time I retired, I had already established myself as an actor and my career was progressing at a fairly good rate. Besides *North Dallas Forty*, I had also appeared in *Caveman* and *Ice Pirates*. I owned my house in Wisconsin, and while I was far from rich, I also wasn't going to starve. For that I counted my blessings. But, still, I felt incomplete. I still missed the game in the worst possible way.

I was stuck in the void.

Every athlete feels it, some worse then others. I took it hard. For eighteen years I had expressed myself on a football field. Every week it gave me something to look forward to, something to get ready for. Game days were always the best, especially when we played against a team like Pittsburgh or Miami. I always got this tremendous rush of exhilaration. I used to love that feeling of challenge, of putting myself out there on the line. It was the purest high in the world—the high of competition. It was habit forming. And like any addiction, it hurt like hell when I had to quit.

More than anything I missed my friends. I missed Phil and Teddy and Kenny and Mickey Marvin and everyone else. For seven months a year, I used to spend six days a week with those guys. They knew me better than anyone. I missed it all, every damn thing—the childish pranks, the beers at the Bamboo Room, the heckling in the locker room. Deep down I guess I even missed practice.

I had forty-eight teammates when I played with the Raiders. Preppies from New England and surfers from Southern California. Blacks, whites and Hispanics, products of the streets and middle-class suburbs. There were streetfighters and intellectuals, players who were deeply religious, others who had never seen the inside of a church or temple. Off the field we were all so different. But when I walked through that tunnel Sunday afternoons, I never felt closer to anyone in my life. You weren't just going out there for yourself, you were going out there for forty-eight other people. You knew the next three hours might be hell, but you wouldn't be out there alone. You were going with your team—people who cared about you, understood you, would protect you, knew exactly how hard you'd worked to get to this point. When you won, there was a beautiful feeling of shared accomplishment. Even when you lost, you lost together.

Sometimes you don't realize how much you care about something until you feel you've lost it. After I retired I understood something, fully, that I never really had grasped when I was playing. That feeling of togetherness, of camaraderie, was extremely important to me. In high school and college—even to some extent at Houston and Kansas City—I thought of myself as a loner. But all that changed when I came to the Raiders. Teddy used to joke that Phil and I were like brothers. Teddy was right. Only it wasn't just me and Phil. All my life I missed having a brother. On the Raiders I found forty-eight of them.

I was beginning to wonder—was that a feeling I could ever replace?

EPILOGUE:
TOOZ GOES TO HOLLYWOOD

In so many ways, what you are is what you do. For eighteen years, football defined my life, it gave me a purpose. I wasn't just John Matuszak, I was John Matuszak the football player. Football was what I was all about. Along with that identity came self-esteem. For eighteen years, football provided me with something that made me feel good about John Matuszak. Where would I get that feeling now?

That type of brooding went on for about eighteen months. Then I got tired. Tired of dwelling on things I couldn't control, tired of living my life in the past. It didn't happen overnight, but gradually I came to an understanding with myself. Football was over. There was nothing I could do about that. But the rest of my life was just beginning. How it unfolded was up to me and no one else. I could be happy or I could be miserable. The choice seemed simple. All I needed was something to fill the void.

Acting was a logical choice. By the time I retired from football, I had already appeared in three feature films, two of which—*North Dallas Forty* and *Caveman*—had enjoyed considerable success at the box office. In both films, my reviews were largely positive. All of that was important—rather than starting from scratch, I already had some credibility. And I knew the profession had a lot more positives than negatives. Unlike football, age was not a critical factor. Acting was something I could do for many years. Because it paid well, I wouldn't have to spend my down time scrambling for other jobs. I could spend it with my family or with my girlfriend Stephanie. Acting would also keep me in the public eye, something I must admit I had grown to enjoy. Most importantly, I could really commit myself to acting. With a cushy desk job, I might have been able to coast. But if I didn't work hard at acting I'd never last a year. I decided to attack it head on.

Today, having a career as an actor is just as important to me as my success as a football player was. I've been at it seven years now; it's no passing fancy. It's what I do—it's how I support myself. But it's not the money that pushes me. It's that need I've always had to compete, to keep on driving. Some people, those who don't know me, might think because I sometimes partied hard, I didn't work hard. Nothing could be further from the truth. My work ethic was ingrained at an early age. When I was young, I watched my father work two jobs just to keep his family afloat. I learned the value of hustling for everything you got. And for everything he did for me and my family, I feel I owe something to my father, if not to be a success, then at least to bust my ass in an effort. Hell, I owe it to myself.

It's funny, I wanted to be an actor even before I ever touched a football. When I was six years old, my cousin Tommy took me to see James Dean in *Rebel Without a Cause*. I didn't really understand it, but I couldn't take my eyes off the screen. I looked at James Dean and I knew he must have had the time of his life getting paid to be so cool. By the time I left the theater, I decided I would someday be an actor. Although that urge was put aside when I got heavily involved in football, my desire to act never left my consciousness entirely. When I was with the Chiefs in 1975, a TV reporter asked me what I planned to do when I left the NFL. I told her I was going to be an actor. She looked at me as if I had said I was going to open a Wendy's franchise on the moon. She practically started laughing at me right on the air. Mentalities like that just made me want it more.

The first film I made was *North Dallas Forty*. When it was released in 1979, many people were shocked. It was the first film about football that was grounded in reality. Players weren't painted as All-American gods; they were depicted as real people with real hangups like anyone else. The movie also revolved heavily around the subject of pain. It went right into the locker room to show players taking painkillers, doing what they had to in order to get out there every Sunday. The realism was hardly a coincidence. It was based on a novel by Peter Gent, a noted author who also played wide receiver for the Dallas Cowboys for five seasons in the 1960s. When the film was made, producers Frank Yablans and Jack Bernstein and director Ted Kotcheff were committed and open-minded enough to surround themselves with actual football people. Fred Biletnikoff was brought in to work specifically with Nick Nolte, the movie's star, and there were nineteen current or former players in the cast. Some of the names you'll probably recognize were Louis Kelcher, Doug France and Harold Jackson. And, of course, John Matuszak.

Actually I was lucky to get into the movie at all. My part was originally offered to Harvey Martin of the Cowboys, but for reasons I'll get to shortly, the Cowboys wouldn't let him take it. It was then presented to Dave Rowe, one of my teammates on the Raiders. Dave declined, turned off by the severity of the language. Dave suggested me, and I received a call one day from Paramount Pictures in Hollywood. They wanted me to come down for an interview. I said I'd be delighted.

When I walked in the office, there were a bunch of other athletes sitting in the room. One guy walked up to me and told me to ask them for a reading. Now I had no idea what a reading was, but it sounded professional to me. When they called my name, I walked into an office where I was introduced to Yablans and Kotcheff. They asked me a few questions and then, out of the blue, I asked them for a reading. Surprised, they asked me if I'd ever acted before. I said I hadn't but I would still like a reading. They smiled at each other and said okay. They handed me some lines from the script and took me to another room. They said to return in ten minutes. My heart was practically beating out of my chest, but I told myself to get a grip. I had always wanted to be an actor—now it was put up or shut up.

Ten minutes later I entered the room. I started reading and even I couldn't believe how good I sounded. They apparently agreed because they later gave me the part. I *was* going to be an actor.

The lines they had me read were lines that would later appear in the actual movie. I'm going to recount them here for a few reasons: Some people, including several players, felt it was the best dialogue in the movie. I also think that scene, among others, did a lot for my career. I was originally to have only those lines, but they came off so well in rehearsal that I was given a much larger role. Finally, this dialogue will give you a true feel for the movie's underlying theme.

Let me set the scene a little first. My character's name was O. W. Shaddock, an offensive lineman. The scene takes place toward the end of the movie. After a heartbreaking loss, Shaddock and his closest friend on the team, an offensive lineman played by Bo Svenson, are dressing in the locker room. Bo's character, Jo Bob Priddy, has been bloodied and humiliated by the other team's star defensive end. Shaddock and Priddy are confronted by the heartless Coach Johnson, who's played by Charles Durning. The coach is ripping Jo Bob for insufficiently studying his opponent's "facts and tendencies" prior to the game. He actually blames him for the loss of the game. Shaddock, enraged that the coach is so callous, and sick of hearing about facts and tendencies, goes wild. Keep in mind that my first few lines are delivered in a semicontrolled rage, but by the end of the scene I'm screaming violently at the top of my lungs. This is virtually the exact piece of dialogue from the finished movie. I left in all the cursing so you'll get the entire effect.

Shaddock: "Aw, shit, you never give us anything to bring to the game except your fucking facts and tendencies. To you it's just a business, but to us it's still got be a sport."

Coach Johnson: "You're supposed to be professionals. You go out there to play football."

Shaddock: "Aw, shit. We'll work harder than anybody to win. But, man, when we're dead tired in the fourth quarter, winning's got to be more than just money."

Coach Johnson: "You're hired to do a job."

Shaddock: "Job, job, I don't want no fucking job. I want to play football, you asshole. I want some feeling, I want some fucking team spirit."

Coach Johnson: "This ain't no high school. You don't have to love each other to play."

Shaddock: "That's just what I mean, you bastard. Every time I call it a game, you call it a business. And every time I call it a business, you call it a game. You and B. A. and all the rest of you coaches are chickenshit cocksuckers. No feeling for the game at all, man. You'll win but it'll just be numbers on a scoreboard. Numbers, that's all you care about. Fuck man, that's not enough for me."

Coach Johnson: "I don't have to listen to this."

Shaddock: "Oh, yes, you do, you got to listen to me for once. All you fucking coaches are chickenshit cocksuckers. You're all chickenshit cocksuckers. God damn you."

I've never said anything like that to a coach in real life, but I have to admit there were times when I would have liked to. So before we made that scene, that's exactly what I did: I pretended I was screaming at a coach. Not the majority, coaches I liked—people like Madden or Stram or Wiggin—but the few coaches I could never stand. It's probably why the scene was so believable.

When the film was released, the response from the Dallas Cowboys was predictable: They hated it. I don't blame them, it was pretty rough on the Cowboys. Gent, in his novel and in helping to write the film, made no effort whatsoever to conceal the fact that his story was adapted—although somewhat exaggerated—from his experiences as a Cowboy. You get that just from the title, but there were obvious references to the Cowboys throughout the movie. The real Cowboys are noted for their use of computers. When Nolte's character, who is probably based on Gent himself, walks into his coach's office, the first thing the coach does is to call up his file on a computer. The Cowboys' real offensive linemen jerk up and then back down while they're at the line of scrimmage. Our movie linemen did the same. The real Tom Landry is thin and sharp-featured and constantly wears a hat. So was the actor who played the head coach.

I could go on and on. I would like to say one thing though. I thought the character inspired by Landry was not representative of the real man. From what I know about Landry, he's a fine person and an excellent coach.

The snipes against the Cowboys were certainly not lost on the Texas powers that be. When the casting of the film was completed, we were all sent to Houston's Rice Stadium to begin working out. We were there less than a week when the filmmakers announced the bad news: The stadium officials had suddenly and inexplicably changed their minds—we could no longer use Rice stadium. We never found out exactly who or what had changed their minds, but we all chalked it up to Texas Money. Regardless of where it came from, the message was perfectly clear: We love our Cowboys. If you have to make a movie that makes them look bad, you aren't going to do it on Texas soil. The rest of the film was shot in Los Angeles.

In their condemnation of the movie, the Cowboys were not alone. The league office didn't like it much either, nor did several individual teams. In fact, and I don't want to mention any names, four or five players who appeared in the movie were cut soon after it was released. Perhaps it was coincidence but I doubt it. To those teams, participating in a film like *North Dallas Forty* was probably considered conduct detrimental to the image of the NFL. The fact that much of it was based on truth didn't seem to matter.

The only thing everyone seemed to agree on was that Nick Nolte was phenomenal, one of the few actors around who was wholly believable as an athlete. Fred Biletnikoff had a lot to do with it. He showed Nick how to *really* play wide receiver—how to run patterns, how to catch, even how Fred himself got ready in the moments before a game. But Nick knew his way around a football field going in. He played on the freshman team at Arizona State, and later played quarterback and punter at Eastern Arizona Junior College. I heard he almost ran a punt back for a touchdown once.

I felt like any other rookie working with an actor like Nolte: half intimidated, half thrilled at the prospect. It took us fourteen weeks to film the movie, and in the twelfth week I was given a week off because Nick was filming some love scenes with his leading lady. I had begun to feel relatively comfortable around the set, but when I returned from my break I felt totally lost. I just didn't feel like an actor. Movies are never shot in the order of their scenes and we were about to film the opening scene, where Nick and I go duck hunting with a few other players. I didn't feel right. I turned to Nick, who was standing next to me.

"Nick, how are we supposed to act in this scene?"

He looked at me with that sleepy smile of his.

"Tooz," he said, "acting is not acting."

I waited for him to expound but he never did. At that time I had no clue whatsoever as to what he meant, but I didn't want to be exposed for the novice I really was. So I smiled at him knowingly, as if he'd just revealed the hidden meaning of life. Later on, when I'd been around, I understood exactly what he meant. Become the character you're portraying. Don't think like an actor, think like the person you're playing. He was telling me to make it real.

Nick eased my fears about Hollywood "stars." He was loose and funny on the set and completely relaxed with his fellow actors. Nick's one of those actors who doesn't like to reveal much of himself to the public, a la Redford or DeNiro. It gives his fans something to wonder about. As part of that mystique, I think Nick likes to give the impression that he couldn't care less about acting, that he basically drifts onto the set, spits out his lines, then blows out of there. It's only an image. Nick's preparation for every scene was impeccable, and he worked his ass off to make himself believable as a jock. He's definitely a dedicated actor, even if he doesn't like to admit it.

Before the film was released, the entire Raiders team was invited to Paramount Studios for a private screening. We were in Los Angeles that week anyway, to play the Rams. Just about every player showed up. Me, Teddy, Kenny, Phil, and a few other players were all sitting in the first row chomping on popcorn. I was biting my nails like a little kid. I had never seen myself on film before and I had no idea what to expect. I didn't want to look like a clown in front of my teammates, not to mention the entire nation when the movie was later released. I stole a few glances at the guys and they seemed to be absorbed in the movie. That was encouraging. But when the movie ended there wasn't any applause. There wasn't any sound at all, just this awkward silence. Everyone kind of shuffled from his seat to the lobby in a daze. I think I know why. It hit too close to home. It's not like they learned anything they didn't know, but that giant screen can have tremendous impact.

The reviews, at least from my teammates, came in a few days later. Almost to a man, they all thought it was excellent. One Raider said it wasn't the best movie made about football, it was the first. As for Al Davis, I don't know if he ever saw it. Either way he never gave me a word of grief. Then again, he's never been a Cowboys fan.

———

In 1980, I got a role in the movie *Caveman*. Movie critics have never confused it with *Gone With the Wind*, but a lot of people who saw it thought it was a fun little movie. It was strictly for laughs, a spoof on prehistoric times in the same way *Airplane* was a send-up of disaster movies. It had a great cast: Ringo Starr, Barbara Bach, Shelley Long, Dennis Quaid and Avery Schreiber. I thought it was funny but could have been better. I don't want to sound egotistical, but I think I should have been in it more. Not because of me so much, but my character. I played a caveman called Tonda, the leader of the Hostile tribe, the bad guys. The movie was filmed two hours from Durango, Mexico, and all the actors in my tribe were Mexican stunt men. These guys were serious bad asses, tough old guys whose faces looked like they'd been chiseled from stone. Ringo was the leader of the Misfit tribe, which was also funny but a whole lot calmer. Most of the critics felt the movie moved much faster when our tribe was on camera. I had to agree with them.

This was in no way an intellectual movie. In fact, in the entire film there are no human words spoken. We all talk in "Caveman," which is roughly the equivalent of animals grunting. Coupled with the fact that my costume in the movie was relatively brief, I frequently got asked if I was worried about getting typecast as just another dumb jock who looked good flexing his muscles. When you're in only your second movie and you're still scared to death, the last thing on your mind is getting typecast. Later in my career I admit the notion crossed my mind. And at first I'm sure there were producers who dismissed me as just another ex-jock trying to be a movie star. I was never confronted with anything tangible, but at times I could sense doubt. I could even understand that, because there have been dozens and dozens of athletes who have tried, unsuccessfully, to make the transition.

Even if my size and history did invite some initial prejudice, I never took it personally. I knew that *anybody* who makes a name in one field, then tries his hand at another, is generally greeted with a measure of skepticism. People think you're just being cocky—who does this guy think he is? You just have to show them you're serious. Besides, why worry about things you can't control? This is the body I've got, for better or for worse. So I'll never star in the Bill Shoemaker story. I'll have to learn to live with it.

The biggest kick I got out of making *Caveman* was working with Ringo Starr. You have to understand, when I was young I wasn't just a casual Beatles fan. I bordered on obsession. I had almost all their records and I could recite the verses to most of their songs. One year I even talked my mom into buying me one of those collarless *Nehru* jackets they wore, the ones that stayed in style for about a week. I kept wearing mine after everyone else's had already been moved to the back of the closet. The neighbors thought I was a little strange. I thought I was the coolest kid on the block.

The first time I met Ringo I was anything but cool. This was big-time stuff, actually meeting one of your childhood heroes. I was excited but not quite sure what to expect. Rock stars aren't known to be the most levelheaded people on earth, and here was one of the biggest of all time. Ringo turned out to be one of the friendliest people I've ever met. I think he could sense he made me nervous and he went out of his way to loosen me up. The night after our first day's shooting, the cast was having a party. This wasn't like hanging around with Teddy and

Phil, who were accomplished in their own right, but were much more familiar to me. These were proven actors and I was still the new kid on the block. I was standing by myself playing wallflower. Ringo walked up and asked me, totally deadpan, if I wanted to dance. I didn't know what the hell to say, so I just stood there looking at him. After thirty seconds of awkward silence, finally he burst out laughing and told me he was only joking. We got along well after that. Ringo had no star hangups whatsoever—he worked as diligently as anyone else. It was a nice feeling to meet a childhood hero who wasn't that different from you.

If I sound like a movie fan, it's because I am. I was the same way when I played football. I used to love to meet people like Joe Namath or Don Shula. They were American heroes and I was standing right next to them. It was a tremendous honor. And I always figured if I listened closely enough, maybe I could learn something. That was one of the best things about working with people like Al Davis and John Madden. They taught me so much about my trade.

Acting has been a learning experience too. Besides the feature films I've made, I've also learned from all the television work I've done. I've appeared in *M*A*S*H, Fall Guy, Trapper John, Matt Houston, Benson, Silver Spoons, Dukes of Hazzard, Hunter, Miami Vice, Amen, Father and Sons,* and *Today's FBI.* I've had parts in four TV pilots: *Stir Crazy, Half Nelson, Command Five* and Aaron Spelling's *Hollywood Beat.* Before it was canceled after thirteen weeks, I was a regular on *Hollywood Beat.* I played a homosexual short order cook. So much for typecasting.

In the course of my career as an actor, I've also met people who showed me what *not* to do. Generally speaking, the life-styles of people in Hollywood are nowhere near as radical as a lot of people are led to believe. If they were you'd never see a movie, because none of them would get finished. But I have met actors and actresses who had their excesses. John Belushi is the saddest and most tragic example.

I met John exactly five days before his death. I was eating at my favorite restaurant, the Imperial Gardens in Hollywood, which is right in front of the Chateau Marmont. That's the hotel where John often stayed and eventually died. I was sitting at a table with my date when John walked in. Naturally I was thrilled. I thought he was one of the funniest men on earth, and at that time I had no idea how severe his problem was. John looked at our table, realized he knew my date, and walked over to say hello. John didn't look good, his face was puffy and his eyes were red. He looked like he needed sleep. I asked John if he was hungry and he said he was. I ordered him a plate of octopus and the waiter laid it in front of him. I tried to strike up a conversation, but John didn't appear to hear a word I said. He seemed to be extremely preoccupied and nervous, and he could barely sit still in his seat. Just then a man stuck his head in the door of the restaurant. He spotted John and said, "Let's go." John stood up from his seat, walked to the door and left. Didn't say thank you or goodbye, didn't even nod his head at us.

That same night I was introduced to Richard Donner. Donner is a close friend of, and frequent collaborator with, Steven Spielberg. He's directed movies like *Superman, The Omen, Ladyhawke* and several others. Sometimes I think back to that night I met Belushi and Donner. I can't help thinking how odd it was to meet two people, in the same night, who were going in such radically different directions.

That meeting with Donner would pay invaluable dividends later in my career. Toward the end of 1984, I was sitting at home one afternoon when I got a call from Charles Stern, my commercial agent. He was so excited he was practically screaming. Richard Donner and Steven Spielberg were making a film called the *Goonies* and they wanted to talk to me. I drove to Warner Brothers and Donner was waiting. He took one look at me and started jumping up and down.

"This is Sloth, this is Sloth," he kept saying.

I didn't know if I should take that personally, but I figured there was something going on I didn't know. Then he took me to the president's office.

"Is this Sloth or what?" Donner asked the president.

"Yeah, yeah," said the president. "You're Sloth."

And just like that, I got the part of Sloth. As Donner explained the part I tried to stay calm and collected, but on the inside I was going wild. Steven Spielberg, I'm sure you know, was and is the number one man in all of Hollywood. Whether he produced it, directed it, conceived it, or bankrolled it, the track record of his films reads like an anthology of Hollywood smashes. *Jaws. Close Encounters of the Third Kind. Raiders of the Lost Ark. Back to the Future. Poltergeist. Gremlins.* And the number one box office hit of all time, *E.T.—The Extraterrestrial.* Steven Spielberg is the Al Davis of Hollywood.

This may sound crazy, but Steven actually reminds me of a young Al Davis. For one thing, he's a giant in his field whose methods a lot of people have tried to emulate. He knows exactly what he wants to do and he has the clout and the expertise to do it. And Steven and Al both have that quiet aura of power. Like Al, Steven doesn't say much when he's unhappy. He just gives you the look.

Don't get me wrong though, Steven is anything but a dictator when he's on the set. Not in the least. The thing I liked best about him was that he was always willing to listen to his actors, not a universal trait among Hollywood superstars. But Steven let us try new things, make our own mistakes. If he didn't like what he saw, he didn't go crazy. When he felt it was appropriate, he'd come in and say, "Well, this is one way you could do it." He's a fair-minded guy who is blessed with a once-in-a-generation gift. And despite his tremendous success, he's never lost that wonder of making movies. As Steven says, he gets paid to be a dreamer.

Some people think life in Hollywood is nothing but limousines and cocktail parties. Let me put it this way: For a job that's supposed to be so glamorous, you sure work your ass off. In that respect, and others, acting is similar to football. Both professions pay extremely well, but also demand extraordinary perserverance. In both professions you have to "play in pain." If you're feeling lousy one day when you're shooting a film, you can't call in sick; you have to get up there and perform your part regardless. And there's always that pressure of producing, not when you're in the mood to produce, but at the precise moment you're called on. The moment the camera rolls, just as when the ball is snapped, you'd better be ready to move.

When I was working on *Goonies,* I would usually get to the set at four or five in the morning and not get home until seven or eight that night. The basic theme of the movie was friendship and sticking together. A group of close friends, adventurous little kids who called themselves the Goonies, are about to be split up because their homes are to be destroyed to make way for a new golf course. On the last weekend before they're to split up, they stumble onto one last adventure. Along the way they run into the Fratelli Gang, a family of bumbling but cutthroat thieves. That's where I come in. I play Sloth, a huge, deformed, Hunchback of Notre Dame kind of creature who is one of the Fratellis' children. The Fratellis keep me locked in chains in a basement, where I'm discovered by the Goonies. The Goonies are frightened and repelled when they first meet me, but they soon see I'm just a little kid like them, trapped in a grotesque body. At the end of the film I become the hero, helping the kids escape my evil family.

According to makeup chief Tom Burman, turning me into Sloth every day was one of the most difficult makeup jobs he's ever done. The mask I wore was amazing. There were fifteen overlapping pieces, including an electronic eye and ears, all of which would move via remote control. I would arrive at the set at five in the morning, and it would take them five hours just to make me up. Even then I couldn't shoot my scenes. Because of child labor laws, the children had to be finished with their work and off the set by a certain time. So while they were doing their scenes, I would spend those six to eight hours doing nothing, lying in a trailer, going nuts. There were so many glues and adhesives used that my skin was breaking out all over. One of my eyes was completely covered by makeup, so I couldn't even read. I also couldn't leave the set because a riot would have started if anyone saw me. It was even worse before they hired Burman. They had another makeup guy for the first two months and it wasn't working out. He'd work on me all morning but when I'd arrive on the set something was always wrong with my mask. We ran two months of those tests before they ever shot a foot of film. It was hard, exhausting work, but everyone else was working just as hard. And it was worth it to work with people like Spielberg and Donner.

––––––––

September, 1984. I was in the dressing room of *Silver Spoons,* the sitcom starring little Ricky Schroeder, when I first spotted Stephanie. One of the makeup artists for Embassy Television, she was working that day on *Silver Spoons.* There were a few other women doing makeup, but I made sure I got Stephanie. We talked, found out we both were single, were both from the Midwest (she's from Fort Wayne, Indiana) and that we liked a lot of the same things. When I asked her out, and she said yes, I just had one of those feelings. Like maybe this was The One.

I went back to Oak Creek for Thanksgiving, called her from there, saw her that Sunday, and we've been together ever since. The courtship moved gradually—our second date, she brought along her sister and cousin—but I realized quickly she was someone special. Stephanie's beautiful and incredibly sexy, but that isn't what sets her apart. She's the kind of person you're proud to be around. She's bright, considerate, sweet natured, well grounded. Also very, very loyal. She always sticks by me, no matter how difficult things might get. She could have taken the easy way out at times, just left, but she withstood the pain right along with me. I owe this woman a lot.

As difficult as it was to leave the game, having someone like Stephanie eased the transition. Rather than dwell only on what I'd lost, having her made me take stock in what I still had. It's true: I've got a lot to be thankful for. I've got a woman who loves me, a wonderful family, an exciting new career. And I've still got the Raiders.

I'll always have the Raiders. I thought when I retired I would drift away from Phil and Teddy, and all the other guys. In a sense I have; since we're spread out all over, it's tough to stay in touch. But Phil and I are working hard to renew our relationship; we make it a point to get together a few times a year. And even with the guys I only talk to over the phone, every time we do, that excitement, that nostalgia, that friendship, is always right there. Hell, we've got history together. For a lot of years, we ate together, worked together, watched each others' backs. That's a bond distance can never break.

Miraculously, with the things I've done and the game I played, I've also got my health. In terms of your body, playing pro football is like beating your head against a wall: It feels real good when you stop. As a pro athlete, I gave my body to the game, to the team. Now I can do with it what I want. No more painkillers, no more black and blue Mondays. I've still got some trouble spots, and there isn't a morning when I'm not reminded I used to play pro football. But on balance I've been fortunate. My back is much stronger than it's been in years. I can still run and lift weights and swim and play basketball. When I get too wound up, when the walls start moving in, I practice my karate, or do a little Mike Tyson on my punching bag. My body feels good, and a lot of former athletes can't say that.

As much as I still miss playing, as much as you have to shut me up once I get reminiscing, leaving the game was good for me. It helped me mature. That's a difficult process when you're an athlete. You're on a pedestal. Everyone tells you how great you played, fusses over you at restaurants, stands in line for your autograph. You're front and center at the head of the parade.

I'd be lying if I said I didn't enjoy that; hell, if I didn't, I never would have gone into acting. Believe me, it was a whole lot better than being ignored. I still love it when people walk up and want to talk about the Raiders. I wouldn't trade my career, my memories, for anything in the world. I'd do it all again— well, most of it—in a minute.

But sometimes being an athlete was also confusing. Part of growing up is having and taking the time to learn about the kind of person you are. Separating the real you from the image people have of you, the roles we all play from the reality. From up on that stage, underneath that spotlight, sometimes it's hard to tell who you really are. I think I've got a pretty good idea now.

Let's get something straight though: I don't have a case of terminal mellow. I don't walk around the house in a baking apron, quoting Alan Alda. I'm still an excitable, emotional person. That's never going to change.

It's just that I've developed a sense of balance now. I don't have to act on every crazy impulse that goes rushing through my head. You can still go cruisin' with the Tooz. But it doesn't have to be in fifth gear.